Fredericksburg City, Virginia

Deed Book

1782–1787

Ruth and Sam Sparacio

HERITAGE BOOKS
2020

HERITAGE BOOKS
AN IMPRINT OF HERITAGE BOOKS, INC.

Books, CDs, and more—Worldwide

For our listing of thousands of titles see our website
at
www.HeritageBooks.com

Published 2020 by
HERITAGE BOOKS, INC.
Publishing Division
5810 Ruatan Street
Berwyn Heights, Md. 20740

International Standard Book Number
Paperbound: 978-1-68034-490-5

FREDERICKSBURG CITY, VIRGINIA
HUSTINGS COURT DEED BOOK A
1782-1787

pp. (On margin: "The Original delivered Mr. ELISHA DICKENSON Feby. 8th 1783")
1- THIS INDENTURE made the twelfth day of September one thousand seven hun-
3 dred and Eighty two Between WILLIAM JACKSON of County of Spotsylvania of
one part and ELISHA DICKENSON of Town of Fredericksburg of other part; Witnesseth that WILLIAM JACKSON for the Rents and Covenants herein mentioned hath granted and to farm lett unto ELISHA DICKENSON his heirs and assigns all that parcel of ground in Town of Fredericksburg & County of Spotsylvania containing one third part of an acre and being a part of the Lotts No. 13 and No. 15 of the first addition to the said Town taken from the Land of HENRY WILLIS Gent., then deceas'd, and are bounded by CAROLINE STREET by Lotts No. 14 and No. 16; by PRINCESS ANN STREET and by (blank) Street between the said Lotts No. 13 and No. 15 and the Lotts No. 33 and No. 34 of the first survey of the Town of Fredericksburg, the said one third part of an acre of ground lying along side the Lott No. 14 and No. 16 and containing Fifty five feet front on CAROLINE STREET and Fifty five feet fron on PRINCESS ANN STREET, Together with all profits To have and to hold unto ELISHA DICKENSON his heirs and assigns from the 31st day of December last passed during term of Twenty one years, paying yearly on the 31st of December the sum or Rent of Eight pounds in Spanish Silver milled Dollars at Six shillings the Dollar or other current Gold or Silver Coin rated in the same proportion, And if any rent be behind for Sixty days that said WILLIAM JACKSON his heirs upon the said Land to reenter and the same to have again at the expiration of the said Term of Twenty one years they will deliver up peaceable possession unto WILLIAM JACKSON his heirs the said ground with all the houses or buildings which may be erected unless decayed by time or destroyed by unavoidable accident; In Testimony whereof the said parties have set their hands and seals

Sealed and delivered in presence of
WILLIAM LOVELL, CHARLES YATES, WILLIAM JACKSON
RICHARD KENNY, WIILLIAM SMOCK
JOHN ATKINSON, WILLIAM JACKSON,
WILLIAM MASSEY, JOHN BENSON

At a Hustings Court held for the Town and Corporation of Fredericksburg the Twenty first of October one thousand seven hundred and Eighty two.

This Lease and Indenture was proved by the oaths of JOHN ATKINSON, WILLIAM MASSEY and JOHN BENSON and ordered to be recorded

Test HENRY ARMISTEAD, Clk.
Truly recorded Test THOMAS SYDNOR, Dp. Clk.

pp. THIS INDENTURE made this Twentieth day of January in year of our Lord one
3- thousand seven hundred and Eighty three between JOHN WELCH of County of
4 Spotsylvania and Bourough of Fredericksburg and NELLEY his Wife of one part
and GODLOVE HEISKELL of County and Borough aforesaid of other part; Witnesseth that JOHN WELCH and NELLEY his Wife of sum of Seven hundred pounds Specie Virginia currency to them paid hath sold unto GODLOVE HEISKELL his heirs and assigns all that part of the Lott numbered in the plan of the said Borough (41) and is the lower part of the Lott the said JOHN WELCH purchased of JOHN WIGLESWORTH formerly belonging to WILLIAM HOUSTON being One hundred and thirty feet on HANOVER STREET and Sixty one feet on CAROLINE STREET up to the lower part of the said lott, which the

aforesaid JOHN WIGGLESWORTH sold to WILLIAM JACKSON, thence Twenty feet along the side of said JACKSONs House, then turning Nine feet outwards toward the LONG ORDINARY and continuing fourteen feet back and twelve feet paralel with the said CAROLINE STREET, thence Ninety eight feet back from thence to run to CAROLINE STREET Eighty four and one half feet; it being now in the possession of the said GODLOVE HEISKILL, and the said JOHN WELCH and NELLEY his Wife agree that they will warrant and forever defend the said Lott against claim of every other persons In Witness whereof the said JOHN WELCH & NELLEY his Wife have hereunto set their hands and affixed their seals JOHN WELCH
NELLEY WELCH

At a Hustings Court held for the Town and Corporation of Fredericksburg on Monday the Twentieth day of January one thousand seven hundred and Eighty three

This Deed indented from JOHN WELCH & NELLEY his Wife to GODLOVE HEISKILL (she being first privately examined) was acknowledged and ordered to be recorded

Truly recorded Test THOMAS SYDNOR Dp. Clk.
Test HENRY ARMISTEAD, Clk.

pp. 4-7 (On margin: ("Septr. 2nd 1783. The Original Deed was delivered unto Mr. JAS: TAYLOR")

THIS INDENTURE made this Twenty sixth day of December in the year of our Lord one thousand seven hundred and Eighty two Between JOHN WELCH and NELLY his Wife of Town of Fredericksburg and County of Spotsylvania of one part and SAMUEL RODDY and JAMES TAYLOR, both of the said Town and County, of the other part; Whereas WILLIAM SIMS, a Subject of Great Britain, was lately seized of a certain Lott in the said Town of Fredericksburg known and described in the plan of the said Town by Number Two hundred and Fifty seven and bounded by CAROLINE STREET and PRUSSIA STREET and Lotts numbered 256, 266 and Two hundred sixty seven, which said Lott became forfeited under the Act of Assembly of this Common Wealth and was sold by CHARLES WASHINGTON Escheator, to JOHN WELSH, as will appear by Letters Pattent signed by THOMAS JEFFERSON and bearing date the tenth day of April MDCCXXXI and registered in the Land Office. Now this Indenture witnesseth that the said JOHN WELSH and NELLY his Wife being seized of the sait Lotts have sold the said Lott unto the said SAMUEL RODDY and JAMES TAYLOR for the sum of Three hundred pounds lawfull money of Virginia, together with all houses and appertenances belonging and the said JOHN WELSH for himself doth covenant that he hath not done any Deed by which the Title to the said Lott may be affected; but the same is free from every other incumbrance and doth warrant the said Lott from him the sd. JOHN WELSH & his heirs and any persons claiming under him; In Witness whereof the said JOHN WELSH and NELLY his Wife have set their hands and seals

Signed sealed and delivered in presence of
EDWARD HERNDON JUNR. JOHN WELCH
JAMES WEIR, JACOB WHITLER NELLY WELCH

At a Hustings Court held for the Town and Corporation of Fredericksburg the Twenty first day of April 1783

This Deed from JOHN WELSH and NELLY his Wife to SAMUEL RODDY and JAMES TAYLOR with the receipt; (she being first privately examined) was acknowledged & ordered to be recorded Test HENRY ARMISTEAD, Clerk pp. 7-9 THIS INDENTURE made the Twenty first day of April in the year of our Lord one thousand seven hundred and Eighty three Between EDWARD SIMPSON & CATHARINE his Wife of one part and JOHN WELCH of the other part; Witnesseth that the said EDWARD SIMPSON & CATHARINE his Wife hath this day sold unto the said JOHN WELCH and his heirs all that parcel of ground containing Fifty five feet in front and One hundred and fifty feet back being one third of that part of the CHURCH LOT in Fredericksburg ordered to be sold by Act of Assembly for the benefit of the Parish of St. George; being on the West side of CAROLINE STREET and in the middle part of said CHURCH GROUND, the part next to the MARKET HOUSE being sold to GEORGE THORNTON Gent., and the lower part lying to the South being sold to ALEXANDER BLAIR and is a Corner lot lying on CAROLINE and GEORGE STREETs, for the sum of Two hundred pounds together with all houses gardens ways and appurtenances belonging; In Witness whereof the said EDWARD SIMPSON and CATHARINE his Wife hath hereunto set their hands & seals

In presence of us — EDWARD SIMPSON

(no witnesses shown) — CATHARINE SIMPSON

At a Hustings Court held for the Town & Corporation of Fredericksburg on Monday the Twenty first day of April one thousand seven hundred & Eighty three

This Deed indented from EDWARD SIMPSON & CATHARINE his Wife to JOHN WELCH (she being first privately examined) was acknowledged & ordered to be recorded

Truly recorded Test HENRY ARMISTEAD, Clk.

pp. 9-12 THIS INDENTURE TRIPARTITE made this day of (blank) in year one thousand seven hundred and Eighty (blank) Between CHARLES WASHINGTON and MILDRED his Wife, late of Town of Fredericksburg of the first part; BURGESS BALL and FANNY his Wife of the second part; And ROBERT FORSYTH of the third part. Whereas CHARLES WASHINGTON Esqr. being seized in fee of two certain lotts of land known in the plan of the Town of Fredericksburg by the numbers (70) and (80) and being so seized for a valuable consideration him thereunto moving make over the two Lotts aforesd. to the aforesaid BURGESS BALL, which said two Lotts the said BURGESS BALL before a Conveyance had from the said CHARLES WASHINGTON for the sum of money hereafter mentioned did agree to sell unto the said ROBERT FORSYTH. Now this Indenture witnesseth that the said CHARLES WASHINGTON and MILDRED his Wife for value received and divers other good causes and the said BURGESS BALL and FANNY his Wife for Two hundred and fifty pounds current money to them paid by ROBERT FORSYTH have granted unto the said ROBERT FORSYTH his heirs and assigns forever; To have & to hold the said two Lotts and premisses with all appurtenances belonging and the said CHARLES WASHINGTON and BURGESS BALL each for himself and his heirs do warrant that the said ROBERT FORSYTH his heirs shall peaceably enjoy the said two Lotts clear from molestation of them and their heirs and every other person. In Witness whereof the said CHARLES WASHINGTON and MILDRED his Wife and BURGESS BALL and FANNY his Wife have sett their hands and seals

Signed sealed and delivered in presence of

JNO: AUGS. WASHINGTON, — CHS: WASHINGTON

GEORGE A. WASHINGTON, — MILDRED WASHINGTON

WILL: DREW, ROB: RUTHERFORD, — BURGESS BALL

JAS: CRANE, — FRANCES BALL

THORNTON WASHINGTON as to F. & B. BALL

At a Hustings Court held for the Town and Corporation of Fredericksburg on Monday the nineteenth day of May one thousand seven hundred and Eighty three

This Deed and receipt was acknowledged by BURGESS BALL and ordered to be recorded And at a Court held on Monday the (incomplete)

pp. (On margin: "July 22d. 1783. This Deed delivered to JNO: WALLACE")
12- THIS INDENTURE made this the Tenth day of May in the year of our Lord one
15 thousand seven hundred and eighty three Between JOHN WELCH and NELLY his Wife of the Corporation of Fredericksburg of the first part and JOHN WALLACE of the said Corporation of the second part; Witnesseth that the said JOHN WELCH and NELLY his Wife for Sixty pounds lawful money of Virginia have granted unto the said JOHN WALLACE one certain Lott of Land known in the plan of the Town of Fredericksburg by (No. 212) Number Two hundred and twelve and adjoining the lands of Colo. LEWIS WILLIS by the Run on the back of the said Town whereon the said JOHN WELCH formerly had a STABLE together with all rights; To have and to hold the said Lott with the premisses unto the said JOHN WALLACE his heirs and assigns and he the said JOHN WELCH for himself and his heirs doth warrant that he the said JOHN WALLACE his heirs shall hold the above described lot clear from the claim of all persons whatsoever; In Witness whereof he the said JOHN WELCH and NELLY his Wife have set their hands and seals

Signed sealed & delivered in presence of JOHN WELCH
(no witnesses shown) NELLY WELCH

At a Hustings Court held for the Town and Corporation of Fredericksburg the third Monday in May one thousand seven hundred and Eighty three

JOHN WELCH acknowledged this Deed and Receipt to JOHN WALLACE and it is ordered to be recorded; And on the Third Monday of July, NELLY WELCH, his Wife, (being first privately examained) acknowledged the same

Test HENRY ARMISTEAD, Clk.

pp. (On margin: "Delivd. WM. SMOCK 16th Novr. 89")
15- THIS INDENTURE made the nineteenth day of May one thousand seven hundred
16 and Eighty three Between WILLIAM CALDWELL, Orphan of JAMES CALDWELL of Town of Fredericksburg, with the approbation of the Court of Hustings of the said Town of Fredericksburg of the one part and WILLIAM SMOCK, Sadler, of the same Town of the other part; Witnesseth that the said WILLIAM CALDWELL with the approbation of the Court doth by these presents untill he shall arrive to the age of Twenty one years during which term the said WILLIAM CALDWELL his said Master shall truly serve, his secrets keep, his lawful commands obey, hurt to his said Master he shall not do or suffer to be done but of the same give nether to his said Master, the goods of his said Master he shall not embezzle nor lend them without his said Masters consent; at dice cards or any other unlawful game he shall not play, Matrimony he shall not contract, the service of his said Master he shall not absent but in all things truly demean himself towards his said Master, And the said WILLIAM SMOCK doth for himself promise to the said WILLIAM CALDWELL & to the Court of Hustings that he will do his utmost endeavor during the said term to teach the said CALDWELL in the business & trade of a Sadler, and promise that he will case the said Apprentice to be taught to read & write, that he will furnish him with proper cloathing, lodging, washing & mending & diet fitting such an Apprentice and at the expiration of the term he will pay to the said WILLIAM CALDWELL the sum of Three pounds ten shillings as Freedom Dues; Witness our hands & seals this 19th day of May 1783

WILLIAM CALDWELL
WILLIAM SMOCK

At a Court of Hustings held for the Town and Corporation of Fredericksburg on Monday the Nineteenth day of May one thousand seven hundred and Eighty three
This Indenture of Apprenticeship between WILLIAM CALDWELL and WILLIAM SMOCK was acknowledged and ordered to be recorded
Test H. ARMISTEAD, Clk.

pp. 17-18 THIS INDENTURE made this 19th May one thousand seven hundred and Eighty three Between JOHN CRUTCHFIELD of County of Spotsylvania of one part and PHILLIP LIPSCOMB of Town and Corporation of Fredericksburg, Bricklayer, of other part; Witnesseth that the said JOHN CRUTCHFIELD of his own free will and by consent of the Corporation Court of Fredericksburg, doth bind himself an Apprentice to the said PHILLIP LIPSCOMB untill he shall arive to age of Twenty one years he being (blank) during which time said JOHN CRUTCHFIELD shall serve the said PHILLIP LIPSCOMB, not absent himself day nor night without leave, nor lend his goods unlawfully, nor frequent taverns or any disorderly meetings, at cards dice or any unlawfull games he shall not follow, nor contract Matrimony, And in all things truly serve his Master willingly obey during the sd. Term and the said PHILLIP LIPSCOMB for his part agree with the said JOHN CRUTCHFIELD that he will teach the said JOHN CRUTCHFIELD in reading writing and Arithmatic and in the Trade of Brick Laying and will provide for him sufficient meat drink washing clothing lodging fitt for an Apprentice; In Witness whereof the parties have set their hands and seals

JOHN CRUTCHFIELD
PHILLIP LIPSCOMB

At a Court of Hustings held for the Town of Fredericksburg on Monday Sixteenth June one thousand seven hundred and Eighty three
This Indenture of Apprenticeship was acknowledged & ordered to be recorded
Test HENRY ARMISTEAD, Clk.

pp. 18-20 THIS INDENTURE made the Sixteenth day of June in year of our Lord one thousand seven hundred and Eighty three Between GEORGE CRUTCHFIELD of County of Spotsylvania of one part and PHILLIP LIPSCOMB of the Town of Fredericksburg, Bricklayer, of the other part; Witnesseth that the said GEORGE CRUTCHFIELD of his own free will and the consent of the Corporation Court of the aforesaid Town doth bind himself Apprentice to the said PHILLIP LIPSCOMB untill he shall arrive to the age of twenty one years he being (blank) during which time the said GEORGE CRUTCHFIELD shall truly serve his said Master, not absent himself unlawfully or without leave of his said Master, not seel or lend the goods of his Master but as a faithful Apprentice give notice of the same to his said Master; Taverns or any other disorderly meetings he shall not frequent, Cards, dice or any other unlawfull games he shall not play, fornication he shall not commit or Matrimony contract within the term of his Apprenticeship, his Masters secrets he shall truly keep and all his lawfull commands gladly obey and in every respect behave himself as a faithfull Apprentice during the said term; And the said PHILLIP LIPSCOMB on his part doth agree to teach reading writing and arithmitic and the art trade and mystery of a Bricklayer, which he the said PHILLIP LIPSCOMB now useth and provide sufficient meet drink washing cloathing lodging and all other necessarys during the said term; In Witness whereof the parties above mentioned have set their hands and seals

GEORGE CRUTCHFIELD
PHILLIPS LIPSCOMB

At a Hustings Court held for the Town and Corporation of Fredericksburg on Monday the Sixteenth day of June one thousand seven hundred and eighty three
This Indenture of Apprenticeship was acknowledged and ordered to be recorded
Test H. ARMISTEAD, Clk.

pp. THIS INDENTURE made the 16th day of June Seventeen hundred and Eighty
20- three Between MARY RISKLE of the City & Town of Fredericksburg and WIL-
21 LIAM McWILLIAM, JAMES SOMERVILLE, CHARLES MORTEMORE & JAMES TAYLOR
Gentlemen Justices of the peace of the aforesaid City and Town and County of Spotsylvania of one part and AUSTIN FARRELL & ANN his Wife of County of CAROLINE of other part; Witnesseth that the said Justices by virtue of their said Office and the authority to them given by the Laws of the Common Wealth of the State of Virginia have bound placed & put her Daughter, MARY RISKLE, as a Servant or Apprentice to the said AUSTIN FARRELL & ANN his Wife to serve them untill the said MARY RISKLE shall arrive to the age of Eighteen years, during which time the said Apprentice her said Mater and Mistress faithfully shall serve, their secrets keep and all their lawful commands gladly obey; In consideration whereof the said AUSTIN FARRELL and ANN his Wife doth hereby covenant themselves to learn their said Apprentice to Spell, Read & Write & to do their true endeavours to instruct her in the art of Spinning, Weaving, Knitting &c., and to find for their said Apprentice good and sufficient diet, clothing, lodging and washing during the time of their Apprentices service &c., In Witness whereof the said parties have set their hands & seals

Signed sealed & delivered in presence of MARY RISKLE
(no witnesses shown) AUSTIN FARRELL

At a Hustings Court held for the Town and Corporation of Fredericksburg on Monday the Sixteenth day of June one thousand seven hundred and eighty three
This Indenture of Apprenticeship between MARY REISKILL and AUSTIN FERROLL was approved of by the Court acknowledged & ordered to be recorded
Test HENRY ARMISTEAD

pp. THIS INDENTURE made the Twenti first day of July one thousand seven hundred
22- & eighty three witnesseth that GEORGE MORE with the approbation of the Court
23 and of his own free will and that of his Brother, hath bound himself Apprentice
to JOHN McKENNY of County of Spotsylvania & Town of Fredericksburg to be taught the trade of a House Carpenter & Joiner which the said JOHN McKENNY now useth and with him as an Apprentice to dwell & serve from the day of the date before mentioned for the term of Six years & six months during all which time the said Apprentice his said Master will faithfully serve, his secrets keep, lawfull commands gladly obey, do no hurt to his said Master nor suffer to be done by other but give notice to his said Master, the goods of his Master he shall not wast nor lend without his consent, matrimony he shall not contract, from the service of his Master he shall not depart or absent himself without leave but in all things behave himself during the said term and the said Master his said Apprentice the said Trade of Carpenter and Joiner shall instruct after the best way and manner he can and will also find his said Apprentice meat drink, washing lodging and apparriel fit for such an Apprentice during the term aforesaid and cause to be taught to Read & Write; In Witness whereof the parties have affixed their hands and seals

JOHN McKENNY
GEORGE MORE

At a Court of Hustings held for the Town and Corporation of Fredericksburg on Monday the Twenty first day of July one thousand seven hundred and Eighty three
This Indenture of Apprenticeship acknowledged and ordered to be recorded
Test H. ARMISTEAD, Clk.

pp. (On margin: "The Original as delivered Mr. W.. WYATT")
23- TO ALL TO WHOM these presents shall come, We BENJAMIN GRYMES, SALLY his
29 Wife, and JUDY ROBINSON of ORANGE County in the Commonwealth of Virginia and WILLIAM WIATT of the Town of Fredericksburg, County of Spotsylvania, in the State aforesaid send Greeting. Whereas PETER ROBINSON late of KING WILLIAM County in the said State, deceased, Father of the said SALLEY & JUDY, seized of the fee simple Estate in the County of YORK in Kingdom of GREAT BRITAIN called BOWLES & EMPECY leaving the said SALLY and JUDY & one other Daughter named LUCY ROBINSON, by which the said Estate descended to the three Daughters as Copartners, And Whereas the said BENJAMIN GRYMES as the Husband of the said SALLY and JUDY ROBINSON, Daughter of the said PETER ROBINSON, are each intitled to an interest of one third part & portion of the said Estate; And Whereas the said BENJAMIN GRYMES hath executed his Bond to the said WILLIAM WIATT conditioned for the selling & making over to the said WIATT & his heirs, all the right and interest of her the said SALLY to the Estate aforesaid; And Whereas the said BENJAMIN GRYMES & SALLY his Wife, JUDY ROBINSON & WILLIAM WIATT being at a considerable distance from the said Estate, and for their own convenience desirous of impowering some proper persons living near to the said Estate to transact their busines in their portions of the same in the said Kingdom of GREAT BRITAIN, Now Know ye that for the special trust which they have in WILLIAM QUINCY & JOHN & THOMAS BACKHOUSE of Town of LIVERPOOL in County of PALATINE of LANCASTER and Kingdom of GREAT BRITAIN, Merchants, have appointed the said WILLIAM QUINCY, JOHN and THOMAS BACKHOUSE their true & lawful Attorney and Agent for them in their own names as they shall be advised, to dispose of and turn into money all their portion in the said Estate for the most money and best price that can be gotten for the same; And also for them to demand and receive from the present tenants or any tenansts all rents and arrears of Rents which are due & owing them and to enter into and upon all said Estate and seize any goods or chattels that shall be found upon the same or to make distress of the premisses or to take such other lawful ways for the recovery thereof as their said Attorney shall think fit, giving unto their said Attorney full power to perform any act that shall be needfull and necessary touching the said lands hereby confirming all their said Attorneys shall in their name lawfully do and the said BENJAMIN GRYMES, SALLY his Wife, JUDY ROBINSON and WILLIAM WIATT do impower the said WILLIAM QUINCY, JOHN & THOMAS BACKHOUSE to retain & reimburse themselves all charges and expences which they may be put to in the execution of these presents; In Witness we have hereunto set our hands and affixed our seals this Eighth day of September in year of our Lord one thousand seven hundred & Eighty three & in the Eighth year of the Independance of America
Signed sealed & delivered in presence of

G. WEEDON, ALEXR; DICK,
DAVID HENDERSON,
GEO: MASSINGBIRD

BENJAMIN GRYMES
SALLY GRYMES
JUDITH ROBINSON
WILLIAM WIATT

At a Hustings Court held for the Town and Corporation of Fredericksburg on Monday the fifteen day of September one thousand seven hundred and Eighty three
This Power of Attorney between BENJAMIN GRYMES, SALLY GRYMES, JUDITH ROBIN-

SON and WILLIAM WYATT and WILLIAM QUINCY & JOHN & THOMAS BACKHOUSE proved by the oaths of GEORGE WEEDON, DAVID HENDERSON and GEORGE MASSINGBIRD and ordered to be recorded

Test HENRY ARMISTEAD, Clk.

pp. 29-32 (On margin: "July 29th 1784 delivered this Deed to JAS: TAYLOR")

THIS INDENTURE made the fourth day of November in year of our Lord one thousand seven hundred & eighty three Between SAMUEL RODDY of Town of Fredericksburg, Mercht., and MARY his Wife of one part and JAMES TAYLOR, Mercht., of other part; Whereas one Lot lying in the said Town of Fredericksburg known in the plan of the said Town by the number Two hundred & fifty seven and bounded by CAROLINE STREET and PRUSSIA STREET and by lots numbered 256, 266 & 267 has been escheated under the Laws of the Commonwealth as the Property of WILLIAM SIMS, a British Subject, and as such sold by CHARLES WASHINGTON Esqr., late Escheator of the County of Spotsylvania, to JOHN WELCH, who in consequence of such sale procured a Grant thereof from THOMAS JEFFERSON Esqr. late Governor of Virginia, dated the tenth day of April in year one thousand seven hundred and eighty one; And Whereas the said JOHN WELCH and NELLY his Wife did afterwards by Deed dated the Twenty sixth day of December 1782 & recorded in the Court of Hustings in the said Borough of Fredericksburg sell the lot to the said SAMUEL RODDY and JAMES TAYLOR as Tenants in Common, And Whereas the said SAMUEL RODDY hath greed to sell all his right in the Lot afd., to the said JAMES TAYLOR, Now This Indenture Witnesseth that the said SAMUEL RODDY & MARY his Wife in consideration of the premisses and the sum of One hundred pounds current money have granted unto the said JAMES TAYLOR his heirs & assigns all his the said SAMUEL RODDYs moiety or one half of the Lot first mentioned and his interest therein and all houses buildings gardens profits belonging; To have and to hold unto the said JAMES TAYLOR his heirs & assigns and the sd. SAMUEL RODDY for himself & his heirs doth grant that he the said JAMES TAYLOR his heirs shall at all times hereafter quietly hold the aforesaid Lot without molestation of him the said SAMUEL RODDY & MARY his Wife; In Witness whereof the sd. SAMUEL RODDY & MARY his Wife have hereunto set their hands and affixed their seals

Sealed & delivered in the presence of

WILLIAM HARVEY, SAM: RODDY
JOHN McCALL, JOHN ANDERSON MARY RODDY

At a Hustings Court held for the Town and Corporation of Fredericksburg the Sixteenth day of February one thousand seven hundred and Eighty four

This Deed indented from SAMUEL RODDY & MARY his Wife (she being first privately examined) to JAMES TAYLOR acknowledged and ordered to be recorded

Test H. ARMISTEAD, Clk.

pp. 32-35 (On margin: "July 23rd 1784. Delivered this Deed to JAMES TAYLOR")

THIS INDENTURE of Partition made second day of November one thousand seven hundred and eighty three Between SAMUEL RODDY of Town of Fredericksburg and MARY his Wife of one part and JAMES TAYLOR of same place; Whereas two lotts in the Town of Fredericksburg known in the plan thereof by the numbers Thirty three and Thirty four, late the Property of MESSRS. COCKRON & COMPY., Merchants, and Subjects of GREAT BRITAIN, have been escheated under the Laws of this Common Wealth as Brittish Property, and as such sold by CHARLES WASHINGTON Esquire, Escheator of Spotsylvania County, to the said SAMUEL RODDY and JAMES TAYLOR, who in consequence of such sale have procured a grant thereof as Jointenants in fee simple from THOMAS JEFFERSON Esquire, late Governor of the Common Wealth of Virginia under the Seal of the same; as by the said Grant may appear dated the first day of February in year one thousand seven hundred and eighty one; And Whereas the said SAMUEL RODDY and JAMES TAYLOR have agreed to make partition and divide the said Lotts between them that each may hold his own part thereof by metes and bounded in the following manner; that is to say, the said JAMES TAYLORs part to begin on CAROLINE STREET at the Corner of the said Lott number Thirty three where it joins the Lott number Thirty five, the Corner to JACOB WHITTEY, running thence sixty five feet and two inches (more or less) along CAROLINE STREET to the corner of the STORE now occupied by the said SAMUEL RODDY and commonly known and called READ'S STORE, thence at right angles by a strait line running paralel to the Lott number Thirty five and Lott number Thirty six, and also paralel to WOOLF STREET till it intersects or runs to PRINCESS ANN STREET, which line is to be the dividing line between the said RODDY and TAYLOR, thence with PRINCESS ANN STREET to the Lott number Thirty six, thence with said Lotts number Thirty six and Thirty five to the beginning; The said SAMUEL RODDY's part to contain the ballance or remainder of said Lotts Thirty three and Thirty four and to begin where the said TAYLORs distance aforesaid on CAROLINE STREET ends, then on the said Street to the corner of said Lot number Thirty three and where CAROLINE STREET intersects WOOLF STREET, thence along WOOLF STREET till it intersects PRINCESS ANN STREET, thence with said Street to the dividing line aforesaid; then with said to the beginning; Now This Indenture Witnesses that the parties aforesaid in consideration of the premisses do grant unto each other respectively their heirs their respective parts of the lotts aforesaid as above laid off and do for themselves their heirs relinquish and give up to each other all right they have to the respective shares as above bounded; To have and to hold to them their heirs without any hindrance of the other party or their heirs; And lastly the said SAMUEL RODDY and his heirs the share of Lotts Thirty three and Thirty four made over to JAMES TAYLOR will warrant from claim of said SAMUEL RODDY & MARY his Wife and their heirs, And also the said JAMES TAYLOR and his heirs the share of the said lotts made over to said SAMUEL RODDY his heirs will warrant and defend from the claim of the said JAMES TAYLOR and his heirs; In Witness whereof the parties have set their hands and seals

In presence of WILLIAM HARVEY, SAMUEL RODDY
JOHN HALL, MARY RODDY
JNO: ANDERSON, JAMES TAYLOR

At a Court of Hustings held for the Town and Corporation of Fredericksburg on Monday the Sixteenth day of February one thousand seven hundred and Eighty four

This Deed of Partition between SAMUEL RODDY and MARY his Wife and JAMES TAYLOR (the said MARY RODDY being first privately examined) was acknowledged by the said SAMUEL & MARY & proved as to the said TAYLOR by the oaths of WILLIAM HARVEY, JOHN HALL & JOHN ANDERSON & is thereupon ordered to be recorded

Test HENRY ARMISTEAD, Clk.

pp. (On margin: "This Deed was sent to Mr. W. HARVEY pr. Order on Novr. 4th 1784")
36- THIS INDENTURE made the twenty first day of November in the year of our
39 Lord one thousand seven hundred and eighty three Between JAMES TAYLOR of
Town of Fredericksburg in County of Spotsylvania of one part and WILLIAM HARVEY of the same Town and County of other part; Witnesseth that the said JAMES TAYLOR for Seven hundred and fifty pounds current money of the State aforesaid hath sold unto the said WILLIAM HARVEY his heirs his portion of the Lotts number Thirty three and Thirty four in aforesaid Town of Fredericksburg bounding on CAROLINE

STREET at the corner of said Lott number Thirty three where it joins the Lott number Thirty five, the Corner to JACOB WHITTER & running thence Sixty five feet two inches more or less along CAROLINE STREET to the corner of the STORE now occupied by SAMUEL RODDY and commonly called READS STORE, thence at right angles by a straight line parallel to WOLFE STREET till it intersects lor runs to PRINCESS ANN STEET which is the dividing line between the said JAMES TAYLOR and SAMUEL RODDY, thence with PRINCESS ANN STREET to the Lott number Thirty six, thence with said Lotts number Thirty six and Thirty five to the beginning, Together with the Mansion or Dwelling House and all structures thereon standing; And all ways paths lights profits to said land belonging; To have and to hold the said land unto the said WILLIAM HARVEY his heirs and assigns forever and the said JAMES TAYLOR for himself his heirs against all persons will warrant and forever defend by these presents; In Witness whereof the parties have hereunto set their hands and seals
Signed sealed and delivered

SAM: RODDY, L. MACKINTOSH, JOHN BROWNLOW. G. C. TUCKER — JAMES TAYLOR

At a Court of Hustings held for the Town and Corporation of Fredericksburg on Monday the 16th day of February one thousand seven hundred and Eighty four

This Deed and Receipt from JAMES TAYLOR to WILLIAM HARVEY was proved by the oaths of GAVIN CORBIN TUCKER, LACKLIN MACKINTOSH & SAML. RODDY and ordered to be recorded Test HENRY ARMISTEAD, Clk.

pp. 40-42 THIS INDENTURE made the Tenth day of January one thousand seven hundred and eighty four Between ROBERT CUNNINGHAM of County of Spotsylvania, Planter, and ANN CUNNINGHAM, Widow and Relict of JAMES CUNNINGHAM, late of the said County, deceased, of one part and JOHN FRAZER of the Town of Fredericksburg, Merchant, of the other part; Whereas the said ROBERT CUNNINGHAM is possessed in two third parts of a Lot No. 127 containing half an acre in the Town of Fredericksburg, And also of the other third part in Revertion expectant on the death of his Mother; And also whereas the said ANN CUNNINGHAM is in immediate possession and occupation of the said other third part of the said lot in right of Dower, Now This Indenture Witnesseth that in consideration of Fifty pounds to him the said ROBERT CUNNINGHAM in hand paid; And in consideration of Six pounds lawful money of this Commonwealth to her the said ANN CUNNINGHAM in hand paid, they the said ROBERT & ANN CUNNINGHAM do grant all their the said ROBERT and ANN CUNNINGHAMs estate unto said JOHN FRAZER his heirs and assigns all their the said ROBERT and ANN CUNNINGHAMs right in the lot of land abovesaid, No. one hundred and twenty seven, containing half an acre in the Town of Fredericksburg, beginning in CHARLES STREET ajoining lot No. One hundred and twenty five running thence to the corner North 24 1/2 degrees West to WILLIAM STEEET, thence South 65 1/2 degrees West to Lot No. one hundred and twenty eight; thence South 24 1/2 degrees East to the corner adjoining Lotts No. one hundred and twenty heigh, one hundred and twenty six and one hundred and twenty five, thence North 65 1/2 degrees East to the beginning in CHARLES STREET, as described in a Deed from FIELDING LEWIS Esquire, deceased, to the aforesaid JAMES CUNNINGHAM of Record in Spotsylvania Court; To have & to hold unto the said JOHN FRAZER his heirs and assigns forever against all other persons whatsoever
Signed sealed and delivered in presents of

EDWD. HERNDON, THOMAS FOX, DAVID HENDERSON, JOHN CHUE — ROBERT CUNNINGHAM, ANN CUNNINGHAM

At a Hustings Court held for the Town and Corporation of Fredericksburg on Monday the Sixteenth day of February one thousand seven hundred and eighty four

This Deed from ROBERT CUNNINGHAM and ANN CUNNINGHAM was proved by the oaths of EDWARD HERNDON and DAVID HENDERSON and ordered to be certified;

And at a Court held for the said Town on Monday the (blank) day of (blank) this Deed was farther proved by the oaths of (blank) and ordered to be recorded

Test HENRY ARMISTEAD, Clk.

pp. 42- KNOW ALL MEN by these presents that we WILLIAM ROBINSON, JOHN ROBINSON, JAMES ALLAN, JNO: STEWARD are firmly bound unto WILLIAM McWILLIAMS, JAMES SOMERVILLE, GEORGE WEEDON, JOHN JULIAN and THOMAS MILLER Gent., Justices of Court of Hustings for Town and Corporation of Fredericksburg in the full sum of Eight thousand pounds current money of Virginia the payment of which we bind ourselves our heirs jointly and severally by these presents; dated this Sixteenth day of February 1784

The Condition of the above obligation is such that if WILLIAM ROBINSON & JOHN ROBINSON, Executors of the last Will & Testament of MICHAEL ROBINSON deceased, do cause to be made a perfect Inventory of all the goods chattels and credits of the said deceased which shall come to the hands of them and the same so made do exhibit unto the Court of Hustings for the Town & Corporation of Fredericksburg as shall be required do well and truly administer according to Law, and further make a true account of their doings therein when required & truely pay all Legacys as far as the goods & credits will extend & as the Law shall charge them, Then this obligation to be void

WILLIAM ROBINSON
JOHN ROBINSON
JAMES ALLAN
JOHN STEWARD

(No recording shown.)

pp. 44-46 TO ALL PEOPLE to whom these presents shall come I JAMES THOMPSON sometimes called JAMES CARTER of STAFFORD County in the State of Virginia in America send Greeting. Whereas my Mother, MARY THOMPSON, late of PINSFORD in SOMERSETSHIRE in that part of the Kingdom of GREAT BRITAIN called ENGLAND departed this life some years ago possessed of a considerable Estate real and personal, And I am informed that by her last Will & Testament she has left me a Legacy of One hundred and fifty pounds Sterling or thereabouts; Now Know ye that I the said JAMES THOMPSON have made SAMUEL JAMES now or late of EMBER COPPER MILLS in the County of SURRY near HAMPTON COURT in that part of the Kingdom of GREAT BRITAIN afsd. my true and lawful Agent & Attorney for me to receive of the Executors or Administrators of my Mother afsd., or any other persons, all legacies left to me by the Will of my Mother afsd., or any Estate, money or other thing which I may be entitled under the Will, or that may have fallen to me by the death of my Mother afsd., and on failure of payment I do empower my said Attorney in my name to sue for the same to recover Judgment for the same and in every respect regarding the premisses to act & do as amply as I could were I personally present; In Witness whereof I have hereunto set my hand and affixed my seal the third day of May in the year of our Lord one thousand seven hundred & eighty four

Sealed and delivered in presence of

EDWD. KNIGHT on the Ship *"THOMASON"*
where there were no Stamps

JAMES THOMPSON

At a Court of Hustings held for the Town and Corporation of Fredericksburg (in the State of Virginia in the Eighth year of the Commonwealth) on Monday the third day of May one thousand seven hundred and eighty four, JAMES THOMPSON came personally into Court and acknowledged this Instrument as his true & lawful Power of Attorney to SAMUEL JAMES which is ordered to be recorded

Test HENRY ARMISTEAD, Clerk

pp. (On margin: August 10th 1785 examd. & delvd. to WM. HARVEY H. A.)
46- THIS INDENTURE made the twenty seventh day of September in year of our Lord
50 one thousand seven hundred & eighty three Between JAMES JEMISON of ORANGE County & LUCY his Wife of the one part and WILLIAM HARVEY of the Borough of Fredericksburg of the other part; Witnesseth that for Forty five pounds current money of Virginia they the said JAMES JEMISON & LUCY his Wife have granted unto the said WILLIAM HARVEY & his heirs all that Lott or half acre of Ground being in the Town of Fredericksburg described in the plan of the said Town by the No. (219) and lies back of the Lot belonging to ANDREW FRAZER on PRINCESS AUGUSTUS and FREDERICK Streets and all houses orchards waters & appurtenances belonging; To have and to hold unto the said WILLIAM HARVEY his heirs and assigns forever; And the said JAMES JEMISON for himself his heirs doth grant the said land now are free from all former grants (the Quit rents hereafter to grow due & payable to the State of Virginia only excepted) And that the said JAMES JEMISON and his heirs unto the said WILLIAM HARVEY will warrant and forever defend by these presents; In Witness whereof the said JAMES JAMISON and LUCY his Wife have set their hands and seals

Sealed & delivered in presence of

G. C. TUCKER, JN: MOALTSON — JAMES JAMESON
JOHN HARDIA, ZACHS: NOWLES — LUCY JAMESON

At a Hustings Court held for Town and Corporation of Fredericksburg on Monday the first day of March 1784

This Deed from JAMES JAMESON & LUCY his Wife was proved by two of the witnesses and ordered to be certified; And at a Court held for the said Corporation on Monday the third day of May 1784, this Deed was further proved by the oath of (blank) and ordered to be recorded Test HENRY ARMISTEAD

Common Wealth of Virginia to JAMES SUMMERVILLE, CHARLES MORTIMORE & JOHN JULIAN Gent., Justices of the Town and Corporation of Fredericksburg; Whereas JAMES JAMESON and LUCY JAMESON his Wife have conveyed unto WILLIAM HARVEY one half acre lot in Fredericksburg and said LUCY JAMESON cannot travel to our Court of Hustings to make her personal acknowledgement, we authorize you to go to the said LUCY and her examine separate from her said Husband whether she doth freely acknowledge the said Indenture and such acknowledgement as she shall make send certified under your hands & seals; Witness HENRY ARMISTEAD, Clerk of our said Court Hustings this Twenty seventh day of September 1783 in the Eighth year of the Common Wealth

HENRY ARMISTEAD, Clerk

At a Hustings Court held for the Corporation of Fredericksburg on Monday the first day of March 1784

This Commission was returned & ordered to be recorded

Test HENRY ARMISTEAD, Clk.

pp. (On margin: Delivd. to JOS: CHRISTIE June 4th 1785)
51- THIS INDENTURE made the first day of March one thousand seven hundred and
53 Eighty four Between WILLIAM JACKSON and FRANCES his Wife of the County of Spotsylvania and Town of Fredericksburg of the one part and JOSEPH CHRISTY of

the same County & Town of the other part; Witnesseth that WILLIAM JACKSON and FRANCES his Wife for Two hundred and fifty pounds current money of Virginia hath sold unto the said JOSEPH CHRISTY and his heirs one parcel of Ground in the County of Spotsylvania and Town of Fredericksburg lying on the South side of CAROLINE STREET and beginning at the lower corner of the House formerly occupied by WILLIAM HOUSTON and purchased by JOHN WIGGLESWORTH of him, since occupied by JOHN GREEN and WILLIAM SMOCK, running along CAROLINE STREET thirty eight feet, thence right angles to the COURT HOUSE Lott, thence along the COURT HOUSE Lott downward seventeen feet, thence right angles toward CAROLINE STREET til it comes within thirty four feet of front of said Street, thence turning downwards paralel with said Street twelve feet, thence turning to sd. CAROLINE STREET fourteen feet, thence downward paralel with said Street nineteen feet, thence turning right angles to the said CAROLINE STREET twenty feet along the side of said House occupied as aforesaid by sd. WILLIAM HOUSTON since by JOHN GREEN & lately by WILLIAM SMOCK to the beginning; including the said House and reference being had to two several Deeds from JOHN WIGGLESWORTH to WILLIAM JACKSON recorded in Spotsylvania Court may more fully appear; To have and to hold to the said JOSEPH CHRISTY and his heirs or assigns against the demand of the said WILLIAM JACKSON and FRANCES his Wife or any other person
Signed sealed acknowledged & delivered in presents of
WILLIAM SMITH, WILLIAM JACKSON
JOHN DAWSON, GODLOVE HEISKELL FRANCES JACKSON

At a Hustings Court held for the Town and Corporation of Fredericksburg on Monday the fifth day of April one thousand seven hundred and eighty four
This Deed was acknowledged by FRANCES JACKSON (she being first privately examd.) and proved by the witnesses as to WILLIAM JACKSON and ordered to be recorded
Test H. ARMISTEAD, Clk.

pp. (On margin: SOMERVILLE to FREDS. LODGE Deld. R. B. CHEW)
53- THIS INDENTURE made the fifth day of April in year of our Lord one thousand
57 seven hundred & eighty four Between JAMES SOMERVILLE of the Borough of
Fredericksburg Gent. of the one part; CHARLES MORTIMER, WILLIAM McWILLIAMS, ALEXANDER DICK, JOHN JULIAN, EDWARD SIMPSON, FRANCIS THORNTON, GEORGE WEEDON, ELIEZER CALLENDER, THOMAS MILLAR and DAVID GALLOWAY JUNR., Gent. of second part, and the FREDERICKSBURG LODGE of FREE MASONS of the Third part; Witnesseth that the said JAMES SOMERVILLE in consideration of the sum of Forty pounds current money to him in hand paid by the said LODGE hath sold unto the said (the names of those listed above) a certain lot of Ground in the said Town & Borough of Fredericksburg known & described in the plan of the said Town by the number 125; Together with all houses buildings ways to the same belonging; To have and to hold the said Lot number 125 with all its appurtenances unto them & their heirs in Trust & to and for the use of the Master, Wardens, Officers, Fellows and Brethern of the said FREDERICKSBURG LODGE and their Successor Members of the said LODGE forever; and for no other use whatsoever; And that the said JAMES SOMERVILLE & his heirs the above sold lot & premisses unto the said Trustees and their heirs for purposes aforesaid against the claim of every person whatsoever will warrant and forever defend by these presents, and do agree that if at any time hereafter they or their heirs shall fail in the performance thereof or shall put the Lot & premisses afsd. to any other use, then as before mentioned without the consent of the said LODGE first had and obtained that then this Deed shall be void; In Witness whereof the said JAMES SOMERVILLE and the Trustees have hereunto set their hands & affixed their seals

ELIEZER CALLENDAR W. McWILLIAMS JAMES SOMERVILLE
DAVID GALLOWAY G. WEEDON CHS. MORTIMER
EDWD. SIMPSON FRANS. THORNTON
JOHN JULIAN THOS: MILLER

At a Court of Hustings held for the Town & Corporation of Fredericksburg April 5th 1784 This Indenture was acknowledged and ordered to be recorded
Test H. ARMISTEAD, Clk.

pp. THIS INDENTURE made the Twenty seventh day of May in year of our Lord one
58- thousand seven hundred & eighty four Between HENRY FLEET of the County of
61 ORANGE & State of Virginia and MILDRED his Wife of the one part and WILLIAM WIATT of the Town of Fredericksburg and State aforesaid on the other part; Witnesseth that for Sixteen pounds Thirteen shillings & Four pence current money of Virginia to HENRY FLEET whereof he hath granted to the said WILLIAM WIATT his heirs & assigns in fee simple for ever all that Lot or half acre of Ground in the said Town of Fredericksburg being the lowermost Lott in the Town on the South West side of PRINCESS AUGUSTA STREET, and is described in the plan of the said Town by the number (206), and all houses buildings orchards ways appertaining to the said Lott; To have and to hold the said lands to the said WILLIAM WIATT his heirs and assigns forever and the said HENRY FLEET and MILDRED his Wife for himself and his heirs tht the said premisses are clear of any incumbrances whatsoever and as will appear by ROGER DIXON & LUCY his Wifes Deed to his Father bearing date the third day of September in the year one thousand seven hundred and Sixty four in the Town of Fredericksburg to WILLIAM FLEET of KING and QUEEN County and acknowledged by the said ROGER DIXON in Spotsylvania County Court in March 5th 1765 and recorded, And by the death of the said WILLIAM FLEET, I the said HENRY FLEET, as heir at Law, became possessed of the Lot & premisses aforesaid; And that the said HENRY FLEET and MILDRED his Wife shall warrant and forever defend by these presents; In Witness whereof the said HENRY FLEET and MILDRED his Wife have set their hands and affixed their seals
Signed sealed & delivered in presence of
DAVID BLAIR, JAMES BROWN, HENRY FLEET
JOHN ANDERSON, WILLIAM ORR MILDRED FLEET

The Commonwealth of Virginia to ZACH: BURNLEY & THOMAS BARBOUR, Gent. Justices of the County Court of ORANGE Greeting; Whereas HENRY FLEET and MILDRED his Wife have conveyed unto WILLIAM WIATT a Lott or half acre of Ground in the Town of Fredericksburg and Whereas the said MILDRED cannot travel to our Court of Hustings to make her personal acknowledgement of the said Indenture, we require you to examine her separate from her Husband whether she freely acknowledges the same and and send certified under your hands and seals without delay sending this Commission; Witness HENRY ARMISTEAD Clk. of our said Court of Hustings this Ninth day of June 1784 in the Eighth year of the Common Wealth
HENRY ARMISTEAD, Clk.

ORANGE County to wit: Pursuant to this Commission, we have examined Mrs. MILDRED FLEET, Wife of HENRY FLEET, and she did freely without the threats of her said Husband acknowledge the said Indenture this 19th day of June 1784
ZACH: BURNLEY
THOMAS BARBOUR

pp. THIS INDENTURE made this third day of June in year of our Lord one thousand
62- seven hundred and eighty four Between JOHN HALL of the Town of Fredericks-
66 burg and JOHN HORNER and PATTY his Wife of one part and JOHN HAWKINS of
the County of CAROLINE of the other part; Witnesseth that for Six hundred and twenty pounds current money of Virginia, they have this day granted unto the said JOHN HAWKINS and his heirs and assigns all that certain parcel of land sold by ROBERT JURDIN being part of a Lott in the said Town of Fredericksburg and numbered in the first plant thereof 43 and bounded as follows; Beginning on Main Street of said Town called CAROLINE STREET at the Intersection of said Street and GEORGE STREET, thence down CAROLINE STREET to the North end of the LONG ORDINARY, thence at a right angle from CAROLINE and parallel with GEORGE STREET, one hundred and thirty two feet to the COURT HOUSE LOTT, thence with the line of the COURT HOUSE LOTT and parallel with CAROLINE STREET to GEORGE STREET and along GEORGE STREET to the beginning, except so much thereof as was sold or intended to be sold to JOHN ATKINSON by GEORGE MITCHELL which is bounded as follows; Beginning on CAROLINE STREET thirty three feet above the North end of the LONG ORDINARY, thence along CAROLINE STREET thirty three feet to the end of the LONG ORDINARY, thence at a right angle from CAROLINE STREET (the second line afore described) one hundred and thirty two feet to the COURT HOUSE LOTT aforementioned; thence with the line of the COURT HOUSE LOTT and parallel with CAROLINE STREET thirty seven and half feet, thence by a direct line to the beginning of this last Dividend; unto the said HAWKINS and his heirs and assigns forever; and the said JOHN HALL, JOHN HORNER and PATTY his Wife for themselves their heirs shall warrant and forever defend by these presents; In Witness whereof the said JOHN HALL, JOHN HORNER and PATTY his Wife have set their hands and seals

In presence of ANTHONY McKITTRICK, JOHN HALL
Evidence to Mr. & Mrs. HORNER acknowledgmt. JOHN HORNER
EDWARD MOORE, WILLIAM TAYLOR, PATTY HORNER
JAMES SOMERVILLE, WILLIAM PORTER

The Commonwealth of Virginia to HARRIS HOE, DANIEL TRIPLITT Gent., Justices of the County of STAFFORD Greeting; Whereas MESSRS. JOHN HALL & JOHN HORNER & PATTY his Wife have sold part of a Lott of Land unto JNO: HAWKINS and Whereas the said PATTY cannot travel to our Court of Hustings of Fredericksburg to make acknowledgement of the same; We give you power to receive her acknowledgement apart from the said JOHN her Husband and that you certify us thereof in our said Court; Witness HENRY ARMISTEAD Clerk at the Courthouse the 4th day of June one thousand seven hundred and eighty four and in the Eighth year of the Common Wealth

HENRY ARMISTEAD, Clk.

STAFFORD to wit: Pursuant to the above Commission, we did go to PATTY HORNER and examined her apart from her Husband and she acknowledged the same to be without his persuasions; Given under our hands and seals this 5th day of June 1784

HARRIS HOOE
DANIEL TRIPLETT

At a Court of Hustings held for the Corporation of Fredericksburg on Monday the second day of August 1784

This Deed from JOHN HALL, JOHN HORNER and PATTY HORNER with a Commission for her privy examination, the said Deed was acknowledged by JOHN HALL and proved as to the said JOHN HORNER by the Oath of WILLIAM TAYLOR, which is ordered to be certified,

And at a Court held the sixth day of December 1784; This Deed was farther proved by the Oaths of WILLIAM TAYLOR, EDWARD MOOR & ANTHY. McKETERICK as to JOHN HORNER which with the Commission annexed is ordered to be recorded

Test HENRY ARMISTEAD, Clk.

pp. TO ALL PEOPLE to whom these presents indented writing shall come, ALEXAN-
67- DER DICK of County of Spotsylvania and Town of Fredericksburg sendeth
68 Greeting; Wheresa the said ALEXANDER DICK is seized and possessed of a considerable Estate both real and personal, consisting of Messuages, Lands, Tenements, slaves, goods & chattels and being about to depart from the Town and County aforesaid to the OHIO, and the lands on the Western Waters, doth therefore by these presents authorize the Honorable JAMES MERCER Esquire of the aforesaid Town & County to seel and dispose of any part of the said Estate and deliver such writing and agreements as proper, And further the said ALEXANDER doth constitute the said JAMES his true and lawfull Attorney and Agent, and doth commit to the said JAMES the care and management of the whole Estate of the said ALEXANDER, to receive all rents duties and the whole profits and in his name discharges for the same; Also to pay any just Debts and execute all lawful acts as shall be needful to be done, giving unto the said JAMES MERCER the said ALEXANDER DICKs full power and holding firm whatever the said JAMES MERCER may do by virtue of these presents as if the said ALEXANDER DICK was personally present; and performed the same himself; In Witness whereof the said ALEXANDER DICK hath set his hand and seal this ninth day of February one thousand seven hundred and eighty four

Sealed and delivered in presence of

JNO: FRAZER, BR: FRAZER, ALEXANDER DICK
WILLM. ZIMMERMAN, GUST. WALLACE;
G. WEEDON

(No recording shown.)

p. This is to Certify that I HENRY HEAD of Spotsylvania County and Corporation of
69 Fredericksburg have this day sold & delivered unto JNO. WEAGLESWORTH of said County one Negro wench Daphney and Child (by name of Henry) which property I warrant and defend unto the said WEAGLESWORTH his heirs &c., from all claims whatever; this seventeenth day of March one thousand seven hundred & eighty four

The Condition of the above obligation is such that if the above bound HENRY HEAD shall pay unto the said WEAGLESWORTH or his heirs &c., the sum of Eighty seven pounds current money on or before the first day of December next ensuing, then the above mentioned Negro wench to become then the property of the said HEAD else remain in full force and virtue

Signed sealed & delivered in presence of

SIMON FRINSLEY, JOHN ATKINSON HENRY HEAD

At a Hustings Court held for the Town and Corporation of Fredericksburg May 1784 This Bill of Sale from HENRY HEAD to JOHN WEGGLESWORTH was acknowledged by the said HEAD and ordered to be recorded

Test HENRY ARMISTEAD, Clk.

pp. (On margin: July 29th 1784 delivered this Deed to JAMES TAYLOR the rect. 308)
70- THIS INDENTURE made the Twenty secon day of November in year of our Lord
73 one thousasnd seven hundred and Eighty three Between WILLIAM HARVEY and FRANCES his Wife of the Town of Fredericksburg in County of Spotsylvania of the one part and JAMES TAYLOR of the same Town and County of the other part; Witnesseth that for the sum of Three hundred and fifty pounds current money of Virginia the said WILLIAM HARVEY and FRANCES his Wife have sold unto the said JAMES TAYLOR his heirs or assigns forever, his portion of the Lotts number Thirty three and Thirty four situate in the aforesaid Town, butting and bounding as following; to wit, Beginning on

CAROLINE STREET at the Corner of the said Lott number Thirty three where it joins the Lott number Thirty five the corner of JACOB WHITLER and running thence thirty five feet two inches more or less along CAROLINE STREET to the Corner of the STORE now occupied by SAMUEL RODDY and commonly called READS STORE, thence at right angles by a straight line parallel to WOLF STREET till it intersects or runs to PRINCESS ANNE STREET to the Lott number Thirty six, thence with the said Lotts number Thirty six and Thirty five to the beginning, Together with the houses and improvements thereon; To have and to hold to the said JAMES TAYLOR his heirs and assigns forever; PROVIDED Nevertheless that if the said WILLIAM HARVEY his heirs do well and truly pay to the said JAMES TAYLOR the sum of Three hundred and fifty pounds current money on or before the Twenty second day of May next ensuing; then this present Indenture shall cease and that in case any default shall happen to be made, it shall be lawful for the said JAMES TAYLOR into all the hereby sold premisses to enter and the same to hold for the only use and behoof of the said JAMES TAYLOR without any denial of him the said WILLIAM HARVEY and FRANCES his Wife; And Lastly it is hereby mutually agreed between the parties that until default shall be made in payment of the said sum, he the said JAMES TAYLOR will permit the said WILLIAM HARVEY his heirs to occupy the said premisses without rendering any account to him the said JAMES TAYLOR; In Witness whereof the parties have set their hands and seals

Sealed & delivered in presence of
SAM: RODDEY, LAC: MACKINTOSH, WM. HARVEY
JOHN BROWNLOW; JOHN BROWN SENR. FRANCES HARVEY

Received this Twenty second day of November one thousand seven hundred and eighty three from JAMES TAYLOR the sum being the consideration money mentioned
Witness SAM: RODDEY, LAC: MACKINTOSH, WM. HARVEY
JOHN BROWNLOW. G. C. TUCKER

At a Court of Hustings held for the Town and Corporation of Fredericksburg on Monday the Seventh day of June one thousand seven hundred and eighty four

This Indenture from WILLIAM HARVEY and FRANCES his Wife to JAMES TAYLOR with the Receipt thereon was proved by the oaths of SAMUEL RODDY, LAC: MACKINTOSH and JOHN BROWNLOW and ordered to be recorded

Test HENRY ARMISTEAD, Clk.

pp. THIS INDENTURE made the fifth day of July in year of our Lord one thousand
73- seven hundred and Eighty four Between ALEXANDER DICK of Town of
Fredericksburg in the County of Spotsylvania Esquire of the one part; & SAMUEL ARRELL & DAVID ARRELL of the Town of ALEXANDRIA in County of FAIRFAX, Merchants, of the other part; Witnesseth that for the sum of Two hundred pounds good & lawful money paid, the said ALEXANDER DICK hath sold unto the said SAMUEL & DAVID ARRELL their heirs one certain peice of land containing about a quarter of an acre; being parcel of one certain Lott of Land being within the limitts of the said Town of Fredericksburg and numberd in the plan of the said Town 5 the said land being bounded on the South East of GEORGE STREET, on the South West by SOPHIA STREET, on the North East by RAPPAHANNOCK RIVER & on the North West by the dividing line of the opposite square on the South West continued to the River, together with all ways waters advantages to the said land; To have and to hold unto the said SAMUEL & DAVID ARRELL as Tenants in Common and not as Jointenants; And their respective heirs and assigns without the lawful hindrance or denial of him the said ALEXANDER DICK or his heirs or any other persons whatsoever; In Witness whereof the said ALEXANDER DICK hath set his hand and seal

Signed sealed & delivered in presence of
(no witnesses shown) ALEXANDER DICK
(Ackd.) See Minutes of 5th July 1784

p. 75 Received of Mr. THOMAS ALLEN one bay Horse for which I acknowledge the Receipt of Two thousand nine hundred pounds of tobacco at Fifteen shillings per Hundred, balance due on a Bond from ALLEN J. ATKINSON now in hand of MESSRS. LAPORT & GALAVAN & COMPANY
June 24th 1782 Test EDWD. SIMPSON ELISHA SMITH
At a Hustings Court held for the Town and Corporation of Fredericksburg on Monday the seventh day of June 1784
This Rect. was proved by the oath of EDWARD SIMPSON & ordered to be recorded
Test HENRY ARMISTEAD, Clk.

p. 76 KNOW ALL MEN by these presents that I HENRY HEAD of the Town of Fredericksburg in the County of Spotsylvania hath granted and sold unto JOHN RICHARDS of the Town and County aforesaid, a certain Negro boy cal'd Charles now about the age of Sixteen years; for the consideration of the sum of Fifty pounds current money to me paid by the said JOHN RICHARDS, which said Negro I warrant and forever defend against the claims of every person whatsoever; of the performance of which I bind my self my heirs by these presents; Sealed with my seal and dated this Fourth day of March one thousand seven hundred and Eighty four
Sealed & delivered in presence of
EDWARD HERNDON, HENRY HEAD
EZEKIEL HAYDON
(No recording shown)

pp. 77-78 KNOW ALL MEN by these presents that I HENRY HEAD of the Town of Fredericksburg in County of Spotsylvania hath sold unto JOHN RICHARDS of the Town and County aforesaid a certain Negro wench cal'd by the name of Daphney now about the age of Eighteen years and her Child cal'd by the name of Harry now about the age of three years for the consideration of Fifty pounds current money to me paid by the said JOHN RICHARDS, which said Negros I will warrant and forever defend against the claim of all persons for the performance of which I bind my self by these presents; Sealed with my seal and dated the Fifth day of March one thousand seven hundred and Eighty four
Sealed and delivered in presence of
JAMES BERRY, HENRY HEAD
ROBT. WALKER
Apl. 29th 1784. In presence of us this day we seen the within named HENRY HEAD deliver a Negro wench named Davney & her Child a boy about three years old by the name of Harry to JOHN RICHARDS & acknowledged them to be the said RICHARDS property, his Wife, the said HEADs, consenting thereto
Witness our hands the day and year first within written EDWARD SIMPSON
THOMAS MILLER
At a Hustings Court held for the Town of Fredericksburg on Monday the (blank) day of (blank) one thousand seven hundred and eighty four
This Bill of Sale from HENRY HEAD to JOHN RICHARDS was acknowledged by the said HENRY HEAD and is ordered to be recorded
Test HENRY ARMISTEAD, Clk.

pp. 78-80 THIS INDENTURE made the tenth day of October in year of our Lord one thousandseven hundred and Eighty two Between DANIEL PAYNE of Town of FALMOUTH in the County of STAFFORD of the one part and WILLIAM JENCKINS of the Borough of Fredericksburg in the County of Spotsylvania of the other part; Witnesseth that the said DANIEL PAYNE for sum of Five shillings current money to him in hand pad by WILLIAM JINCKINS hath let and to farm let unto the said WILLIAM JENKINS one Lot of Ground in the said Borough of Fredericksburg whereon the said WILLIAM JINKINS now dwells, and particularly described in the plan of the said Borough by the number 56 Together with all benefits and advantages belonging; To have and to hold unto the said WILLIAM JENKINS from the day of the date hereof and during the term of Nine years to commence on the first day of January in the year one thousand seven hundred and Eighty three, the said WILLIAM JINKINS paying unto the said DANIEL PAYNE his heirs the sum of Sixteen pounds specie or hard money in every year during the term foresaid (to wit) Eight pounds on the first day of July one thousand seven hundred and Eighty three and the further sum of Eight pounds on the first day of January one thousand seven hundred and eighty four, and so to continue his two regular payments on the first day of July and first day of January that happens in each of the Eight following years, the specie or hard money to be in silver dollars at Six shillings each dollar as in other Silver or Gold coin in proportion thereto, together with all taxes charges and incumbrances that shall become due on the said Lot of Ground and the said WILLIAM JENKINS further agrees that he will not sell rent or dispose of this Lease without the consent of the said DANIEL PAYNE his heirs; In Witness whereof the parties have set their hands and seals
Signed sealed and delivered in presence of
CHS: YATES, RICHARD KENNEY, DANL. PAYNE
THOS: KENNEY WILLIAM JENKINS
At a Hustings Court held for the Town and Corporation of Fredericksburg on Monday the (the recording was not completed)

pp. 80-81 THIS INDENTURE made the Twenty second day of October one thousand seven hundred and eighty four Between ALEXANDER DICK of the Town of Fredericksburg in the County of Spotsylvania, Gentleman, of the one part and LAURENCE SLAUGHTER of the County of CULPEPER & State aforesaid, Gentleman, of the other part; Witnesseth that the said ALEXANDER DICK for sum of Five hundred pounds hath sold unto the said LAURENCE SLAUGHTER his heirs & assigns forever all that Lott being partly within and partly without the present limits of the said Town of Fredericksburg commonly known by the name of the MEADOW LOTT of said DICK containing Ten acres more or less bounded to wit; on the North East by ALLIN TOWN, on the South East by the land of WILLIAM JACKSON, on the South West by the land of LEWIS WILLIS and on the North West by the land of JOHN LEWIS, with all the rights of him the said ALEXANDER DICK; To have and to hold unto the said LAURENCE SLAUGHTER his heirs and assigns forever against him and his heirs and all persons whatsoever will warrant & forever defend by these presents; In Witness whereof the said ALEXANDER DICK hath set his hand and seal
Sealed & delivered in presence of
WILLM. WADDLE, ALEXR: DICK
ABNER VERNON, G. BOSWELL
At a Court of Hustings held for the Town & Corporation of Fredericksburg on Monday the first day of November one thousand seven hundred and eighty four
This Deed indented from ALEXANDER DICK to LAURENCE SLAUGHTER was proved by the

oaths of WILLIAM WADDLE & GEORGE BOSWELL and ordered to be recorded; And at a Court held the Sixth day of December 1784, this Deed was farther proved by the Oath of ABNER VERNON and ordered to be recorded

Test HENRY ARMISTEAD, Clk.

pp. 82-84 (On margin: Deliv. to JAMES SOMERVILLE 9th Nov. 1785)

THIS INDENTURE made the Sixteenth day of October in the year of our Lord one thousand seven hundred and eighty four Between ROBERT JOHNSTON of the Town of PORT ROYAL, Merchant, and JANE his Wife of the one part and JAMES SOMERVELLE of the Town of Frederickburg, Merchant, of the other part; Witnesseth that the said ROBERT JOHNSTON & JANE his Wife in consideration of the sum of Thirty pounds current money to them paid hath granted unto the said JAMES SOMERVELLE his heirs & assigns a tract of Ground in the said Town of Fredericksburg known in the plan of the said Town by the number Two hundred & seventy four; which moiety the said ROBERT JOHNSTON purchased of JOHN MITCHELL and the part thereof which is hereby intended to be conveyed is described and bounded Beginning on WATER STREET at the distance of Twenty seven feet from the Lowermost corner of said Lot at the intersection of FREDERICK & WATER STREETs, and running thence up WATER STREET twenty seven feet, thence to the RIVER RAPPAHANNOCK on a line parallel to FREDERICK STREET aforesaid; thence down the River twenty seven feet or half way between the last mentioned corner and the lowermost corner of the said Lot on the River side; thence a straight line through the middle of a WAREHOUSE built on the said Lott at the joint expence of the said JOHNSTON & SOMERVILLE to the first beginning; so as to include one full half of the WAREHOUSE afd., Together with all houses buildings ways waters to the same belonging To have and to hold unto the said JAMES SOMERVILLE his heirs and assigns to hold and enjoy without the hindrance of said ROBERT JOHNSTON & JANE his Wife and their heirs; And it is further agreed between the said parties for themselves their heirs that they & each of them may at all times hereafter as Tenants in Common enjoy & make use of the Passage of Eight feet running through the Middle of the WAREHOUSE afsd., without any interruption from the other party for the purpose of taking in & delivering out goods & merchandizes, but that either party his heirs or assigns shall have the liberty of running up a Partition along the middle of the Passage so as to leave an equal space on each side, and this to be done at the joint expence of both parties their heirs; And Whereas the said ROBERT JOHNSTON holds twenty seven feet below & twenty eight feet & one half above the aforesaid parcell of Ground sold to the said JAMES SOMERVILLE, it is hereby agreed that the said SOMERVILLE may at all times hereafter be allowed a free passage along the River side upon the said JOHNSTONs part of the said Lot, wide enough for a Waggon to pass with ease and that the said ROBERT JOHNSTON his heirs shall have the same liberty & passage along the River upon the peice of ground above sold to the said JAMES SOMERVILLE, In Witness whereof the said parties have set their hands and seals

Sealed and delivered in presence of

JAMES ALLAN, GARL: THOMPSON, AARON McCLINTOCK

ROBT. JOHNSTON
JAMES SOMERVILLE

At a Court Hustings held for the Town and Corporation of Fredericksburg on Monday the first day of November one thousand seven hundred and eighty four

This Deed of Partition between ROBERT JOHNSTON and JAMES SOMERVILLE was acknowledged by the said SOMERVILLE and proved as to ROBERT JOHNSTON by GARLAND THOMPSON and JAMES ALLEN and is ordered to be recorded; And at a Court held the sixth day of December 1784; This Deed was further proved by the Oath of AARON McCLINTOCK and is ordered to be recorded Test HENRY ARMISTEAD, Clk.

pp. KNOW ALL MEN by these presents that I JAMES ALLAN SENR. of the Borough of
85- Fredericksburg in the State of Virginia in America have made WILLIAM
86 CLELAND, Doctor of Physick, of ARCEHINLEE near the Town of HAMILTON in that
part of GREAT BRITAIN called SCOTLAND my true and lawfull Attorney for my use to sell in any manner that shall be thought proper and most for my advantage a peice of Land lying in the Haugh of HAMILTON aforesaid; supposed to contain one acre lying now in the possession of his Grace, the DUKE of HAMILTON, and which descended from my Brother, JOHN ALLAN, and is commonly called by the name of the SMITHLAND BUTTS and do hereby empower him to make legal Deeds of Conveyance to the purchaser for the same in fee simple agreeable to the Laws and Customs of the said County in which the land lies; and to receive the purchase money therefore, and on payment to give good discharges so as to be binding on me my heirs and in every respect to do as fully as I could were I personally present, hereby confirming whatever my said Attorney shall legally do in the premises; In Witness whereof I have set my hand and affixed my Seal the seventh day of February in the year of our Lord one thousand seven hundred and Eighty five

Sealed and delivered in presence of
(no witnesses shown) JAMES ALLAN

p. (On margin: Delivd. to JA: SOMERVILLE Novr. 9, 1785)
86 KNOW ALL MEN by these presents that I JAMES WEIR of the Corporation of
Fredericksburg Virginia for the sum of Three hundred and twenty pounds, Five shillings and three pence Sterlg., to me in hand paid by JAMES SOMERVILLE of said Corporation, Merchant, have sold the following slaves, to wit, Moll, Jeaney, Jeaney the Child of Moll, Patty, Fanny the Child of Patty, George the Child of Phillis and Isaac, To have and to hold all the said slaves with their future increase unto JAMES SOMERVILLE his heirs against all persons will warrant and forever defend by these presents; In Witness whereof I have set my hand & seal this thirteenth day of July one thousand seven hundred and Eighty four

Sealed & delivered in presence of
JAMES DUNLAP JAMES WEIR

pp. (On margin: Delivd. Nov. 9th 1785 to Mr. JAS. SOMERVILLE)
87- THIS INDENTURE made the Sixteenth day of October in year of our Lord one
87- thousand seven hundred and eighty four Between JAMES SOMERVELLE of the
Town of Fredericksburg, Merchant, of the one part and ROBERT JOHNSTON of the Town of PORT ROYAL, Merchant, of the other part; Witnesseth that the said JAMES SOMERVELLE for sum of Thirty pounds current money have sold unto the said ROBERT JOHNSTON his heirs and assigns, a part of the moiety of a Lott of Ground in the Town of Fredericksburg known in the plan of the said Town by the number Two hundred & seventy four; which moiety the said SOMERVELLE purchased of JOHN MITCHELL and the part or dividend thereof which is hereby intended to be conveyed is described & bounded as follows, Vizt., Beginning on WATER STREET at the distance of Eighty two and one half feet from the lowermost corner of said Lott at the intersection of FREDERICK & WATER STREETs, and running thence up WATER STREET seven feet; thence to the RIVER RAPPAHANNOCK on a line paralel to FREDERICK STREET aforesaid; thence down the River seven feet; thence in a streight line to WATER STREET the beginning, together with all houses buildings wasy to the same belonging; To have and to hold unto the said ROBERT JOHNSTON his heirs & assigns without the molestation of the said JAMES SOMERVILLE and his heirs or any person claiming under him; And it is hereby further agreed

between the said parties that they as Tenants in Common be allowed a free passage along the River side from the said ROBERT JOHNSTONs upper line to the remaining parts of said Lott belonging to the said JAMES SOMERVILLE wide enough for a Waggon to pass with ease and that the said ROBERT JOHNSTON his heirs shall have the same liberty and passage along the River side upon the Ground of twenty seven feet from part of the said Lott which the said SOMERVILLE purchased of the said ROBERT JOHNSON, In Witness whereof the said parties have set their hands and seals

Sealed & delivered in presence of

JAMES ALLEN, JAMES SOMERVILLE

GARL: THOMPSON, AARON McCLINTOCK ROBT. JOHNSTON

At a Hustings Court held for the Town and Corporation of Fredericksburg on Monday the first day of November one thousand seven hundred and eighty four

This Deed indented of Partition between JAMES SOMERVILLE and ROBERT JOHNSTON acknowledged by the said JAMES SOMERVILLE and porved as to ROBERT JOHNSTON by the oaths of GARLAND THOMPSON and JAMES ALLEN and ordered to be Certified

At a Court of Hustings held for the Town and Corporation of Fredericksburg on Monday the Sixth day of December 1784

This Deed Indented of Partition was farther proved by the Oath of AARON McCLINTOCK and ordered to be recorded

Test HENRY ARMISTEAD, Clk.

pp. (On margin: The Original delv. E. SIMPSON June 30 1785)

89- THIS INDENTURE made the Seventh day of April in year of our Lord one thou-

95 sand seven hundred and Eighty four between JOHN THORNTON of CULPEPER & JANNY his Wife of one part and JOHN LEWIS, Son & Heir of RICHARD LEWIS deced. of another part; MANN SOWELL and ELIZABETH his Wife, a Daughter of the said RICHARD LEWIS of another part; THOMAS SOWELL & ANNE his Wife, another Daughter of the said RICHARD LEWIS of the Fourth part & EDWARD SIMPSON of the Town of Fredericksburg of the Fifth part; Whereas the said JOHN THORNTON did agree to sell to the said RICHARD LEWIS in his the said RICHARDs life time the one half or moiety of a Lot in the Town of Fredericksburg known in the plan of the said Town by the number Thirty nine, but never executed Deeds of Conveyance for the same; And Whereas the said RICHARD LEWIS afterwards by his last Will & Testament dated the 5th of April one thousand seven hundred and seventy seven among other things desired that the said moiety after the decease of his Wife, ANNE, should be sold and the money arising therefrom should be equally divided among his Six Children; JOHN, ELIZABETH, MARY, ANN, SARAH & HANNAH, two of whom, MARY & SARAH, are since dead without issue & intestate, the said HANNAH is under the age of Twenty one; And Whereas the said THOMAS SOWELL hath purchased of the said MANN SOWELL all his interest in the said Lot which he had in right os his Wife, ELIZABETH, and is also become entitled to the said JOHN LEWIS his part therein by purchase from the said MANN SOWELL who bought the same of WILLIAM CRAIGHILL who purchased it of the said JOHN, but the Deeds for transferring these respective interests are perhaps not legally authenticated & properly recorded, And Whereas the said THOMAS SOWELL hath agreed to sell unto the said EDWARD SIMPSON and his heirs as well the said THOMAS his interest in the premisses which he has in the same by virtue of his marriage with the said ANNE, one of the Daughters & Devisees of the said RICHARD LEWIS, as the respective shares of the said JOHN LEWIS & MANN SOWELL amounting in the whole to three fourths of the moiety of the Lot aforesaid; And Whereas the said EDWARD SIMPSON is in possession of the premisses by virtue of a Lease thereof from the said ANNE LEWIS, Widow of the said Testa-

tor, the said ANNE is still living; Now this Indenture witnesseth that the said JOHN THORNTON & JENNEY his Wife for Five hundred pounds current money to them in hand paid have sold unto the said EDWARD SIMPSON & his heirs all their claim in the moiety of the Lot aforesaid lying on the Main or CAROLINE STREET, being the lower half of the said Lot number Thirty nine; Together with all houses gardens wasys belonging; To have and to hold unto the said EDWARD SIMPSON his heirs & assigns forever freed from all incumbrances done by each of them (the claim and interest of the said ANNE LEWIS the Widow and the said HANNAH, the Daughter of said RICHARD LEWIS only excepted) and will warrant and forever defend by these presents; In Witness whereof the parties have hereunto set their hands and affixed their seals

Sealed & delivered in presence of
(On part of JNO: THORNTON & JOHN LEWIS)
SAML. TODD, JAMES BROWN,
JOHN ANDERSON, JAMES GELLIES
(On the part of J. T.)
FRAS. THORNTON, PHIL: JACOB IRION,
WM. C. BROWN
(On part of JOHN LEWIS) JOHN TINSLEY
THOMAS TOWLES (as to MANN & THOMAS SOWELL)
BEVY: STUBBLEFIELD (as to ditto)
H. DAWSON (as to ditto)
TURNER SOUTHALL, W. FOUSHEE, JOHN BENSON (as to ELIZABETH & ANN SOWELL)

JOHN THORNTON
JANE THORNTON
JOHN LEWIS
MANN SOWELL
ELIZABETH SOWELL
THOMAS SOWELL
ANN SOWELL

Commonwealth of Virginia to WILLIAM BROWN, HENRY HILL and WILLIAM WALKER Gent., Justices of the County of CULPEPER Greeting; Whereas JOHN THORTON and JENNY his Wife, JOHN LEWIS, MANN SOWELL and ELIZABETH his Wife, THOMAS SOWELL and ANN his Wife have conveyed unto EDWARD SIMPSON of the Town of Fredericksburg half a Lott in the Town of Fredericksburg, And Whereas the said JENNY THORNTON cannot travel to our Court to make her personal acknowledgement of the Indenture, we authorize you to go to the said JENNY THORNTON and examine her apart from her said Husband whither she doth freely acknowledge the said Indenture without the threats of her Husband and send under your hands & seals without delay sending therewith this Commission; Witness HENRY ARMISTEAD Clerk of our said Court Hustings this Second day of April 1784 in the Seventh year of the Common Wealth

HENRY ARMISTEAD, Clk.

CULPEPER Sc. Pursuant to the Commission we did this day privily examine Mrs. JENNY THORNTON, Wife of JOHN THORNTON, and the said JENNY THORNTON did freely acknowledge the said Indenture & declared she did the same without the persuasion of her said Husband; Certified under our hands and seals this Seventh day of April one thousand seven hundred and eighty four

WILLIAM BROWN
HENRY HILL

Commonweath of Virginia to TURNER SOUTHALL, RICHARD ADAMS & WILLIAM FOUSHEE, Gent. Justices of the peace of the County of HENRICO Greeting; Whereas JOHN THORNTON and JENNY his Wife, JOHN LEWIS, MANN SOWELL and ELIZABETH his Wife, THOMAS SOWELL and ANN his Wife have conveyed unto EDWARD SIMPSON of the Town of Fredericksburg half a Lott in the Town of Fredericksburg, And Whereas the said ELIZABETH & ANN SOWELL cannot travel to our Court of Hustings for the Town to make their personal acknowledgements, we do authorize you to go to the said ELIZABETH & ANN SOWELL and them examined and when you have received their acknowledgement without delay sending therewith this Commission; Witness HENRY ARMISTEAD Clerk of our said Court this Twenty sixth day of June 1784 and in the Eighth year of the Common Wealth

HENRY ARMISTEAD, Clk.

Pursuant to the within Commission, we did this day examine ELIZABETH SOWELL & ANN SOWELL and they freely acknowledge the said Indenture and declared that they did the same without the threats of their said Husbands; Certified under our hands and seals this first day of July 1784 TURNER SOUTHALL
W. FOUSHEE

At a Hustings Court held for the Town and Corporation of Fredericksburg on Monday the first day of November one thousand seven hundred and eighty four
This Deed indended with a Commission for the Examination of Mrs. THORNTON & a Commission also for the Examination of ELIZABETH and ANN SOWELL was acknowledged by JOHN THORNTON and proved as to JOHN LEWIS by the oaths of SAMUEL TOOD and JAMES BROWN and ordered to be Certified; And at a Court held the Sixth day of December 1784, This Deed was proved as to MANN and THOMAS SOWELL by the oaths of BEVERLEY STUBBLEFIELD, JOHN BENSON and WILLIAM DAWSON and ordered with the Commissions to be recorded Test HENRY ARMISTEAD, Clk.

p. Fredericksburg June 6th, 1785
95 Received from Mr. JAMES TAYLOR One hundred and twenty pounds in full of all demands against the late Houses of RODDEY & TAYLOR and JAMES TAYLOR & COMPY., except what may concern the Account of the Sloops *PORT ROYAL & JOLLY MILLER;* Witness our hands this day and year above mentioned
N. B. Should any error appear in Tobacco will at any time rectify it
CALLENDER & HENDERSON

pp. (On margin: October the 12th 1785, the Original delivd. to Mr. JNO: LEGG)
96 THIS INDENTURE between JOHN FRAZER and BETTY FRAZER his Wife of the
97 County of Spotsylvania and Town of Fredericksburg of the one aprt and JOHN LEGG of the same Town and County of the other part Witnesseth that JOHN FRAZER and BETTY his Wife for the sum of Sixty five pounds current money hath granted unto the said JOHN LEGG and his heirs and assigns forever a Lott of Ground in the Town of Fredericksburg containing half an acre numbered 127 beginning in CHARLES STREET adjoining Lot 125 running thence to the Corner, North 24 1/2 degrees West to WILLIAM STEET, thence South 65 1/2 degrees West to Lott No. 128, thence South 24 1/2 degrees East to the corner adjoining Lotts No. 128, 126 & 125; thence North 65 1/2 degrees East to the beginning; being the Ground purchased by the said JOHN FRAZER of ROBT. & ANN CUNNINGHAM as by Deed recorded in the Court Hustings of Fredericksburg may appear, To have and to hold to the said JOHN LEGG and his heirs and assigns peaceably against the claim of the said JOHN FRAZER and BETTY his Wife or any other person whatsoever unto the said JOHN LEGG and his heirs and will warrant and forever defend by these presents; In Witness whereof the said JOHN FRAZER & BETTY FRAZER his Wife hereunto set their hands and seals this Ninth day of December one thousand seven hundred and Eighty four
Signed sealed acknowledged in presence of
THOS: RYAN, CHARS. TURNER, JOHN FRAZER
JAMES DICKENSON, NATHL: FOX BETTY FRAZER

Commonwealth of Virginia to CHARLES MORTIMER & GEORGE FRENCH, Gent. Justices of the Corporation of Fredericksburg greeting; Whereas JOHN FRAZER and BETTY his Wife have conveyed unto JOHN LEGG one Lott of Ground in the said Town and whereas the said BETTY cannot travel to our Court Hustings to make her personal acknowledgement, these are to require you to go to the said BETTY and examine her apart from her said Husband whether she doth freely acknowledge the said Indenture and such acknowledgement send certified with this Commission; Witness HENRY ARMISTEAD Clerk of our said Court this 29 day of January 1785 in the Ninth year of the Common Wealth

HENRY ARMISTEAD, Clerk

Corporation of Fredericksburg to wit: Pursuant to the within Commission we did this day examine Mrs. BETTY FRAZER and she did acknowledge the said Indenture and declared she did the same without the threats of her said Husband; Certified under our hands & seals this seventh dy of March 1785

CHARLES MORTIMER
GEORGE FRENCH

At a Hustings Court held for the Corporation of Fredericksburg on Monday the third ay of January one thousand seven hundred and Eighty five

This Deed from JOHN FRAZER & BETTY his Wife (with a Commission of her privy examination) was proved by the oaths of THOMAS RYAN & CHARLES TURNER at February Court 1785 and was further proved by the oath of JAS: DICKINSON & is ordred to be recorded Test HENRY ARMISTEAD, Clerk

pp. 98-100 KNOW ALL MEN by these presents that I JAMES ALLAN of the Town and Borough of Fredericksburg in the State of Virginia in Ameria have made MESSRS. ANDREW BLACKBURN & PETER BLACKBURNE, Merchants of GLASGOW, my Attornies to sell for the best price two acres of Land in the Hough of HAMILTON in the Parish of HAMILTON and Shire of LAUNACK in that part ofthe Kingdom of Great Britain called SCOTLAND, one of which acres lies in that part of the Hough called SOUTHLAND BUTTS and is bounded by the lands of JOHN CLERKE, Writer, on the North, the lands of JOHN REIVE on the South, the Common Haugh on the East and the Long Lan on the West; & is now in possession of his Grace, the DUKE of HAMILTON, and the other acre of land in that part of the said Haugh called the WINDFORD betwixt the lands now belonging to JOHN SEMPLE on the East, and the lands of JOHN REIVE on the West parts, which acre is one of the acres of land annexed & appertaining to that Tenement called LITSTERS TENEMENT, both which acres of Land were formerly the property of my Father, JAMES ALLAN, Merchant, sometime Baillie in the Town of HAMILTON, deced., and by him given to my Brother, JOHN ALLAN, late of Fredericksburg afsd. deced., who gave the same to me by his Last Will, but which have now for many years been in possession & occupation of my Mother, CHRISTIAN ALLAN, late of HAMILTON afsd., deced., or of her Tenements holding under her, and by this said CHRISTIAN ALLAN given to me by her Last Will & Testament registered in the Court of the Shereff of LANNARHSHIRE of sd. and I do hereby authorize the said ANDREW BLACKBURNE & PETER BLACKBURNE my Attornies to make a Deed of Sale for the two acres of land to the purchasers agreeable to the Laws prevailing and made use of within that part of the said Kingdom of Great Britain called SCOTLAND, and I do authorize my said Attornies to receive the purchase money agreed to be given and make proper receipts & releases for the same, and in my respect to do as fully as I should were I personally present, In Witness whereof I have hereunto set my hand & affixed my Seal at Fredericksburg afsd. the fourth day of July in the year of our Lord one thousand seven hundred and eighty five

JAMES ALLAN

At a Hustings Court held for the Town and Corporation of Fredericksburg on Monday the Fourth day of July one thousand seven hundred and eighty five

This Power of Attorney from JAMES ALLAN to MESSRS. ANDREW BLACKBURN and PETER BLACKBURN was by him in open Court acknowledged and declared to be his Power of Attorney and was ordered to be recorded; And is recorded

Test HENRY ARMISTEAD, Clk.

pp. (On margin: August 8th 1785. This Deed was examd. & delivd. to CHS.
101- MORTIMER H. A. C. C. F.)
104 THIS INDENTURE made the thirtieth day of April in the year of our Lord one thousand seven hundred and eighty five and in the ninth year of the Independence of the United States of America Between JOHN WELCH of the Corporation of Fredericksburg in the State of Virginia, Gentleman, and NELLY his Wife of the one part and CHARLES MORTIMER of the same place and State Esquire of the other part; Whereas the said JOHN WELCH by his Bond became bound to the said CHARLES MORTIMER in the penal sum of Eight hundred and eighty pounds Specie (at the rate of Six shillings per dollar) with a condition thereunto written that if the said JOHN WELCH should pay to the said CHARLES MORTIMER the sum of Four hundred and forty pounds like money in manner following, (to wit), One hundred and ten pounds on or before the thirtieth day of April in the year one thousand seven hundred and eighty six, one hundred and ten pounds on or before the thirtieth day of April in the year one thousan seven hundred and eighty seven, one hundred and ten pounds on or before the thirtieth day of April in year one thousand seven hundred and eighty eight, and one lhundred and ten pounds before the thirtieth day of April in year one thousand seven hundred and eightynine with legal interest on the same, then the said obligation to be void or else to remain in full force; Now this Indenture witnesseth that the said JOHN WELCH and NELLY his Wife as well for the better securing the payment of the said sum as also for Five shillings to the said JOHN WELCH in hand paid by CHARLES MORTIMER they have granted unto CHARLES MORTIMER his heirs all that parcel of land containing Fifty four feet in front and one hundred and fifty feet in depth being one third part of that part of the CHURCH LOT situated in the Corporation of Fredericksburg aforesaid, ordered to be sold by virtue of an Act of Assembly for the benefit of the Parish of St. George, the said land on CAROLINE STREET in the occupation of JACOB KUGH and in the middle part of the said CHURCH LOT, the part next to the MARKET HOUSE being sold to GEORGE THORNTON late deceased, and the lower part to ALEXANDER BLAIR is a corner lot lying on CAROLINE and GEORGE STREETs which peice of land containing Fifty five feet in front on CAROLINE STREET aforesaid and extending One hundred and fifty feet therefrom was conveyed by JOHN LEWIS to JOHN CRAIG and ELIZABETH his Wife, & by the said JOHN CRAIG and ELIZABETH his Wife conveyed to EDWARD SIMPSON and by the said EDWARD SIMPSON and CATHARINE his Wife conveyed to the said JOHN WELCH, together with the houses and improvements thereon; To have and to hold to the only proper use of said CHARLES MORTIMER his heirs forever; Provided Always that if the said JOHN WELCH shall truly pay the said sum in manner follwoing with legal Interest on the same, that then thereafter he the said CHARLES MORTIMER will transfer all the premisses unto the said JOHN WELCH his heirs and assigns; In Witness whereof the said parties have to these presents set their hands and seals
Sealed and delivered in presents of

JOHN STAMPER, ALEXANDER VAUNE (Witness) JOHN WELCH
JOS: WOOD JUNR. NELLY WELCH's mark

At a Court held for the Town and Corporation of Fredericksburg on Monday the second day of May one thousand seven hundred and eighty five
This Mortgage between JOHN WELCH & NELLY his Wife (she being first privately examined) and CHARLES MORTIMER was acknowledged by the said JOHN WELCH and NELLY his Wife and ordered to be recorded Test HENRY ARMISTEAD, Clk.

pp. (On margin: 1785 Octr. 8th. Deld. this Deed to Messrs. CALLENDER & HENDERSON)
104- THIS INDENTURE TRIPARTITE made the Twenty seventh day of August one
106 thousand seven hundred and Eighty four Between SUSANNA HEATH of the Town of Fredericksburg and County of Spotsylvania of one part, JOSIAS PEAK ADAM, late of the same place but now of the County of CULPEPER of the second part; both of the State of Virginia, and MESSRS. REID & FORD, Merchants and Partners, of the City of PHILADELPHIA and State of PENSYLVANIA of the third part; Whereas the said SUSANNA HEATH (being possessed of a peice of a Lott of Ground in the Town of Fredericksburg in County of Spotsylvania number Forty three) as may appear by a Deed from JOHN HAWKINS and ANNA GAIBREILLA his Wife dated the seventh day of August one thousand seven hundred and eighty four; recorded in the Hustings Court of said Town, reference being had thereto, did sell the same unto the said JOSIAS PEAKE ADAMS for the sum of Eight hundred pounds which he hath since paid to her but never had any Conveyance of the same; And the said JOSIAS PEAKE ADAMS hath agreed to sell the said Lott unto the said MESSRS. REID and FORD, Merchants and Partners, for the sum of Twelve hundred pounds current money of Virginia; Now this Indenture Witnesseth that for the sum of Eight hundred pounds by the said JOSIAS PEAKE ADAMS paid to the said SUSANNA HEATH and for the sum of Twelve hundred pounds the said MESSRS. REID and FORD, Merchants and Partners, have paid to the said JOSIAS PEAKE ADAMS (satisfied by his being a party to and delivering these presents) and for the further sum of Five pounds by the said MESSRS. REID and FORD, Merchants, paid to the said SUSANNA HEATH, sold unto the said MESSRS. REID and FORD, Merchants, their heirs the Lott or part of a Lott of Ground numbered Forty three and bounded; Beginning on the Main Street of the said Town of Fredericksburg called CAROLINE STREET at the intersection of said Street and GEORGE STREET, thence down CAROLINE STREET to the Corner of JOHN ATKINSONs House, thence at right angles from CAROLINE STREET and parallel with GEORGE STREET one hundred and thirty two feet to the COURT HOUSE LOTT, thence with the lines of the COURT HOUSE LOTT and parallel with CAROLINE STREET to GEORGE STREET; thence down GEORGE STREET to CAROLINE STREET and the beginning; To have and to hold to the said MESSRS. REID & FORD, Merchants, against the claim of her the said SUSANNA HEATH and JOSIAS PEAKE ADAMS or their heirs; In Witness whereof the said SUSANNA HEATH and JOSIAS PEAKE ADAMS hath set their hands and seals
Signed sealed acknowledged and delivered in presence of
JAMES HOWORTH, THOMAS McKIM, SUSANNA HEATH
DAVID HENDERSON, JAMES HEATH JOSIAS P. ADAMS
At a Hustings Court held for the Corporation of Fredericksburg on Monday the Third day of January one thousand seven hundred and eighty five
This Deed indented from SUSANNA HEATH and JOSIAS PEAKE ADAMS was proved by the oaths of JAMES HOWART, THOMAS McKIM and DAVID HENDERSON and ordered to be recorded Test HENRY ARMISTEAD, Clerk

pp. THIS INDENTURE made the 31st day of January one thousand seven hundred and
107- eighty five Between ROBERT WALKER & DOROTHEA his Wife of the one part and
109 JOSEPH WALKER of the other part, all of the Town and Corporation of Fredericksburg, Witnesseth that the said ROBERT WALKER and DOROTHEA his Wife for the sum of Two hundred and fifty pounds current money of Virginia to them paid hath granted unto the said JOSEPH WALKER his heirs and assigns forever a Lott of Ground in the said Town of Fredericksburg and by plan of said Town is known by the number of Ninety one, and is on the Lotts purchased by the said ROBERT WALKER of JAMES and MARY DUNCANSON, as by their Deed of Release bearing date the second day of October

one thousand seven hundred and seventy and recorded in the County Court of Spotsylvania reference being had may appear; To have and to hold to the said JOSEPH WALKER and his heirs against the claim of them the said ROBERT WALKER and DOROTHEA his Wife; In Witness whereof the said ROBERT WALKER and DOROTHEA his Wife have set their hands and seals

Signed sealed & delivered in presence of
JOHN HAIDEA, ROBERT WALKER
WM. McWILLIAMS, THOMAS MILLER DOROTHEY WALKER

The Commonwealth of Virginia to WILLIAM McWILLIAM & THOMAS MILLER Gent., Justices of the Court of Hustings for the Town of Frederickburg Greeting; Whereas ROBERT WALKER and DOROTHEA his Wife have conveyed land in Town of Fredericksburg unto JOSEPH WALKER and the said DOROTHEA cannot travel to our said Court to make acknowledgement of the same; We require you to go to DOROTHEA WALKER and examine her apart from her Husband and when you have received her acknowledgement that you certifiy under your hand and seal; Witness HENRY ARMISTEAD, Clerk of our said Court this 29th day of January 1785 and in the Ninth year of the Commonwealth

HENRY ARMISTEAD, Clk.

Corporation of Fredericksburg, to wit; Pursuant to the within Commission we did examine Mrs. DOROTHEA WALKER and she did freely acknowledge the said Indenture; Certified under our hands and seals this 31st day of January 1785

WILLIAM McWILLIAMS
THOMAS MILLER

At a Hustings Court held for the Corporation of Fredericksburg on Monday the Seventh day of February one thousand seven hundred and eighty five
This Deed from ROBERT WALKER and DOROTHEA his Wife (with a Commission of her privy examination) was acknowledged to JOSEPH WALKER and ordered to be recorded

Test HENRY ARMISTEAD, Clerk

pp. THIS INDENTURE witnesseth that CHRISTOPHER BLACKBURN doth put himself
109- Apprentice to WILLIAM GRIMES of Fredericksburg, Taylor, to learn the Art and
110 with him after the manner of an Apprentice to serve from the date hereof untill he shall retain the again of Twenty one years; during which term the said Apprentice his said Master shall serve, his secrets keep, his commands gladly do, do no damage to his said Master or see it done by others, but give waring of the same; he shall not waste goods of his Master nor lend them to any, he shall not commit fornication nor contract matrimony; he shall not play at cards dice or any other unlawful games, he shall not absent himself from his Masters service day or night but in all things as a faithful Apprentice he shall behave himself and the said Master his said Apprentice in the same Art which he useth by the best means that he can shall teach; finding unto the said Apprentice meat drink apparel lodging and to cause him to be taught to read and write and other necessarys during the said term; In Witness whereof we the sd. above named have put our hands and seals this 7th day of March one thousand seven hundred and Eighty five

WM. GRIMES
CHARLES BLACKBURN

At a Hustings Court held for the Corporation of Fredericksburg on Tuesday the Eighth day of March one thousand seven hundred and eighty five
This Indenture between WILLIAM GRYMES and CHRISTOPHER BLACKBURN (with the approbation of the Court) was acknowledged and is ordered to be recorded

Test HENRY ARMISTEAD, Clk.

pp. 110-111 THIS INDENTURE witnesseth that JAMES JONES doth put himself Apprentice to WILLIAM GAINES of Fredericksburg, Taylor, to learn his Art & with him after the manner of an Apprentice to serve from day of the date hereof untill he shall retain the age of Twenty one years during which term the said Apprentice his said Master faithfully shall serve, his secrets keep, his lawfull commands gladly do, he shall do no dammage to his said Master nor see it to be done of others; but that he shall forthwith give warning to his said Master of the same; he shall not waste the goods nor lend them unlawfully to any; he shall not commit fornication nor contract matrimony within the term; he shall not play at cards or dice or any other unlawful games; he shall not absent himself from his Masters service day or night unlawfully, but in all things as a faithful Apprentice he shall behave & himself toward his said Master; and the said Master his said Apprentice the same Art which he useth by the best means that he can shall instruct, finding unto the said Apprentice meat, drink, apparel, lodging and teach or cause him to be taught to read and write and all other necessarys, during the said term; In Witness whereof we the above named have put our hands & seals this 7th day of March one thousand seven hundred and eighty five

WILLIAM GRIMES
JAMES JONES

At a Hustings Court held for the Corporation of Fredericksburg on Tuesday the Eighth day of March one thousand seven hundred and eighty five
This Indenture between WILLIAM GRYMES and JAMES JONES (with the approbation of the Court) was acknowledged and ordered to be recorded
Test HENRY ARMISTEAD, Clk.

pp. 112-113 THIS INDENTURE made in the year of our Lord one thousand seven hundred and Eighty five between ALEXANDER DICK of the Town of Fredericksburg of the one part and JOHN FRAZER of the said Town of the other part; Witnesseth that the said ALEXANDER DIX for Five shillings paid hath sold unto the said JOHN FRAZER his heirs and assigns all that Land in the Town of Fredericksburg number One hundred and Thirty five, bounded on the South by Lot number one hundred and Thirty three, on the West by Lot number one hundred and Thirty six, and being opposite Lot number One hundred seven, whereon MRS. WASHINGTON now Dwells, containing one half acre together with all houses buildings and profits thereof; To have and to hold unto the said JOHN FRAZER his heirs and assigns forever against him the said ALEXANDER DICK his heirs and assigns, In Witness whereof the said ALEXANDER DICK hath set his hand and seal this seventh day of March in the year above mentioned
Signed sealed and delivered in presents of
WM. SYMMES, THOMAS WHITTING, ALEXANDER DICK
ELGAN CHAPMAN, ELISHA DICKENSON

At a Hustings Court held for the Town and Corporation of Fredericksburg on Tuesday the Eighth day of March one thousand seven hundred and eighty five
This Deed was proved by the oaths of WILLIAM SYMMES, THOMAS WHITTING & ELGAN CHAPMAN & ordered to be recorded Test HENRY ARMISTEAD, Clk.

pp. 114-115 THIS INDENTURE made in the year of our Lord one thousand seven hundred and eighty five Between ALEXANDER DICK of the Town of Fredericksburg of the one part and ELISHA DICKINSON of the said Town of the other part; Witnesseth that the said ALEXANDER DICK for the sum of Five shillings to him paid hath sold unto the said ELISHA DICKENSON his heirs all that Lot of land in the Town of Fredericksburg number One hundred thirty six, bounded on the south by lot number one hundred and thirty four, on the East by lot number one hundred and thirty five, lying opposite number One hundred and eight on the North, and one hundred fortty seven on the West, containing an hald acre; To have and to hold the said lot with the appertenances unto ELISHA DICKENSON his heirs and assigns forever against him the said ALEXANDER DICK his heirs and assigns and the said ALEXANDER DICK his heirs will forever warrant and defend by these presents; In Witness whereof the said ALEXANDER DICK hath set his hand and seal this seventh day of March in the year above mentioned

Signed sealed and delivered in presence of
WM. SYMMES, THOMAS WHITING, ALEXANDER DICK
ELGAN CHAPMAN, JOHN FRAZER

At a Hustings Court held for the Corporation of Fredericksburg on Tuesay the Eighth day of March one thousand seven hundred and eighty five
This Deed from ALEXANDER DICK to ELISHA DICKENSON proved by the oaths of WILLIAM SYMMES, THOMAS WHITING and ELGAN CHAPMAN & ordered to be recorded
Test HENRY ARMISTEAD, Clk.

pp. 115-116 THIS INDENTURE made this Twentyeth day of February one thousand seven hundred and Eighty five Between GEORGE JENKINS of the one part and JAMES SMOCK of the Town of Fredericksburg, Saddler, of the other part; Witnesseth that the said GEORGE JENKENS of his own free will and with approbation of the Corporation Court of Fredericksburg doth put and bind himself an Apprentice to the said JAMES SMOCK for the term of One year and six months, during which time the said GEORGE JENKINS will serve the said JAMES SMOCK, not absent himself day or night without leave, nor lend his good to any, not frequent taverns or disorderly meeting, at cards dice or any other unlawfull games he shall not follow; nor contract matrimony and in all things as an Apprentice he shall serve, the lawfull commands of his Mster willingly obey and the said JAMES SMOCK for his part doth bind himself that he will teach the said GEORGE JENKINS the Trade of a Saddler, and will find him sufficient meat drink washing clothing and loding fitting for an Apprentice during the time aforesaid; Also the said SMOCK doth agree that the said GEORGE JENKINS shall be learned the rule of Division; In Witness whereof the parties have hereunto set their hands and seals

JAMES SMOCK
GEORGE JENKINS

At a Hustings Court held for the Corporation of Fredericksburg on Tuesday the Eighth day of March one thousand seven hundred and Eighty five
This Indenture (with the approbation of the Court) was acknowledged and ordered to be recorded Test HENRY ARMISTEAD, Clerk

pp. 116-119 THIS INDENTURE made at GLASGOW in the Kingdom of GREAT BRITAIN the Eighteenth day of June in the year of our Lord one thousand seven hundred and Eighty two between GEORGE McCALL of the City of GLASGOW, Merchant, and MARY his Wife, ARCHIBALD SMELLIE of the said City, Merchant, & CHRISTIAN his Wife, RICHARD SMELLIE of the said City, Merchant & ANNE his Wife & HENRY MITCHELL late of Fredericksburg, Virginia, Merchant, of one part and ROBERT JOHNSTON of the Town of PORT ROYAL and Colony of Virginia, Merchant, of the other part; Witnesseth that for the sum of One thousand pounds Sterling money of Great Britain to the sd. HENRY MITCHELL (in behalf of the account of the said GEORGE McCALL, ARCHIBALD SMELLIE, RICHARD SMELLIE & HENRY MITCHELL) they have sold unto ROBERT JOHNSTON and his heirs two lotts of land in the Town of Fredericksburg and County of

Spotsylvania in Virginia on the Main Street and being half of the square on which LEWIS WILLIS Esquire did live & were conveyed to the said GEORGE McCALL, &c. by HENRY MITCHELL by Deed of Lease and Release recorded in the County Court of Spotsylvania and all houses buildings; To have and to hld unto the said ROBERT JOHNSTON his heirs and assigns forever; In Witness whereof the said GEORGE McCALL & MARY his Wife, ARCHIBALD SMELLIE & CHRISTIAN his Wife, RICHARD SMELLIE & ANN his Wife and HENRY MITCHELL have set their hands to this their act and deed written upon three pages of Stampt. paper by the said HENRY MITCHELL consenting likewise to the segestration thereof in the books of Council & Session or any other Competent in North Britain or Virginia for the better preservation of the same and for that efect constitute
Sealed & delivered in presence of us

ANDREW JOHNSTON	GEORGE McCALL	MARY McCALL
JOHN LOVE	ARCHD. SMELLIE	CHRISTIAN SMELLIE
JOHN BUCKANAN,	RICHD. SMELLIE	ANNE SMELLIE
WILLIAM REID	HENRY MITCHELL	

At the City of GLASGO in the Kingdom of Great Britain the Fourth day of July one thousand seven hundred and eighty two in the presence of PATRICK COLQUHOUN Lord Provost and Cheif Magistrate of the said City of GLASGOW, appeared the above named GEORGE McCALL of the said City, Merchant, & MARY his Wife, ARCHIBALD SMELLIE of the said City, Merchant, & CHRISTIAN his Wife; RICHARD SMELLIE of the said City, Merchant, and ANNE his Wife and the said HENRY MITCHELL, late of Virginia, now of GLASGOW, when they severally acknowledged the annexed Deed of Bargain & Sale that they delivered the same to the use of ROBERT JOHNSTON of PORT ROYAL in Virginia, Merchant and agreed the same might be recorded in the Honourable the General Court of Virginia; The Court of the County of Spotsylvania, or any other Court agreeable to the Laws of Virginia, And I the said PATRICK COLQUHOUN certify that MARY McCALL, Wife to the said GEORGE McCALL, CHRISTIAN SMELLIE Wife to the said ARCHIBALD SMELLIE & ANNE SMELLIE Wife to the said RICHARD SMELLIE (parties to the said Deed) privately & apart from their said Husbands when they severally also declared they signed & now acknowledged the said Deed without the persuasion of their said Husbands, and were willing the same should be recorded in any Court in Virginia according to the Laws of use & usage there; In Testimony whereof I have subscribed my name & caused the Seal of the City of GLASGOW to be affixed thereto the day month and year first above written

PATRK: COLQUHOUN

At a Hustings Court held for the Town and Corporation of Fredericksburg on Monday the second day of May one thousand seven hundred and eighty five
This Deed (with certificate of PATRICK COLQUHOUN) was acknowledged by HENRY MITCHELL to ROBERT JOHNSTON and ordered to be recorded

Test HENRY ARMISTEAD, Clk.

pp. 120-122 THIS INDENTURE made the twenty eighth day of June in the year of our Lord one thousand seven hundred and eighty five and in the ninth year of the Independence of the United States of America, Between Mr. ROGER DIXON of the Town of Fredericksburg in the State of Virginia, Gentleman, of the one part and MARY SULLIVAN of the same place and State, Spinster, of the other part; Witnesseth that the said ROGER DIXON for the sum of Three hundred pounds in hand paid doth grant unto the said MARY SULLIVAN her heirs and assigns forever all that part of a lot of land numbered 258 situate on the North East side of CAROLINE STREET in the Town aforesaid; containing Seventy two feet in front on the said Street and extending one hundred and thirty two feet in depth from the same, bounded on the North West by part

of a lot of land purchased by JOHN WELCH of BENJAMIN JOHNSTON on the South East by part of a lot of land the property of the late JAMES HUNTER deceased, and on the North East by the lot of land now in the occupation of the said MARY SULLIVAN; Together with all the houses buildings and improvements; To have and to hold unto the said MARY SULLIVAN her heirs and assigns forever without the molestation of him the said ROGER DIXON his heirs or any one claiming under him, Except a certain Lease granted to JOHN WELCH by the said ROGER DIXON of part of the said premisses for the term of Seven years eight months and ten days under the yearly grant of Three pounds (which said Rent is intended to pass hereby) In Witness whereof the said parties have set their hands and seals
Signed sealed and delivered in presents of
JOS: WOODS JUNR., ROGER DIXON
JOHN COAKLY, COLLIN FRAZER
At a Hustings Court held for the Corporation of Fredericksburg on Monday the Fourth day of July one thousand seven hundred and eighty five
This Deed was proved by the witnesses and ordered to be recorded
Test HENRY ARMISTEAD, Clk.

p. THIS INDENTURE made the Fourth day of April one thousand seven hundred and
123 Eighty five between JOSEPH WALKER of the Town of Fredericksburg, Carrage Maker, of one part and JOHN SMITH of the aforesaid Town on the other part; Witnesseth that the said JOHN SMITH of his own free will and by the consent of the Court of Hustings doth bind himself Apprentice to the said JOSEPH WALKER untill he shall arive to the age of Twenty one years; he being Thirteen years old the Twelfth day of December last, during which time the said JOHN SMITH will sereve the said JOSEPH WALKER, not absent himself from his Masters service, nor lend his goods to any, not frequent taverns or any disorderly meetings, at cards dice or any unlawfull games he shall not follow nor contract matrimony and in all things as an Apprentice he shall truly serve and lawfull commands of his Master will obey, and the said JOSEPH WALKER for his part doth agree that he will teach the said SMITH in the Trade of making Carrages and will provide sufficient meat drink washing cloathing and lodging fitting for an Apprentice during the time aforesaid; also teach the said JOHN SMITH to read and write; In Witness whereof the parties have set their hands and seals
JOSEPH WALKER
JOHN SMITH

(No recording shown)

pp. (On margin: This Deed delivered to ISABELLA MERCER March 7th 1786
124- THIS INDENTURE made the twenty second day of June in year of our Lord one
126 thousand seven hundred and eighty five and in the Ninth year of the Independence of the United States of America Between ISABELLA MERCER, GEORGE WEEDON and JOHN TENNENT, Executors of the Last Will and Testament of HUGH MERCER, late of Fredericksburg in the State of Virginia, Practictioner of Physic, deceased, of the one part and JOSEPH WOOD the Younger of Fredericksburg aforesaid, Attorney at Law, of the other part; Witnesseth that the said HUGH MERCER by his said Last Will and Testament bearing date the Sixth day of February in the year one thousand seven hundred and Seventy six did direct that the following part of his Estate should be sold, (Vizt.) the houses and lots which the said HUGH MERCER purchased of JAMES HUNTER and adjoining the Lot of CHARLES DICK and in which houses the Family of the said HUGH MERCER resided; also the Lot which the said HUGH MERCER purchased of DOCTOR JOHN

SUTHERLANDs Estate adjoining to the lot of JAMES ALLEN, likewise the House on the Main Street on CHAPMANs Lot which House the said HUGH MERCER leased of JOHN DALTON, and whereas the said ISABELLA MERCER, GEORGE WEEDON and JOHN TENNANT in pursuance of the Last Will and Testament of the said HUGH MERCER have sold to the said JOSEPH WOOD the several lots of land appertaining, Now This Indenture Witnesseth that the said ISABELLA MERCER , GEORGE WEEDON and JOHN TENNANT for the sum of One thousand pounds paid or secured to be paid sell unto the said JOSEPH WOOD his heirs and assigns all that Lot of Land which the said HUGH purchased of JAMES HUNTER and known in the plan of the said Town by the number Fifty, And also that lot known by the number Sixty three, And also that lot known by the number one hundred and Twenty three, together with the houses buildings and improvements also all the right of the said HUGH MERCER to the said House on the Main Street of Fredericksburg which the said HUGH MERCER leased of the said JOHN DALTON; To have and to hold the said lots of land unto JOSEPH WOOD his heirs and assigns forever; In Witness whereof the said parties have set their hands and seals

Sealed and delivered in presents of

T. D. CAMP,	ISABELLA MERCER
SAML. K. BRADFORD,	GEORGE WEEDON
JAMES FISHER	JOHN TENNENT

At a Hustings Court held for the Corporation of Fredericksburg on Monday the Fifth day of September one thousand seven hundred and Eighty five

This Deed indented was proved as to ISABELLA MERCER and JOHN TENNANT by SAMUEL K. BRADFORD as a witness thereto, and acknowledged by GEORGE WEEDON and ordered to be recorded Test HENRY ARMISTEAD, Clk.

pp. (On Margin: Deld. to WM. SMITH Janry: 10th 1786)
127- THIS INDENTURE made the fifth day of December in year of our Lord one thou-
129 sand seven hundred and Eighty five Between JOHN WIGGLESWORTH of County of
Spotsylvania Gent., and PHILADELPHIA his Wife of the one part and WILLIAM SMITH of the same County and Town of Fredericksburg of the other part; Witnesseth that the said JOHN WIGGLESWORTH and PHILADELPHIA his Wife for Three hundred pounds Specie have sold unto the said WILLIAM SMITH his heirs and assigns forever, part of the LONG ORDINARY LOTT in the Town of Fredericksburg; adjoining the said WILLIAM SMITH's new house now occupied by Mr. PAINE, containing Fifty four feet seven inches in front and on the Main Street, and to extend back its full breadth to the COURT HOUSE LOTT, Together with all buildings and trees; To have and to hold unto the said WILLIAM SMITH his heirs and assigns without disturbance of JOHN WIGGLESWORTH and PHILADELPHIA his Wife their heirs or any other persons whatsoever; In Witness whereof the said JOHN WIGGLESWORTH and PHILADELPHIA his Wife have set their hands and seals

Sealed and Delivered in presence of

WM. LOVELL, GODLOVE HEISKELL,	JOHN WIGGLESWORTH
JOSEPH CHRISTY, WM. SMOCK	PHILADELPHIA WIGGLESWORTH

The Commonwealth of Virginia to GEORGE WEEDON, THOS: MILLER, CHARLES MORTIMER, WILLIAM McWILLIAMS and JAMES SOMVERVILLE Gent., Justices of the Corporation of Fredericksburg; Whereas JOHN WIGGLESWORTH and PHILADELPHIA his Wife by Indenture have conveyed unto WILLIAM SMITH a lott in the Town of Fredericksburg and Whereas the said PHILADELPHIA cannot travel to our Court to make acknowledgement of the same, these are to require you to go to the said PHILADELPHIA and examine her whether she doth freely acknowledge the said Indenture without the threats of her said Husband, and send certified under your hands and seals; Witness HENRY ARMIS-

said Husband and send certified under your hands and seals; Witness HENRY ARMISTEAD Clerk of our said Court the nineteenth day of December one thousand seven hundred and Eighty five in the Tenth year of the Common Wealth

HENRY ARMISTEAD, Clk.

Corporation of Fredericksburg to wit; Pursuant to this Commission we did examine Mrs. PHILADELPHIA WIGGLESWORTH apart from her Husband who declared that she acknowledged the said Indenture of her own free will; Certified under our hands andseals this Nineteenth day of December one thousand seven hundred and Eighty five

THOS: MILLER
CHS. MORTIMER

At a Hustings Court held for the Corporation of Fredericksburg on Monday the fifth day of December one thousand seven hundred and eighty five
This Deed was in open Court acknowledged to WILLIAM SMITH & is ordered to be recorded and on the Second day of January one thousand seven hundred and Eighty six a Commission with a Certificate of the privy Examination of the said PHILADELPHIA was returned & is ordered to be recorded

Test HENRY ARMISTEAD

pp. THIS INDENTURE made third day of December one thousand seven hundred and
130- eighty five Between GABRIEL J. JOHNSTON of County of Spotsylvania of the one
132 part and CHARLES YATES of Town of Fredericksburg on the other part; Witnesseth that the said GABRIEL J. JOHNSTON for Five shillings doth sell all that parcel of ground in ALLEN TOWN adjoining and within the jurisdiction of the Corporation of Fredericksburg, which is numbered by a plan of the said Town "Eight" and which my Father, BENJAMIN JOHNSTON, bought of Mr. JOHN BENGER his Exrs. and Admrs. and sold in my minority by Deed to EVEN CLEMENT who sold to WILLIAM HUNTER, who sold to Colo. ALEXANDER SPOTSWOOD, who sold it to the said CHARLES YATES without recollecting or having due regard to the Deed from Mr. JOHN BENGERs Executors or Administrators, being made to me in my Infancy although the consideration for it was settled by my said Father, BENJAMIN JOHNSTON, Together with all houses stables gardens belonging; To have and to hold unto the said CHARLES YATES and the said GABRIEL J. JOHNSTON agre that he will warrant and forever defend the land unto the said CHARLES YATES against the claim of any person whatsoever; In Witness whereof the said GABRIEL J. JOHNSTON hath set his hand and seal
Sealed & delivered in presence of
WM. LOVELL, G. J. JOHNSTON
WILLIAM ORR, JAMES MAURY

At a Hustings Court held for the Town and Corporation of Fredericksburg on Monday the fifth day of December one thousand seven hundred and eighty five
This Deed and Receipt was acknowledged in open Court by the said GABRIEL JONES JOHNSTON and is ordered to be recorded

Test HENRY ARMISTEAD, Clk.

pp. KNOW ALL MEN by these presents that I JOHN ATKINSON of Fredericksburg
132- for the sum of One hundred & twenty pounds Virga: currency do sell unto
133 ARCHD. McCALL my Negro wench Venas & her two boys, Fielding & Jack, and their increase; To have & to hold the said Negroes unto the said ARCHD. McCALL & his heirs and do warrant the said Negroes from me & my heirs from the claim of all persons whatsoever as Witness my hand & seal this Fourth December 1784
Witness RICHARD SIMCOCK, NEWMAN BARNES JOHN ATKINSON

Memdn. I do agree that Mr. ATKINSON may sell any person the above Negroes provided they pay me the money down for them

ARCHD. McCALL

At a Hustings Court held for the Town and Corporation of Fredericksburg on Monday the seventh day of March one thousand seven hundred and eighty five this Bill of Sale from JOHN ATKINSON to ARCHD. McCALL was proved by the witnesses and ordered to be recorded Test HENRY ARMISTEAD, Clerk

pp. (On margin: Sent this Deed August 1786 to Mr. SMITH by T. WHITHURST)
133- THIS INDENTURE made the twenty third day of April in the year of our Lord
137 one thousand seven hundred and eighty five and in the Ninth year of the Independence of the United States of America, Between SAMUEL RODDY of the Corporation of Fredericksburg in the State of Virginia, Gentleman, of the one part and JOHN SMITH of BALTIMORE TOWN in the State of MARYLAND, Merchant, of the other part; Whereas the said SAMUEL RODDEY by his certain Bond or obligation bearingd ate the twenty third day of May in the year of our Lord one thousand seven hundred and eighty one acknowledged himself to be firmly bound to the said JOHN SMITH his certain Attorney and assigns in the penal sum of Three thousand six hundred and six pounds and five shillings Sterling money of Great Britain; with a condition thereunder written that if the said SAMUEL RODDEY his heirs should pay the full sum before the first day of November next ensuing the sate thereof with legal Interest for the same; And Whereas the said SAMUEL RODDEY is indebted to HARRY BARTLETT of the County of Spotsylvania in the said State of Virginia, Gentleman, in the sum of Six hundred and Fifty pounds fourteen shillings and one penny current money of the said State of Virginia with legal Interest from the Second day of December in the year of our Lord one thousand seven hundred and Eighty which said sum the said JOHN SMITH hath agreed to advance to the said HARRY BARTLETT for the said SAMUEL RODDEY, And Whereas the said SAMUEL RODDEY and JAMES TAYLOR his late copartner were seized as joint tenants in fee of the Lotts number Thirty three and Thirty four in the said Corporation of Fredericksburg with the buildings improvements belonging; And Whereas the said SAMUEL RODDEY and JAMES TAYLOR did by Indenture recorded in Court of said Corporation make partition of the said Lotts number Thirty three and Thirty four in manner following (to wit) the said JAMES TAYLOR to begin on CAROLINE STREET at the corner of the said Lot number Thirty three where it joins Lott number Thirty five the property of JACOB WHITLER, running thence sixty five feet and two inches (more or less) along CAROLINE STREET to the Corner of the STORE occupied by the said SAMUEL RODDEY known by the name of REEDS STORE, thence at right angles straight line running parallel to the said Lott number thirty five and thirty six and also parallel to WOOLF STREET till it intersects on PRINCESS ANN STREET, which line is to be the deviding line between the said SAMUEL RODDEY and the said JAMES TAYLOR, thence with the Lotts number Thirty five and Thirty six to the beginning; The said SAMUEL RODDEYs part to contain the ballance of the Lotts number Thirty three and Thirty four and to begin where the said JAMES TAYLOR distance aforesaid on CAROLINE STREET ends; thence up the said Street to the corner of the said Lot number Thirty three and where CAROLINE STREET intersects WOOLF STREET, thence along WOOLF STREET to the dividing line aforesaid, thence with the said line to the beginning; And Whereas SAMUEL RODDEY is desirous to secure to the said JOHN SMITH the payment of the before written obligation as also the amount the said JOHN SMITH doth agree to advance SAMUEL RODDEY as likewise any sums which the said JOHN SMITH may advance in order to prosecute a suit which the said SAMUEL RODDEY hath instituted in the High Court of Chancery of the

State of Virginia against the said HARRY BARTLETT; Now This Indenture Witnesseth that SAMUEL RODDEY for the consideration before mentioned as well as the sum of Five shillings hath sold unto the said JOHN SMITH his heirs and assigns all that parcel of land before described; To have and to hold unto the said JOHN SMITH his heirs and assigns, Provided Always and it is agreed between the parties that if the said SAMUEL RODDEY his heirs shall pay unto the said JOHN SMITH (the sums above mentioned) on or before the first day of January in the year of our Lord one thousand seven hundred and Eighty eight that then he the said JOHN SMITH will transfer the premisses unto the said SAMUEL RODDEY and the said SAMUEL RODDEY for himself doth grant he will pay the said sums of money; In Witness whereof the said parties have set their hands and seals
Sealed and delivered in presence of

JOS: WOOD JUNR., JOSEPH BERRY, SAMUEL RODDEY
SOSELART SABASTIN

At a Hustings Court held for the Corporation of Fredericksburg on Monday the Sixth day of June one thousand seven hundred and Eighty five
This Deed was proved by the witnesses and ordered to be recorded
Test HENRY ARMISTEAD, Clk.

pp. (On margin: Delivd. this Deed to JNO: MERCER 7th March 1786)
137- THIS INDENTURE made the twenty second day of June in the year of our Lord
139 one thousand seven hundred and Eighty five and in the Ninth year of the Independence of the United States of America, Between JOSEPH WOOD of Fredericksburg in the State of Virginia, Attorney at Law, of the one part and ISABELLA MERCER of the same place and State, Widow and Relict of HUGH MERCER deceased, of the other part; Witnesseth that JOSEPH WOOD for the sum of One thousand pounds paid or secured to be paid by the said ISABELLA MERCER, he the said JOSEPH WOOD doth grant unto ISABELLA MERCER her heirs and assigns all that Lot of Land in Fredericksburg aforesaid numbered in the plan of the same, Fifty, and also all the Lot numbered One hundred and Twenty three; Together with all the houses buildings and improvements of which several lots of land were part of the real estate of the said HUGH MERCER and purchased by the said JOSEPH WOOD from the said ISABELLA MERCER and GEORGE WEEDON and JOHN TENNANT, Executors of the Last Will and Testament of the said HUGH MERCER, in pursuance of certain powers vested in the said Executors, And the said JOSEPH WOOD for the said sum doth hereby transfer unto the said ISABELLA MERCER all his right to a House being on the Main Street of Fredericksburg aforesaid on a Lot called CHAPMANs, which the said HUGH MERCER leased of JOHN DALTON, and which Lease was assigned by the said ISABELLA MERCER, GEORGE WEEDON and JOHN TENNANT to the said JOSEPH WOOD in pursuance of the Will of the said HUGH MERCER; To have and to hold the said several lots of land unto the said ISABELLA MERCER without the hinderance of said JOSEPH WOOD or any other person; In Witness whereof the said parties have set their hands and seals
Sealed and delivered in presence of

JAMES FISHER JOSEPH WOOD JUNR.
AMB: CAMP, SAMUEL K. BRADFORD

At a Hustings Court held for the Corporation of Fredericksburg on Monday the Fourth day of July one thousand seven hundred and Eighty five
This Deed of Sale and Assignment was acknowledged and ordered to be recorded
Test HENRY ARMISTEAD, Clk.

pp. (On margin: Deld. to HENRY FITZHUGH Decr. 1st 1786)
140- THIS INDENTURE made the Tenth August one thousand seven hundred & Eighty
141 Five between JOHN LEWIS at present of the Borough of Fredericksburg, Gent., of one part and HENRY FITZHUGH of KING GEORGE County, Gent., of the other part; Witnesseth that JOHN LEWIS for the sum of Two hundred & fifty pounds hath granted HENRY FITZHUGH his heirs and assigns three Lotts in the Town and Borough of Fredericksburg known in the plan of the said Town by the numbers One hundred and seventy seven; one hundred and seventy eight and one hundred and eighty, number One hundred and seventy seven and one hundred & seventy eight being on CAROLINE STREET and number one hundred & eighty on SOPHIA STREET, the three lotts adjoin each other; Together with all houses buildings waters profits to the same belonging; To have and to hold unto the said HENRY FITZHUGH his heirs and assigns without molestation of said JOHN LEWIS and free from all incumbrances (the Taxes hereafter growing due excepted) In Witness whereof the said JOHN LEWIS hath set his hand & affixed his seal

Signed sealed and delivered in presence of
THS: STRACHAN, JAMES MAURY, JOHN LEWIS
SAML. K. BRADFORD, WILLIAM ZIMMERMAN,
JAMES ALLEN, JONAS INGHUM

At Hustings Court held for the Corporation of Fredericksburg on Monday the Fifth day of September one thousand eight hundred & Eighty five
This Deed was proved by the oaths of JAMES ALLEN, SAML. K. BRADFORD & JAMES MAURY and ordered to be recorded Test HENRY ARMISTEAD; Clk.

pp. THIS INDENTURE made the Fourth day of April one thousand seven hundred and
142- eighty five Between JOHN WELCH of the Town of Fredericksburg in County of
143 Spotsylvania of the one part and BENJAMIN SEBASTIAN of the same Town and County of the other part; Witnesseth that the said JOHN WELCH for the sum of Five shillings current money hath lett and to farm lett unto the said BENJAMIN SEBASTIAN one parcel of Ground in the said Town of Fredericksburg on CAROLINE STREET beginning at the corner of MICHL. ROBINSONs Shop, running along the Street twenty two feet & to contain all the Ground by running parallel line from each Corner on the Street to the back of the Ground held by the said WELCH & all houses gardens and appurtenances to the same belonging; To have and to hold unto said BENJAMIN his heirs from the date of the date hereof during the Lives of JOHN DALTON and WALTER DALTON, his Son, formerly inhabitants of this Town, now of PETERSBURG, the said BENJAMIN SEBASTIAN paying annually on the first day of January unto the said JOHN WELCH his heirs (or within thirty days after the expiration of any one year) the sum of Twenty pounds currency of Virginia; Provided Nevertheless that if the said BENJAMIN SEBASTIAN shall fail him or his heirs to pay the said Rent within thirty days after becoming due and demanded then this Instrument shall be void and the Ground and premisses shall revert the same as this Instrument had never been made; In Witness whereof the parties have set their hands and seals

In presence of (no witnesses shown) JOHN WELCH

At a Hustings Court held for the Town and Corporation of Fredericksburg the Fourt day of April one thouand seven hundred and eighty five
This Lease was acknowledged and ordered to be recorded
Test HENRY ARMISTEAD, Clk.

pp. (On margin: 28th March 1786. Delivered this Deed to Mr. N. McCAUL)
143- THIS INDENTURE made the twenty fifth day of March one thousand seven hun-
147 dred and eighty five betwixt DAVID GALLOWAY JUNR. and MARGARET his Wife
of the County of Spotsylvania of one part and NIEL McCOULL of the said County of the other part; Witnesseth that the said DAVID GALLOWAY JUNR. and MARGARET his Wife for the sum of Four hundred and fifty pounds specie current money of Virginia hath granted unto the said NIEL McCOULL one half acre lot of Ground No. (blank) in the Town of Fredericksburg and bounded by the Lotts of PHILIP ERVENS and JOHN LEWIS on two sides and on the others by two Streets; Together with all the buildings to the same belonging; To have and to hold unto the said NEIL McCOULL his heirs from the claim of all other persons whatsoever; In Witness whereof the said DAVID GALLOWAY and MARGARET his Wife have set their hands and seals this Twenty fifth day of March one thousand seven hundred and eighty five

Signed sealed and delivered in presence of

ROBT. RITCHIE, JOHN LEGG, DAVID GALLOWAY JUNR.
ROBERT LILLY, ALEXR. DUNCAN MARGARET GALLOWAY

The Commonwealth of Virginia to GEORGE WEEDON, THOMAS MILLER and JAMES SOMERVILLE Gent., Justices of the Peace for the Town & Corporation of Fredericksburg Greeting (Commission for the privy Examination of MARGARET, the Wife of DAVID GALLOWAY JUNR.) Witness HENRY ARMISTEAD Clerk of our said Court this thirtyeth day of March one Thousand seven hundred and Eighty five in the Ninth year of the Commonwealth

HENRY ARMISTEAD, Clerk

Corporation of Fredericksburg, to wit; (The return of the Certificate for the privy Examination of MARGARET GALLOWAY) THOMAS MILLER
JAMES SOMERVILLE

At a Hustings Court held for the Corporation of Fredericksburg on Monday the Second day of May one thousand seven hundred and Eighty five
This Deed with the receipt thereon endorsed was acknowledged by DAVID GALLOWAY & ordered to be recorded; And a Commission of the Privy Examination of MARGARET GALLOWAY, Wife of the said DAVID GALLOWAY, was at the same time returned and is ordered to be recorded Test HENRY ARMISTEAD, Clerk

pp. (On margin: Delivd. Apl. 19th 1786 to Mr. EDD. ROSS)
148- THIS INDENTURE made the third day of July in the year of our Lord one thou-
150 sand seven hundred and Seventy nine Between WILLIAM WIAT & CATHARINE
his Wife of the County of Spotsylvania and Town of Fredericksburg of the one part and EDWARD ROSS of the same County and Town of other part; Witnesseth that the said WILLIAM WIAT & CATHARINE his Wife for the sum of Three hundred pounds current money do grant unto the said EDWARD ROSS his heirs and assigns all that Lot or half acre of land in the Town of Fredericksburg on PRINCESS MARY STREET on the West side thereof & numbered in the plan of the said Town One hundred & Ninety six and adjoins the Lot number One hundred Ninety eight which two lotts were formerly the property of Mr. JOHN WALLER (since deceased), and by him conveyed to JOHN MITCHELL and by the said MITCHELL conveyed to PETER TALIAFERRO and by the said TALIAFERRO conveyed to THOMAS ALLEN and by the said THOMAS ALLEN conveyed to (JAMES WARD) & the said WILLIAM WIATT, party to these presents; each seperately, all which Deeds are duly recorded in the County Court of Spotsylvania; Now this Indenture witnesseth that the said WILLIAM WIAT and CATHERINE his Wife doth make over unto the said EDWARD ROSS forever in fee simple, all that one half acre or Lott with all ways woods trees fences rail gardens orchards belonging free and clear from the claim of them

their heirs, warranting the same unto the said EDWARD ROSS; In Witness whereof the said WILLIAM WIAT and CATHERINE his Wife hath set their hands and seals
Signed sealed & delivered in presence of
LAC: MACKINTOSH, WILLIAM WIATT
JOHN STAMPER, WM. HOPSON
At a Hustings Court held for the Town and Corporation of fredericksburg the Fourth day of July one thousand seven hundred and Eighty five
This Deed indented with the receipt thereon was acknowledged and ordered to be recorded Test HENRY ARMISTEAD, Clerk

pp. (On margin: Delvd. to EDD. ROSS, Apl. 19th 1786)
150- THIS INDENTURE made the thirtyeth day of April in the year of our Lord one
153 thousand seven hundred & seventy nine Between JAMES WARD and JEAN his Wife of County of Spotsylvania and Town of Fredericksburg of one part and EDWARD ROSS of the same County & Town of the other part; Witnesseth that the said JAMES WARD and JEAN his Wife for the sum of Three hundred pounds current money to them in hand paid hath granted unto EDWARD ROSS his heirs and assigns all that one lot or half acre of land in the Town of Fredericksburg situate on PRINCESS MARY STREET on the West side thereof and numbered in the plan of the said Town One hundred & ninety eight, and adjoins the Lott number One hundred & ninety six, which two lots were formerly the property of Mr. JOHN WALLER (since deceased) & by him conveyed to JOHN MITCHELL & by the said MITCHELL conveyed to PETER TALIAFERRO and by the said TALIAFERRO conveyed to THOMAS ALLEN & by the said ALLEN conveyed the said Lott to JAMES WARD, party to these presents, Now This Indenture Witnesseth that the said JAMES WARD and JEAN his Wife doth make over unto the said EDWARD ROSS his heirs and assigns forever in fee simple all that one half acre of Ground with trees woods orchards minerals benefits belonging free of the claims of them the said JAMES WARD and JEAN his Wife or any other persons; To have and to hold without interruption of them or any other persons; In Witness whereof the said JAMES WARD and JEAN his Wife hath set their hands and seals
Signed sealed and delivered in presence of
RICHARD KENNEY, JAMES WARD
LAC: MACKINTOSH, JAMES BROWN
TO ALL whom these presents shall come, I JANE WARD, Widow of JAMES WARD deceased sendeth Greeting; Whereas by the within deed my deceased Husband JAMES WARD hath conveyed the lott of land described in the said Deed; to which conveyance I was named a party, but not being applied to for the purpose he have never yet released my Title to the premisses; These presents therefore witnesseth that from the regard to the memory of my deceased Husband and for the sum of Five shillings current money to me paid by EDWARD ROSS and in vertue thereof release all right which I now have or claim to the within conveyed Lott of land; And I do hereby covenant that I have done no act to impeach the Title of the within conveyed premisses & lastly that I am willing this my Release may be recorded with this Deed; In Testimony whereof I have set my hand and seal this fifteenth day of October one thousand seven hundred and Eighty four
Sealed and delivered in the presence of
LAC: MACKINTOSH, (no signature)
G. C. TUCKER, JACOB WHITLER
At a Hustings Court held for the Town and Corporation of Fredericksburg on Monday the Fourth day of July one thousand seven hundred and Eighty five

This Deed was proved by the oath of LAC: MACKINTOSH & JAMES BROWN & ordered to be certified; And a Memorandum thereon endorsed signed by JANE WARD was proved by the oath of LAC: MACKINTOSH & JACOB WHITLER and ordered to be recorded

At a Court held for the said Corporation on Monday the first day of August one thousand seven hundred and eighty five This Deed was further proved by the oath of RICHARD KENNEY & ordered to be recorded

Test HENRY ARMISTEAD, Clerk

pp. 153-154 THIS INDENTURE of Apprenticeship Between ELIZABETH MURRAY, HUGH ALDERS, her Son, of the one part and TULLY WHITHURST of the Town of Fredericksburg of the other part; Witnesseth that the said ELIZABETH MURRAY with the consent of the Court of Hustings of Fredericksburg do place and bind her Son, the said HUGH ALDERS, an Apprentice to the said TULLY WHITHURST with him to serve untill he shall arrive to the age of Twenty one years during which time the said HUGH ALDERS shall truly serve the said TULLY WHITHURST in all things behave as a faithful Apprentice, and the said TULLY WHITHURST on his part doth promise that he will cause him to be instructed & taught in the Art and profession he now useth of a Taylor that he will find him sufficient cloathing diet & lodging for such an Apprentice, morevoer that he will cause him to be taught to read & write and treat him as an Apprentice ought to be; Witness our hands and seals this Third day of December One thousand seven hundred and Eighty five

Witness JAMES EDMONDSON, ELIZABETH MURRAY
TULLY WHITHURST

At a Hustings Court held for the Town and Corporation of Fredericksburg on Monday the Fifth day of December one thousand seven hundred and Eighty five
This Indenture of Apprenticeship was proved as to ELIZABETH MURRAY and acknowledged by TULLY WHITHURST and ordered to be recorded

Test HENRY ARMISTEAD, Clerk

pp. 154-156 THIS INDENTURE made the twenty six day of June in the year of our Lord one thousand seven hundred and eighty five and in the ninth year of the Independence of the United States of America Between ROGER DIXON of Fredericksburg in the State of Virginia, Gentleman, of the one part and JOHN WELCH of the same place and State, Gentleman, of the other part; Witnesseth that the said ROGER DIXON for the yearly rents and covenants herein after reserved hath demised and to farm letten unto the said JOHN WELCH his Executors and assigns part of a Lot of Land being in the Town of Fredericksburg aforesaid on the Main Street thereof and is known in a plan of the said Town by the number Two hundred & fifty eight; which part of the said Lott is laid off in a parallelogram or long square containing Thirty six feet in front & one hundred and forty two feet in depth and is the North West or upper part of the said lott with all the houses outhouses buildings and improvements; To have and to hold the said Lott of Land unto the said JOHN WELCH from the date of these presents during the term of seven years eight months and ten days thence next ensuing; paying the yearly rent of three pounds current money on or before the twenty sixth day of June in each year; And so in proportion for the remaining Eight months and ten days of the said term and if it shall happen the yearly rent be behind by space of twenty eight days it may be lawful for ROGER DIXON to have and enjoy as in his former estate right and the said JOHN WELCH for himself his heirs doth grant that he will well and truly pay the said yearly rent; In Witness whereof the said parties have set their hands and seals

Sealed and delivered in presence of

JOS: WOOD JUNR. ROGER DIXON

JOHN COAKLEY, COLLIN FRAZER JOHN WELCH

At a Hustings Court held for the Corporation of Fredericksburg on Monday the Fourth day of July one thousand seven hundred and eighty five

This Indenture of Lease proved by the oaths of JOSEPH WOOD, JOHN COAKLEY & COLLIN FRAZER & ordered to be recorded Test HENRY ARMISTEAD, Clerk

pp. THIS INDENTURE made the Tenth day of October in the year of our Lord one
157- thousand seven hundred & eighty five Between JOHN SPOTSWOOD of the County
160 of ORANGE & State of Virginia of the one part and WILLIAM McWILLIAMS of the County of Spotsylvania & Borough of Fredericksburg of the other part; Wheresa ANN BRAYNE, late of DARTMOUTH STREET in the City of WISTMINSTER in the Kingdom of GREAT BRITAIN, Spinster, in her last Will & Testament in Writing bearing date on or about the twenty eighth day of April in the year one thousand seven hundred & seventy four and by a Codicil thereto bearing date on or about the Twentieth day of May in the year of our Lord one thousand seven hundred & seventy four (among other things) gave all the residue of her personal Estate unto her Nieces and Nephews, DOROTHEA DANDRIGE, ANN THORNTON and WILLIAM THOMPSON, her Niece ANN HIPKINS & her Great Nephew JOHN SPOTSWOOD, thereby revoking the Bequest which she had made thereof by her said Will for the Benefit of Mrs. ANN CATHARINA MOORE and of her said Will appointed JOHN NORTON Esqr. since deceased, and WILLIAM BRAY, Esqr., Executors, who duly proved the same in the Prerogative Court of the Arch Bishop of CANTERBERRY, And Whereas the said ANN BRAYNE was intituled to the principal sum of Two hundred pounds secured by an old Mortgage of certain lands at SHEIR in the County of SURRY in the Kingdom of GREAT BRITAIN aforesaid, with some arrear of Interest thereon, And Whereas the said WILLIAM McWILLIAMS hath agreed with the said JOHN SPOTSWOOD for the purchase of all the share and interest of the said JOHN SPOTSWOOD of and in the said principal sum of Two hundred pounds, and the Interest due to grow due thereon, at & for the sum of Forty pounds Sterling money of Great Britain; This Indenture Witnesseth that for Forty pounds lawfull money of Great Britain to the said JOHN SPOTSWOOD by the said WILLIAM McWILLIAMS paid which sum said JOHN SPOTSWOOD doth acknowledge and doth hereby release the said WILLIAM McWILLIAMS his Exrs. and assigns, hath sold unto the said WILLIAM McWILLIAMS every part of the said principal sum of Two hundred pounds, and of the Interest due & to grow due thereon (being part of the residue of the personal Estate & effects of the said ANN BRAYNE deceased, to which the said JOHN SPOTSWOOD is intituled under the said recited Will of the said ANN BRAYNE) and all Estate right of him the said JOHN SPOTSWOOD to the same; To have and to hold all and every such parts of the said JOHN SPOTSWOOD to the said principal sum of Two hundred pounds & interest unto the said WILLIAM McWILLIAMS as his own property and the said JOHN SPOTSWOOD hath appointed the said WILLIAM McWILLIAMS his Executor and Administrator true and lawful Attorney in the name of the said JOHN SPOTSWOOD to receive from the personal Representative of the said ANN BRAYNE all sums of money as shall belong to the said JOHN SPOTSWOOD and that his Right thereto is now actually subsisting as aforesaid and so continue and be unto the said WILLIAM McWILLIAMS according to the true meaning of these presents, In Witness whereof I hve set my hand and affixed my Seal

Signed sealed and delivered in the presence of

JOHN BROOKE, BENJA: DAY, JOHN SPOTSWOOD

WM. FRENCH, FRENCH GRAY

(No recording shown)

(Page 161 is blank.)

pp. 162-165 THIS INDENTUREA made the Third day of December in the year of our Lord one thousand seven hundred & eighty five Between FRANCIS THORNTON and ANN THORNTON his Wife of the State of Virginia & County of Spotsylvania of one part, and GEORGE FRENCH, Doctor of Physic, & WILLIAM McWILLIAMS, Merchant, of the State of Virginia & Borough of Fredericksburg of the other part; Whereas ANN BRAYNE late of DARTMOUTH STREET in the City of WESTMINSTER in the Kingdom of Great Brittain, Spinster, by her last Will and Testament in writing bearing date the twenty eighth day of April one thousand seven hundred & seventy four, and a Codicil bearing date the twentieth day of May one thousand seven hundred & seventy four amongst other things gave all the residue of her personal Estate unto her Nieces & Nephew, DOROTHY DANDRIGE, ANN THORNTON & WILLIAM THOMPSON, her Niece ANN HIPKENS and her Great Newphew, JOHN SPOTSWOOD, thereby revoking the Bequest which she had made thereof by her first Wil for the benefit of Mrs. CATHARINE MOORE and of her said Will appointed JOHN NORTON Esqr., since deceased, & WILLIAM BRAY Esqr. Executors, who duly proved the same in the Prerogative Court of the Arch Bishop of CANTERBURY, And Whereas the said ANN BRAYNE was intitled to the principal sum of Two hundred pounds, secured by an old Mortgage of certain lands in County of SURRY in the Kingdom of Great Brittain as aforesaid, And Whereas the said GEORGE FRENCH and WILLIAM McWILLIAMS hath agreed with the said FRANCIS THORNTON and ANN THORNTON in the principal sum for the price of Forty pounds, Now This Indenture Witnesseth that for the sum paid the said FRANCIS THORNTON and ANN his Wife doth release the said GEORGE FRENCH and WILLIAM McWILLIAMS & hath sold all their share to grow due thereon, being part of the residue of the personal estate and effects of the said JOHN BRAYNE deceased (to which the aforesaid ANN THORNTON is entitled under the recited Will of the said ANN BRAYNE as aforesaid), To have and to hold unto the said GEORGE FRENCH and WILLIAM McWILLIAMS their heirs from henceforth as their own property they the said FRANCIS THORNTON and ANN THORNTON hath appointed the said GEORGE FRENCH and WILLIAM McWILLIAMS their true and lawful Attornies in the name of the said FRANCIS THORNTON and ANN THORTON to demand from the personal representation of the said ANNE BRAYNE deceased, all sums of moneys as shall belong to the said FRANCIS THORNTON and ANN THORNTON, In Witness whereof we have set our hands and affixed our seals this third day of December in the year of our Lord one thousand seven hundred and Eighty five

FRANCIS THORNTON
ANN THORNTON

At a Hustings Court held for the Corporation of Frederickburg on Monday the Sixth day of February one thousand seven hundred and Eighty six
This Deed of Assignment and Release was proved by the oaths of GUSTAVUS B. WALLACE and WILLIAM GLASSELL two of the witnesses thereto and ordered to be recorded

Test HENRY ARMISTEAD, Clk.

pp. 166-168 THIS INDENTURE made the eighth day of July in the year of our Lord one thousand seven hundred and Eighty five and in the Tenth year of the Independence of the United States of America between MARY GIBBS of the Corporation of Fredericksburg in the State of Virginia, Widow and Relict of RICHARD PEACOCK, late of the same place and State, Gentleman, deceased, and RICHARD PEACOCK, Son and heir at Law of the said RICHARD PEACOCK deceased of the one part and ELISHA DICKENSON of the Corporation and State aforesaid Gentleman of the other part; Witnesseth that the said MARY GIBBS and RICHARD PEACOCK for the sum of One hundred and twenty pounds do grant unto the said ELISHA DICKENSON his heirs and assigns all that lot of land being in the Corporation aforesaid and known in the plan thereof by the number (blank) bounded in front on PRINCESS AUGUSTA STREET and on the upper side by WOOLF STREET, Together with all houses and improvements; To have and to hold the said Land unto the said ELISHA DICKENSON his heirs and assigns; And the said MARY GIBBS and RICHARD PEACOCK the said Land against all persons whatsoever will warrant and forever defend by these presents; In Witness whereof the parties have set their hands and seals

Sealed and delivered in presence of

JNO: FRAZER, MARY x GIBBS,
G: HEISKELL, TULLY WHITHURST RICHARD PEACOCK

WHEREAS there is a parcel of the within mentioned Lot of Land umber Seven(blank) appropriated to the use of a Burial Place in which the body of the within named RICHARD PEACOCK is deposited, And Whereas the within named RICHARD PEACOCK, his Son and heir at Law, is desirous to retain the said burial place, It is mutually agreed and the said ELISHA DICKENSON for himself his heirs dot agree to and with the said RICHARD PEACOCK his heirs that the said burial place being a square of Ten feet shall ( ) the said RICHARD PEACOCK his heirs and assigns anything contined in the within Deed to the contrary thereof notwithstanding; In Witness whereof the said parties have to these presents set their hands and seals

Sealed and delivered in presence of

JNO: FRAZIER, RICHARD PEACOCK
G: HEISKELL, TULLY WHITHURST ELISHA DICKENSON

(No recording shown.)

pp. (On margin: 2nd day of June 1786; Delivered to Mr. JOHN ROBINSON)
169- THIS INDENTURE made the Twenty fifth day of May in the year of our Lord one
171 thousand seven hundred and Eighty five between RICHARD KENNEY, Merchant, of the one part and Town of Fredericksburg and County of Spotsylvania and JOHN ROBINSON of the other part and Town & County aforesaid; Witnesseth that the said RICHARD KENNEY for the sum of Five shillings current money hath let and to farm lett unto the said JOHN ROBINSON a certain piece of Ground in the said Town of Fredericksburg bounded, Beginning one hundred and five feet from the Corner of HAWKE STREET and the House now occupied by THOMAS COCKRAN, Merchant, thence running along CAROLINE STREET thirty two feet, thence right angles one hundred and twenty feet back, thence upward toward HAWKE STREET thirty two feet, thence right angles to the beginning; And it is still further covenanted and agreed between the parties to these presents that at the end of the one hundred and twenty feet above mentioned that a Lane of Fifteen feet wide shall be kept opened for the benefit and advantage of the several Tenements on the before mentioned CAROLINE STREET (that is to say) Beginning at the Cross Street, thence extending on a Strait line to ZACHARIAH LUCASSes Lott, together with the ways unto the said piece of ground belonging; To have and to hold unto the said JOHN ROBINSON during the term of Twenty one years to commence on the fourteenth day of February one thousand seven hundred and eighty five, the said JOHN ROBINSON paying the sum of Nine pounds specie (or hard money) in every year during the term aforesaid, (to wit), on the fourteenth day of February one thousand seven hundred and eighty six and to continued his annual payments of Rents on the Fourteenth day of February in every year during the term of Twenty one years, together with all Taxes and incumbrances that may become due; And the said JOHN ROBINSON doth covenant for himself his heirs that the end of the term aforesaid, the

said RICHARD KENNEY his heirs may enter and take possession of the Ground without any hindrance, and enjoy the same as in his former Estate; In Witness whereof the parties have set their hands and affixed their seals
Signed sealed acknowledged and delivered in presence of
JOHN FORNEYHOUGH, RICHARD KENNEY
THOS: MILLER, THOS: COCKRAN JOHN ROBINSON
At a Hustings Court held for the Corporation of Fredericksburg the Six day of February one thousand seven hundred and Eighty six
This Lease was acknowledged & ordered to be recorded
Test HENRY ARMISTED, Clerk

pp. (On margin: This Deed delivered to Mr. D. BLAIR 26th Apl. 1786)
171- THIS INDENTURE made the Ninth day of September in year of our Lord one
173 thousand seven hundred and Eighty five Between CHARLES YATES of Fredericks-
burg, Merchant, of the one part and DAVID BLAIR of Fredericksburg (for himself) and as Executor & Surviving Partner of ISAAC HESLOP, late of WHITEHAVEN, Merchant deceased, on the other part; Witnesseth that the ssid CHARLES YATES for the sum of Two hundred and fifty pounds Sterling money hath granted unto the said DAVID BLAIR his heirs a certain lot or half acre of Ground in the Town of FREDERICKSBURG lying on the River side and is known in the plan of the said Town by the number Two hundred and Seventy three; together with all houses buildings profits to the same belonging; To have and to hold unto him the said DAVID BLAIR his heirs and assigns forever from the claim of him the said CHARLES YATES his will and will warrant & forever defend by these presents; In Witness whereof the said CHARLES YATES has set his hand and seal
in the presence of (No witnesses shown) CHARLES YATES
At a Hustings Court held for the Corporation of Fredericksburg the Seventh day of November one thousand seven hundred and eighty five
This Deed was personally acknowledged by the said CHARLES YATES and ordered to be recorded Test HENRY ARMISTEAD, Clerk

pp. THIS INDENTURE TRIPARTITE made the Thirteenth day of May in the year of
173- our Lord one thousand seven hundred and Eighty five Between JESSE SLAVEN
175 of the County of STAFFORD and MARTHA his Wife of the first part; WILLIAM
JACKSON of the Town of Fredericksburg and County of Spotsylvania & FRANCES his Wife of the second part and EDWARD HERNDON JUNIOR of the Town and County aforesaid of the third part; Whereas JOHN HARLEGROVE and FRANCES his Wife, now FRANCES JACKSON party hereto by their Indenture bearing date the eleventh day of December one thousand seven hundred and seventy eight did for the consideration mentioned sell lunto the said JESSE SLAVEN all that part of a Lott of Ground in the said Town of Fredericksburg numbered Fifty three in the plan of the said Town particularly bounded in the said Indenture as by the same duly proved & recorded in Spotsylvania Court the Eighteenth day of February one thousand seven hundred and Seventy nine; reference being had may appear, And Whereas although the said FRANCES was a party to the said Deed and signed and sealed the same yet not having been in the lifetime of the said JOHN HARLEGROVE privily examined touching her consent to the same & making a legal relinquishment according to the Act of Assembly in such case provided, she therefore was not devested of her interest therein and having survived her husband, the said JOHN HARLEGROVE, she had as right to claim her endowment in the premisses conveyed by the said Indenture; And Whereas the said JESSE SLAVEN hath sold

the said part of a Lott to the said EDWARD HERNDON JUNIOR, and the said WILLIAM JACKSON and FRANCES his Wife, have also consented to convey all their right of the said FRANCES, This Indenture Witnesseth that the said JESSE SLAVEN and MARTHA his Wife for the sum of Three hundred and twelve pounds current money of Virginia and the said WILLIAM JACKSON and FRANCES his Wife for the sum of Five pounds of the like money to them paid, they the said JESSE SLAVEN and MARTHA his Wife and the said WILLIAM JACKSON and FRANCES his wife with the consent of the said JESSE SLAVEN have granted the aforesaid part of a lott and all the right of them the said JESSE SLAVEN and MARTHA his Wife and the said WILLIAM JACKSON and FRANCES his Wife; To have and to hold the said Lott of Ground unto the said EDWARD HERNDON JUNIOR his heirs & assigns against them their heirs and assigns and claims of all other persons
In Witness whereof the parties have set their hands & affixed their seals
Sealed and delivered in presence of

JNO: RICHARDS,	JESSE SLAVEN
LAUR: ATHERTON, JNO: M. HERNDON	MARTHA × SLAVEN
RHD. MAURY	WILLIAM JACKSON

At a Hustings Court held for the Corporation of Fredericksburg on Monday the seventh day of November one thousand seven hundred and eighty five
This Deed indented Tripartite the acknowledgement of the said JESSE SLAVEN & WILLIAM JACKSON was proved by the oaths of JOHN RICHARDS, JOHN M. HERNDON & RICHARD MAURY, and is ordered to be recorded

Test HENRY ARMISTEAD, Clerk

The Commonwealth of Virginia to CHARLES MORTIMER, JAMES SOMERVILLE and GEORGE FRENCH, Gent., Justices of the Town and Corporation of Fredericksburg (The Commission of Dedimus of MARTHA SLAVEN and FRANCES JACKSON) Witness HENRY ARMISTEAD Clerk of our said Court this ninth day of February one thousand seven hundred and Eighty seven and in the Eleventh year of the Commonwealth

HENRY ARMISTEAD, Clk.

Pursuant to the above Commission, we did this day privily examined Mrs MARTHA SLAVEN, Wife the the within named JESSE SLAVEN, and FRANCES JACKSON, Wife of the within named WILLIAM JACKSON, and they the said MARTHA SLAVEN & FRANCES JACKSON did freely acknowledge the said Indenture & declared they did the same without the threats of their said Husbands; Certified under our hands and seals this Ninth day of February one thousand seven hundred and eighty seven

MARTHA SLAVEN legally complied with the Commission directed but FRANCES JACKSON refused to Consent. Witness our hands and seals February the Ninth one thousand seven hundred and Eighty seven. CHARLES MORTIMER
GEORGE FRENCH

pp. 176-178 THIS INDENTURE made the twenty secon day of December in the year of our Lord one thousand seven hundred and Eighty five Between ADAM HUNTER of STAFFORD County Esqr., of the one part and JOHN BENSON of the Town of Fredericksburg of the other part; Whereas ELIZABETH WILKENSON & MARY SULLIVAN purchased of BENJAMIN JOHNSTON certains lots & parcels of Ground in the said Town of Fredericksburg which were conveyed by the said BENJAMIN JOHNSTON to the said WILKENSON & SULLIVAN as Tenants in Common by Deed dated the first day of January in the year one thousand seven hundred and Seventy nine; & Recorded in the Court of Spotsylvania County; And Whereas the said ELIZABETH WILKENSON in order to secure the payment of a sum of money owing by her to JAMES HUNTER Esqr., late of the said County of STAFFORD, deceased, did by her Deed dated the Fifth day of December in

the year of our Lord one thousand seven hundred & Eighty two, sell their moiety of the lots, houses unto the said JAMES HUNTER for the purpose aforesaid; And by the same Deed did empower the said JESSE HUNTER to sell her moiety aforesaid for the most that he could be got and to make a good title to the purchaser for the same; And Whereas the said JAMES HUNTER in his life time by virtue of such authority did sell the said ELIZABETH WILKENSONs moiety or one half of the lots & parcels of Ground unto the said JOHN BENSON in fee simple for the consideration of One thousand pounds current money of Virginia, and did also by his last Will and Testament after sundry specifick legacies give the residue of his Estate to the said ADAM HUNTER & his heirs subject to the payment of his Debts & Legacies in the said Will mentioned; And died without making any conveyance of the moiety aforesaid to the said JOHN BENSON as he intended to have done. Now This Indenture Witnesseth that the said ADAM HUNTER in consideration of the premisses and of the sum of One thousand pounds current money to him paid hath sold unto the said JOHN BENSON his heirs & assigns all the said moiety of the Lotts, houses Ground & premisses aforesaid, together with all buildings streets ways belonging & all the estate & demand of the said ELIZABETH WILKENSON, JAMES HUNTER and the said ADAM HUNTER to the same; To have and to hold unto the said JOHN BENSON his heirs & assigns forever to hold without the molestation of the said ELIZABETH WILKINSON and ADAM HUNTER their heirs or any person claiming under them; In Witness the said ADAM HUNTER hath hereunto set his hand & affixed his seal
Signed sealed & delivered in presence of
THOMAS MOFFATT, ADAM HUNTER
HENRY MITCHELL, GEORGE HUTCHESON

At a Hustings Court held for the Corporation of Fredericksburg on Monday the Sixth day of February one thousand seven hundred and eighty six
This Deed proved by the witness and ordered to be recorded
Test HENRY ARMISTEAD, Clerk

pp. 178-179 KNOW ALL MEN by these presents that I ADAM HUNTER, Surviving Partner of JAMES & ADAM HUNTER of the County of STAFFORD and State of Virginia have made JOHN DONALDSON & WILLIAM COX JUNR. by the firm of DONALDSON & COX of the City of PHILADELPHIA & State of PENSYLVANIA my lawfull Attorneys for me to receive all such of money and other demands which are due and belonging to me or detained from me by JOHN BROWN of the Town of PROVIDENCE & State of RHODE ISLAND, granting unto my Attorneys my full power about the premisses to use all lawful means for the recovery thereof; And upon receipt of any such Debts discharges for me to make and generally every other things & devices in the Law necessary to be done to perform as fully as I might do if I were personally present; In Witness whereof I have set my hand & seal this Twenty eighth day of April in the year of our Lord one thousand seven hundred and Eighty six
Sealed and delivered in the presence of
HENRY MITCHELL, ADAM HUNTER
THOS: STONE Surviving Partner of sd JAMES & ADAM HUNTER

At a Hustings Court held for the Corporation of Fredericksburg on Monday the first day of May one thousand seven hundred and Eighty six
This Power of Attorney was acknowledged in open Court personally by the said ADAM HUNTER and is ordered to be recorded & is truly recorded; In Testimony whereof I have caused the Seal of my Office to be hereto affixed HENRY ARMISTEAD, Cl, C. C. F.

pp. 180-182 THIS INDENTURE made the Twenty sixth day of June in the year of our Lord one thousand seven hundred and eighty five and in the Tenth year of the Independence of the United State of America Between ROGER DIXON of Fredericksburg and the State of Virginia, Gentleman, of the one part and JOHN WELCH of the same place and State, Gentleman, of the other part; Witnesseth that the said ROGER DIXON for the yearly Rents herein reserved hath granted and to farm letten unto the said JOHN WELCH his heirs & assigns, part of a Lot of Land being in the Town of Fredericksburg on the Main Street distringuished in a Plan of the said Town by the number Two hundred and fifty eight, which part of the said Lott is laid off in a parallelogram or long square contining thirty six feet in front and one hundred and forty two feet in depth, and is the North West or upper part of the said Lot numbered Two hundred & fifty eight; together with all the houses and improvements; To have and to hold from the date of these presents during the term of Seven years eight months and ten days thence next ensuing paying therefore yearly during the said term unto the said ROGER DIXON his heirs the yearly rent of Three pounds current money on or before the Twenty six day of June in each year and so in proportion for the remaining eight months and ten days of the said term; And if it shall happen the said yearly rent to be behind and unpaid by the space of Twenty eight days next after the said days appointed for the payment thereof, then it shall be lawful for the said ROGER DIXON his heirs or assigns into the said premisses to reenter and the same to have again, And the said JOHN WELCH for himself doth grant that he will truly pay the said yearly Rents at the days above expressed clear of all Taxes rates and payments whatsoever; In Witness whereof the said parties to these presents set their hands & seals
Sealed and delivered in presence of

JOS: WOOD JUNR., ROGER DIXON
JOHN COAKLY, COLLIN FRASER JOHN WELCH

At a Hustings Curt held for the Corporation of Fredericksburg on Monday the Fourth day of July one thousand seven hundred and Eighty five
This Lease was proved by the oaths of JOSEPH WOOD, JOHN COAKLEY and COLLIN FRASER & ordered to be recorded Test HENRY ARMISTEAD, Clerk

pp. 182-183 TO ALL PEOPLE to whom this presents writing shall come, I WILLIAM BLYTHE of the County of Spotsylvania and Town of Fredericksburg send Greeting; Know ye that I the said WILLIAM BLYTHE for the natural love and affection which I do bear unto my Son in Law, JOSHUA McWILLIAMS, and MARY his Wife, as well for the said JOSHUA McWILLIAMS and MARY his Wife finding for and providing me the said WILLIAM BLYTHE and my Eldest Daughter, PEGGY BLYTHE, a sufficient maintenance of meat drink washing lodging and apparel during our and each of our lives suitable to our qualitie and for the said JOSHUA McWILLIAMS pay and discharging all my just Debts, have given unto the said JOSHUA McWILLIAMS and MARY his Wife all the tract of land whereon I now live containing One half acre being in the County and Town aforesaid, it being the Lott I bought of JAMES MARYE by Deed bearing date the Sixteenth day of May, one thousand seven hundred & seventy one; and duely proved and recorded in the Court of Spotsylvania County; To have and to hold the sasid Lott of Land and all its rights forever, And also I the said WILLIAM BLYTHE have given all my other Estate now in my possession or that shall accrue to me, and further, Know ye that I the said WILLIAM BLYTHE have this day before the signing & sealing of these presents put the said JOSHUA McWILLIAMS & MARY his Wife in quiet possession of the lands within mentioned together with all my other Estate of every sort whatsoever; In Testimony whereof I have set my hand and affixed my seal this Third day of February one thousand seven hundred and Eighty six

Signed sealed & acknowledged in the presence of
EDWARD HERNDON, WILLIAM BLYTHE
GODLOVE HEISKELL, WILLIAM MALLORY
(No recording shown)

pp. 184-187 THIS INDENTURE made the Seventh day of November in year of our Lord one thousand seven hundred and Eighty five and in the Tenth year of the Independence of the United States of America Between JOHN FRAZER of Fredericksburg in the State of Virginia, Merchant, and BETTY his Wife of the one part and GEORGE FRENCH of the same place and State, Practitioner of Physic, of the other part; Witnesseth that the said JOHN FRAZER and BETTY his Wife for the sum of Three hundred and twenty pounds current money of the State aforesaid, have granted all that lot of land in Fredericksburg aforesaid and known in the plan of the same by the number One hundred and thirty five; Together with all houses buildings and improvements belonging; To have and to hold unto the said GEORGE FRENCH his heirs and assigns forever; In Witness whereof the said parties aforesaid have to these presents set their hands and seals JOHN FRAZER
BETTY FRAZER

The Commonwealth of Virginia to CHARLES MORTIMER, THOMAS MILLER and JAMES SOMERVILLE Gent., Greeting (The Dedimus & examination of BETTY FRAZER). this seventh day of November one thousand seven hundred and Eighty five

Corporation of Fredericksburg (to wit) Pursuant to this Commission, we did this day examine Mrs. BETTY FRAZER (Certificate of Examination) this seventh day of November one thousand seven hundred and eighty five CHARLES MORTIMER
THOMAS MILLER

At a Hustings Court held for the Corporation of Fredericksburg on Monday the seventh day of November one thousand seven hundred and eighty five;
This Deed was personally acknowledged by the said JOHN FRAZER which with a Commission and Certificate of the privy Examination of the said BETTY being returned, is ordered to be recorded Test HENRY ARMISTEAD, Clk.

pp. 187-190 THIS INDENTURE made the sixth day of February in the year of our Lord one thousand seven hundred and Eighty six and in the Tenth year of the Independence of the United State of America Between JOHN LEGG of the Corporation of Fredericksburg in the State of Virginia, Merchant, and LUCY his Wife & ROBERT YOUNG of the same place and State, Merchant, of the one part and the Honorable JAMES MUNROE of the County of KING GEORGE in the State aforesaid Esquire of the other part; Witnesseth that the said JOHN LEGG and LUCY LEE his Wife and the said ROBERT YOUNG for the sum of One hundred and five pounds to the said ROBERT in hand paid doth sell unto the said JAMES MUNROE his heirs and assigns all that Lot of Land in Fredericksburg aforesaid and known in the plan thereof by the number One hundred and twenty seven bounded on front by CHARLES STREET and on the North West or upper side by WILLIAM STEEET, together with all the houses edifices and improvements belonging; To have and to hold the said Lot of Land known by the number One hundred and twenty seven and all the premisses unto the said JAMES MUNROE his heirs and assigns forever; to possess without the molestation of them the said JOHN LEGG and ROBERT YOUNG, their heirs or any other persons claiming under them; In Witness whereof the said parties have set their hands and seal
In presence of (no witnesses shown) JOHN LEGG
LUCY LEE LEGG
ROBERT YOUNG

Commonwealth of Virginia to GEORGE WEEDON, WILLIAM McWILLIAMS & JAMES DUNCANSON Gent., Greeting. (Request for the private Examination of LUCY LEE LEGG) Witness HENRY ARMISTEAD Clerk of our said Court this sixth day of February one thousand seven hundred and eighty six in the Tenth year of the Common Wealth
HENRY ARMISTEAD, Clerk

Corporation of Fredericksburg (to wit); Pursuant to the within Commission (Certificate of execution of the Commission) this Fifth day of February one thousand seven hundred and Eighty six
GEORGE WEEDON
WM. McWILLIAMS

At a Hustings Court held for the Corporation of Fredericksburg on Monday the Sixth day of February one thousand seven hundred and eighty six
This Deed was acknowledged by JOHN LEGG and ROBERT YOUNG and a Commission with a Certificate of the said LUCY LEE LEGG acknowledgement being returned, the said Deed and Commission are ordered to be recorded Test HENRY ARMISTEAD, Clk.

p. 191 THIS INDENTURE made the twenty fourth day of June in the year of our Lord one thousand seven hundred and Eighty five and in the Ninth year of the Independence of the United States of America, Between ROGER DIXON, Son & Heir at Law of ROGER DIXON, late of the Town of Fredericksburg in State of Virginia, Gentleman, deceased, of the one part and RICHARD PEACOCK of the same place and State, Gentleman, of the other part; Witnesseth that the said ROGER DIXON for the sum of Fifty pounds hath granted unto the said RICHARD PEACOCK his heirs and assigns all that parcel of land containing One hundred and seventy one and a half feet in front on CAROLINE STREET in the Town of Fredericksburg aforesaid, being the North West part of the lot numbered Sixteen in the plan of the same and extending (blank) feet in depth from CAROLINE STREET aforesaid to the Lott number fourteen; Together with all the houses and buildings to the same belonging; To have and to hold unto the said RICHARD PEACOCK his heirs and assigns and the said ROGER DIXON will warrnt and forever defend by these presents; In Witness whereof the said parties have set their hands and seals
Sealed and delivered in presence of
JOS: WOOD JUNR., ROGER DIXON
JOHN COAKLEY, COL: FRAZER

At a Hustings Court held for the Corporation of Fredericksburg the Fourth day of July one thousand seven hundred and eighty five
This Deed was proved by the oaths of JOSEPH WOODS JUNR., JOHN COAKLEY and COLLIN FRAZER and ordered to be recorded
Deld. RICHD. PEACOCK Test HENRY ARMISTEAD, Clk.

(Page 192 is blank.)

pp. 193-196 (On margin: Delivered this Deed 17th July 1786 to CHS., LEEMAN)
THIS INDENTURE made the Nineteenth day of November in the year of our Lord one thousand seven hundred and eighty five and in the Tenth year of the Independence of the United States of America Between JOHN REED and STANDISH FORDE of the City of PHILADELPHIA in the State of PENSYLVANIA, Merchants, of one part and CHARLES LEEMAN of the Corporation of Fredericksburg in the State of Virginia, Mercht., of the other part; Whereas the said JOHN REED and STANDISH FORD have by their certain Bond bearing even date with these presents acknowledged themselves their heirs to be firmly bound unto the said CHARLES LEEMAN his heirs Executors and assigns in the penal sum of One thousand four hundred and sixty pounds current money of the State of Virginia with a condition thereunder written that if the said JOHN

REED and STANDISH FORD well and truly pay the certificates issued or acknowledged by the States of NEW HAMPSHIRE, MASSACHUSETTS, CONNECTICULT, RHODE ISLAND, NEW YORK, NEW JERSEY, PENSYLVANIA, DELAWARE, MARYLAND or Virginia or public claims or services which Certificates should be funded or on which the said States have paid Interest at the rate of Six per centum per annum at one third part of the sum expressed in the said Certificates as also the Interest that may be due thereon in the same proportion to the amount of Seven hundred and thirty pounds Currt. money of the said State of Virginia on or before the Seventh day of June in the year one thousand seven hundred and Eighty six the said Bond or Obligation to be void or to remain in full force; Now This Indenture Witnesseth that the said JOHN REED and STANDISH FORDE as well to secure the payment of the said sum before mentioned as also for Five shillings to them in hand paid by the said CHARLES LEEMAN have sold unto the said CHARLES LEEMAN all tht Lott of Land being on CAROLINE STREET in the Corporation of Fredericksburg aforesaid bounded to the North Westward by GEORGE STREET and known in the plan of the Town of Fredericksburg by the number Forty Three; Together with all the houses and improvements belonging; To have and to hold the said Land unto the said CHARLES LEEMAN his heirs & assigns forever; Provided nevertheless that if the said JOHN REED and STANDISH FORDE or their heirs truly pay to the said CHARLES LEEMAN or his Executors on or before the Twentieth day of June in the year one thousand seven hundred and Eighty six the before mentioned sum then this Indenture and every part shall be void and of no effect; In Witness whereof the parties have set their hands and seals

JOHN REED
STANDISH FORDE

Sealed & Delivered by the said STANDISH FORDE as well for and in his own behalf as for and in behalf of the said JOHN REED by virtue of a Letter of Attorney authorizing him so to do in the presence of

JOSHUA PAINE, SAML. PAINE,
ALEXANDER ROANE, JOS: WOOD, JUNR.

At a Hustings Court held for the Corporation of Fredericksburg on Monday the third day of April one thousand seven hundred and eighty six
This Deed of Mortgage was proved by the oaths of JOSHUA PAYNE and ALEXANDER ROANE & ordered to be recorded & is truly recorded

Test HENRY ARMISTEAD, Clk.

pp. (On Margin: Delivered to MICHL. RYAN July 18th 1786)
197- THIS INDENTURE made the fourteenth day of April in the year of our Lord one
201 thousand seven hundred and eighty six Between CHARLES MORTIMER of the Town of Fredericksburg and SARAH G. MORTIMER his Wife of the one part and MICHAEL RYAN of the Town of ALEXANDRIA of the other part; Witnesseth tht the said CHARLES MORTIMER and SARAH his Wife for the sum of Five shillings have granted unto the said MICHAEL his heirs and assigns forever, all that part of the tract or parcel of Land known by the name of SLIGO (except as is herein after excepted) containing under the following lines or bounds vizt., Beginning at ELISHA DICKENSONs corner adjoining to MANN PAGEs line, from thence along the said line to the mouth of HAZLE RUN, thence up the said Run and a Miery Gut to the corner of the said MORTIMERs Meadow fence, thence along said fence on the side of a Hill to JOHN GLASSELLs line (as laid off in a Plott made by JAMES TUTT), and by said GLASSELLs line to JAMES FRAZERs corner and from said Corner across to ELISHA DICKENSONs corner containing twenty acres also all land & trees except out of these presents always reserved a Road of Twenty feet wide as laid off in the above mentioned plott, from the HAZEL RUN through SLIGOE

to the Main Road or a Free Passage by a Street from the Road to the River and also except and out of these presents reserved a Road or Way nine feet wide from the Main Road along JOHN GLASSELLs line to the Meadow of the said CHARLES MORTIMER, and the said CHARLES and SARAH have further granted unto the said MICHAEL his heirs and assigns forever the lower part of that tract called & known by the name of KENNEADEYs POINT containing One hundred yards up the said Point and HAZLE RUN to a Stone Wall thence across a Muddy Gut in a direct line to SLIGOE LAND, containing by estimation one acre with all the lands profits to the same belonging; To have and to hold the said several parcels of land (except as before excepted) unto the said MICHAEL RYAN his heirs and assigns and the said CHARLES and SARAH for them and their heirs the several tracts of land against them and their heirs and all persons will warrant and forever defend by these presents; In Witness whereof we have set our hands and seals
Signed sealed and Delivered in presence of CHS: MORTIMER
(No witnesses shown) SARAH G. MORTIMER

The Commonwealth of Virginia to GEORGE FRENCH, GEORGE WEEDON and ELEAZER CALLANDER Gent., Justices of the Corporation of Fredericksburg, Greetin; ((The Commission for the private examination of SARAH G., Wife of CHARLES MORTIMER), Witness HENRY ARMISTEAD Clerk of our said Court this ninth day of June 1786 and in the Eleventh year of the Commonwealth HENRY ARMISTEAD, Clerk

Corporation of Fredericksburg, Sc. Pursuant to this Commission (Certificate and return of the private examination of SARAH G. MORTIMER) Certified under our hands and seals this 23d day of June one thousand seven hundred and eighty six
G. WEEDON
GEO: FRENCH

At a Hustings Court held for the Corporation of Fredericksburg on Monday the third day of July one thousand seven hundred and eighty six
This Deed & Memorandum (with a Commission of the privy Examination) was acknowledged by the said CHARLES MORTIMER Gent., and is ordered to be recorded; and is truly recorded Test HENRY ARMISTEAD, Clerk

pp. (On margin: Delivered to CHS. YATES July 18th 1786)
201- THIS INDENTURE made the Twenty fifth day of February in the year of our
204 Lord one thousand seven hundred and eighty one Between JOHN THOMPSON of the County of CULPEPER of the one part and CHARLES YEATES of Fredericksburg in County of Spotsylvania of other part; Witnesseth that for the sum of Thirty five pounds current money the said JOHN THOMPSON hath granted unto the said CHARLES YATES and his heirs all the Lott of Land in ALLEN TOWN and adjoining the said CHARLES YATES Garden, which descended to me from my Father, the Reverend MR. JOHN THOMPSON and for which I possest a Bond of Mr. JAMES HEATH to convey to him, or his order, before my Marriage, which Bond is now delivered up to me by the said YATES who purchased Mr. HEATH's right therein, with all houses orchards profits belonging and all the title; To have and to hold unto the said CHAS. YATES his heirs and assigns forever; In Witness whereof the said JOHN THOMPSON hath set his hand and seal
Signed sealed and delivered in presence of
JOHN STRODE, MORDA: BARBOUR, JOHN THOMPSON
ROB: GREEN LANE, THOS: STRODE

At a Hustings Court held for the Corporation of Fredericksburg the Sixth day of March one thousand seven hundred and eighty six
This Deed was proved by the oaths of JOHN STRODE and MORDECAI BARBOUR and ordered to be recorded; And at a Court held the third day of July one thousand seven hundred

and eighty six the same was farther proved by the oath of THOS: STRODE and ordered to be recorded and is truly recorded Test HENRY ARMISTEAD, Clk.

pp. (On margin: This Deed delivered to CHS: URQUHART July 18th 1786)
204- This Indenture made the second day of January in the year of our Lord one
206 thousand seven hundred and Eighty six Between RICHARD KENNEY of the Town of Fredericksburg and State of Virginia of the one part and JOSIAH WATSON of the Town of ALEXANDRIA and State aforesaid of the other part; Witnesseth that the said RICHARD KENNEY for Eleven thousand and fifty pounds of tobacco to him in hand paid hath sold unto the said JOSIAH WATSON his heirs and assigns a certain peice of land in the aforesaid Town of Fredericksburg on the Street called SOPHIA STREET being part of the Lott known by the number 77 in the plan of the said Town of Fredericksburg and bounded, Beginning at a Locust tree where the sasid Lott corners with the Lott No. 75 on SOPHIA STREET belonging to the Estate of Colo. JOHN TAYLOE deceased, thence up the said Street one hundred and twenty five feet, thence at right angles with the said Street and parallel with said TAYLOEs line one hundred and twenty feet to a Division pailing now standing; including the said pailing, thence at right angles to the line dividing the Lotts 75 & 77 one hundred and twenty five feet; and from thence to the beginning, making an oblong figure of one hundred and twenty five feet by one hundred and twenty; To have and to hold the said Ground with all the profits unto the said JOSIAH WATSON his heirs and assigns forever; In Witness whereof the parties have hereunto set their hands and seals

RICHARD KENNEY

At a Hustings Court held for the Corporation of Fredericksburg on Monday the Second day of January one thousand seven hundred and Eighty six
This Deed was personally acknowledged in open Court by the said RICHARD KENNEY and was ordered to be recorded & is truly recorded

Test HENRY ARMISTEAD, Clk.

pp. (On margin: This Deed Delivd. to Rt. B. CHEW July 19th 1786)
206- THIS INDENTURE TRIPARTITE made this Twentieth day of November in the year
210 of our Lord one thousand seven hundred and Eighty five Between ROBERT GILCHRIST and JOHN GRAY of the Town of PORT ROYAL and JAMES SOMERVILLE of the Town of Fredericksburg of the first part; JOHN MITCHELL and SUSANNA his Wife of the County of Spotsylvania of the second part and ROBERT BEVERLEY CHEW of the Town of Fredericksburg, Merchant, of the third part; Witnesseth that the said ROBERT GILCHRIST and JOHN GRAY & JAMES SOMERVILLE for the sum of Two hundred and forty one pounds current money of Virginia paid by ROBERT BEVERLEY CHEW; And the said JOHN MITCHELL and SUSANNA his Wife for the sum of Five shillings of like money to them paid by the said ROBERT BEVERLEY CHEW and for divers other good causes they the said ROBERT GILCHRIST, JOHN GRAY, JAMES SOMERVILLE, JOHN MITCHELL & SUSANNA in this behalf especially moving, hath granted unto the said ROBERT BEVERLEY CHEW his heirs and assigns forever all that piece of Ground known by the number One in the Advertisement No. 1 adjacent to the Old Town of Fredericksburg and adjoining the Lott No. 32 of the said Town, beginning at the upper corner of the said Lott No. 32; upon CAROLINE STREET, thence along the line of CAROLINE STREET twenty three feet and one half to LEWIS STREET, thence down LEWIS STREET one hundred and thirty two feet, thence to the division line or pailing between No. 32 & upon JOHN JULIANs lott, twenty three and one half feet, thence along MITCHELLs & MILLERs upper line on Lott No. 32 one hundred and thirty two feet to the beginning on CAROLINE STREET comprehending

one half of the piece of Ground which the aforesaid JOHN MITCHELL purchased of the late Colo. FIELDING LEWIS, as will appear by a Deed dated the Fourth day of December one thousand seven hundred and Fifty and recorded in Spotsylvania Court, To have and to hold all the said Ground unto the said ROBERT BEVERLEY CHEW his heirs and assigns and the said ROBERT GILCHRIST, JOHN GRAY, JAMES SOMERVILLE and JOHN MITCHELL and SUSANNA his Wife for him and herself severally and apart, and not jointly, and for his and her several heirs doth severally and apart, and not jointly, grant with the said ROBERT BEVERLEY CHEW his heirs that he may enjoy all the said premisses without molestation of them; In Witness whereof the parties have set their hands and seals
Sealed & delivered in presence of

WM. MILLER, GEO: CATLETT,
THOS: MOFFATT, ROBT. YOUNG
JOSEPH BROCK, JAMES LEWIS, JOSEPH CHEW
(as to Mr. MITCHELL

ROBERT GILCHRIST
JOHN GRAY
JAMES SOMERVILLE
JOHN MITCHELL
SUSANNA MITCHELL

The Commonwealth of Virginia to JOSEPH BROCK, EDWD. HERNDON and JAMES LEWIS Gent., Justices of the County Court of Spotsylvania (The Commission for the privy examination of SUSANNA, the Wife of JOHN MITCHELL); Witness HENRY ARMISTEAD, Clerk of our said Court this seventh day of March 1786 and in the Tenth year of the Common Wealth
HENRY ARMISTEAD, Clerk

At a Hustings Court held for the Corporation of Fredericksburg on Monday the Sixth day of March one thousand seven hundred and eighty six
This Deed was proven as to R. GILCHRIST, JNO: GRAY & JAS. SOMERVILLE acknowledgement by the oaths of THOMAS MOFFATT and ROBERT YOUNG, And at a Court held on Monday the third day of April it was farther proved as to the said GILCHRIST, GRAY & SOMERVILLE by the oath of WILLIAM MILLER which on their part with a Commission now returned of the acknowledgement & privy Examination of SUSANNA MITCHELL are ordered to be recorded; And at a Court held on Monday the first day of March one thousand seven hundred and eighty six the said Deed as to JOHN MITCHELLs acknowledgement was proved by the oaths of JOSEPH BROCK, JNO: LEWIS and JOSEPH CHEW & ordered to be rcorded & is truly recorded Test HENRY ARMISTEAD, Clerk

pp. 210-212 THIS INDENTURE made the twenty second day of March in the year of our Lord one thousand seven hundred and eighty six Between JOHN HARDIN and CLARIA his Wife of the one part and WILLIAM ALEXANDER of the other part; Witnesseth that the said JOHN HARDIN and CLARIA his Wife for the sum of Seventy pounds specie doth sell unto the said WILLIAM ALEXANDER his heirs and assigns forever, one half of his Lot No. 252 in the Borough of Fredericksburg adjoining the Lott Doctor CHARLES MORTIMER now occupies and bounded on the other sides by the Main Street and the said JOHN HARDINs Lotts and to extend the full breadth back; Together with all buildings and trees; To have and to hld the said lott and premisses with the appurtenances unto the said WILLIAM ALEXANDER his heirs and assigns against the claim of all persons whatsoever; In Witness whereof the said JOHN HARDIN and CLARIA his Wife have set their hands and seals
In presence of WM. LOVELL,
WM. ORR; THOS: SIMPSON

JOHN HARDIN
CLARISSA HARDIN

Memdn. The half Lott sold to WILLIAM ALEXANDER is that half which joins DR. MORTIMER

Received of Capt. WILLIAM ALEXANDER seventy pounds specie being the consideration money within mentioned this 22d day of March 1786

Test WM. LOVELL, JOHN HARDIN
WM. ORR, THOS: SIMPSON

At a Hustings Court held for the Corporation of Fredericksburg
This Deed indented & Receipt proved by the oaths of WM. LOVELL, WM. ORR & THOS: SIMPSON and ordered to be recorded & is truly recorded
Test HENRY ARMISTEAD, Clk.

pp. (On margin: This Deed Delivd. to Mr. THO: COCKRAN November 17th 1786)
213- THIS INDENTURE made this Sixteenth day of January in the year of our Lord
215 one thousand seven hundred and Eighty six Between JOHN WIGLESWORTH of the County of Spotsylvania, Gent., and PHILADELPHIA his Wife of one part and HUGH THOMPSON of WILMINGTON in the State of DELAWARE and THOMAS COCKRAN of the Town of Fredericksburg and County of Spotsylvania of the other part; Witnesseth that the said JOHN WIGGLESWORTH and PHILADELPHIA his Wife for the sum of One hundred and fifty pounds special sell unto the said HUGH THOMPSON and THOMAS COCKRAN their heirs and assigns forever a Lott of Ground in the Town of Fredericksburg known by the name and being part of the LONG ORDINARY LOTT, and is adjoined on the South side by Mr. WILLIAM SMITHs Ground and containing Thirty one feet in the front on CAROLINE STREET and from the said Street extending with said Breadth one hundred and thirty two feet Westward where it is adjoined by the COURT HOUSE LOTT, Together with all buildings gardens and trees; To have and to hold the said Lott and premisses unto the said HUGH THOMSON and THOMAS COCKRAN their heirs and assigns forever; And the said JOHN WIGLESWORTH and PHILADELPHIA his Wife willl warrant and forever defend the said lott against the claim of all persons whatsoever; In Witness whereof the said JOHN WIGLESWORTH and PHILADELPHIA his Wife have set their hands and seals
Sealed and delivered in the presence of
GEO: FRENCH, JOS: CHRISTY, JOHN WIGLESWORTH
WILLIAM SMITH, THOS: MILLER PHILADELPHIA WIGLESWORTH

The Commonwealth of Virginia to GEORGE FRENCH and JAMES SOMMERVILLE Gent., Greeting (The Commission for the privy Examination of PHILADELPHIA, the Wife of JOHN WIGLESWORTH) Witness HENRY ARMISTEAD Clerk of our said Court this first day of March one thousand seven hundred and Eighty six and in the eleventh year of the Commonwealth HENRY ARMISTEAD, Clerk

Corporation of Fredericksburg (Certification and return of the privy Examination of PHILADELPHIA WIGLESWORTH), Certified under our hands and seals this twentieth day of May one thousand seven hundred and eighty six JAMES SOMERVILLE
GEORGE FRENCH

At a Hustings Court held for the Corporation of Fredericksburg on Monday the Sixth day of February one thousand seven hundred and Eighty six
This Deed was proved by the oaths of THOMAS MILLER, GEORGE FRENCH and WILLIAM SMITH and ordered to be recorded.
Truly copyed Test HENRY ARMISTEAD, Clerk

pp. (On margin: Delivered to LEEMONS Feby. 16th 1787)
215- THIS INDENTURE made this Fifteenth day of May one thousand seven hundred
218 and Eighty six Between RICHARD KENNEY of the County of Spotsylvania of the one part and TERRASSON BROTHERS & CO., Merchants in PHILADELPHIA, of the other part; Whereas the said RICHARD KENNEY upon an Account made up between him and the said TERRASSON BROTHERS & CO., stands indebted unto them in the sum of One hundred and twenty nine pounds eleven shillings Virginia currency for ballance of the same Account; Now This Indenture witnesseth that the said RICHARD KENNEY for

the better securing the payment of the said sum with Interest and in consideration of Five shillings to the said RICHARD KENNEY in hand paid by the said TERRASSON BROTHERS & CO., hath sold unto the said TERRASSON BROTHERS & CO., and to their heirs & assigns forever, all that moiety of a lot and tenement being in the Town of Fredericksburg and now in the tenure of THOMAS COCKRAN being Sixteen feet in front and one hundred and twenty six feet breadth and comprehended in the South West corner of the square number (blank), allso all houses buildings gardens orchards to the said land belonging; To have and to hold the said moiety of a Lot and Tenement and all the premisses unto the said TERRASSON BROTHERS & CO., their heirs and assigns, Provided always and it is agreed between the said parties that if the said RICHARD KENNEY his heirs truly pay unto the said TERRASSON BROTHERS & CO., the full sum with Interest from the above date in Virginia currency on or before the fifteenth day of May in the year one thousand seven hundred and eighty eight without any deduction for taxes assessments or any other impositions either Ordinary or Extraordinary, that then from thence forth these presents shall cease and be void any thing herein contained to the contrary and the said RICHARD KENNEY for himself doth grant that he will truly pay the said full sum with interest on or before the fifteenth day of May in the year one thosuand seven hundred & eighty eight without any deduction and also that they the said TERRASSON BROTHERS & CO., shall at all times after default shall be made in performance of the conditions herein contained peaceably enter into hold and enjoy the said premisses without the lott of him the said RICHARD KENNEY his heirs or assigns and lastly it is covenanted and agreed upon by and between the said parties and it is hereby declared that the said RICHARD KENNEY his heirs and assigns may at all times until default shall be made peaceably and quietly hold and enjoy the said premisses and take the rents and profits thereof to his own use; In Witness whereof the said RICHARD KENNEY hath hereunto set his hand and seal

Signed sealed & delivered in presence of

JOSH: WILLIAMS, RICHARD KENNEY

ARCHD. McCALLEY, JAS: HANSBOROUGH

At a Hustings Court continued and held for the Corporation of Fredericksburg on Tuesday the Eighth day of August one thousand seven hundred and Eighty six

This Indenture of Mortgage was acknowledged by the said RICHARD KENNEY and ordered tob e recorded Test HENRY ARMISTEAD, Clerk

pp. 219-221 THIS INDENTURE made this first day of September one thousand seven hundred and eighty six Between RICHARD KENNEY of the Town of Fredericksburg on the one part and JAMES TOOLE, Merchant of BALTIMORE, on the other part; Witnesseth that the said RICHARD KENNEY for the sum of Nine thousand four hundred and twenty pounds of tobacco to him in hand paid doth sell unto the said JAMES and to his heirs and assigns forever all that messuage and tenement being in the Town of Fredericksburg and now in the Tenure of EDWARD WELLS, containing Twenty four feet front upon CAROLINE STREET and extending One hundred and twenty feet back making an area of Twenty four feet by one hundred and twenty feet and lying between the houses occupied by ZACHARIAH LUCAS, together with all gardens stables houses easements; To have and to hold unto the said JAMES TOOLE his heirs and assigns, Provided always and it is agreed between the said parties that if the said RICHARD KENNEY his heirs shall well and truly pay unto the said JAMES TOOLE the full sum of tobacco with legal Interest from the Thirtieth day of June one thousand seven hundred and Eighty four on demand without any deduction for Taxes or other impositions whatsoever that then & from thence these presents and everything herein contained shall cease and be

void, and the said RICHARD KENNEY for himself his heirs doth grant tht he will truly pay the sum with Interest without any deduction that he the said JAMES may at all times after default shall be made quietly enter into hold and enjoy the said Tenement without trouble of him the said RICHARD KENNEY; And lastly it is agreed that the said RICHARD KENNEY his heirs shall and may at all times until default shall be made hold and enjoy the said premisses above and receive the profits thereof, In Witness whereof the said RICHARD KENNEY hath hereunto set his hand & seal
Signed sealed & delivered in presence of
(no witnesses shown) RICHD. KENNEY

At a Hustings Court held for the Town and Corporation of Fredericksburg on Monday the Sixth day of November one thousand seven hundred and eighty six
This Deed of Mortgage was acknowledged in open Court by the said RICHARD KENNEY and ordered to be recorded Test HENRY ARMISTEAD, Clerk

pp. 222-224 THIS INDENTURE TRIPARTITE made the Twelvth day of November in the year of our Lord one thousand seven hundred and Eighty five Between WILLIAM JACKSON of the County of Spotsylvania Gentleman of the first part; MESSRS. LEEMAN AND WILLEMS of the Town of Fredericksburg and Partners of the second part; and ELISHA DICKENSON of the said Town of Fredericksburg of the third part; Whereas it was agreed between the said WILLIAM JACKSON and the said LEEMAN and WILLEMS that the said WILLIAM JACKSON should let and demise to the said LEEMAN & WILLEMS a certain parcel of ground in said Town and described as hereinafter mentioned; for the sum of Eight pounds specie per year and under such agreements as herein after declared, And Whereas before any conveyance or Deed of Lease was made for the same, the said LEEMAN & WILLEMS for a valuable consideration sold and assigned their right to the said Grounds unto the said ELISHA DICKENSON; Now This Indenture Witnesseth that for the Rents and Covenants herein after declared which was to be paid and performed on the part of the said LEEMAN and WILLEMS and which in their place is to be paid by the said ELISHA DICKENSON, and also for the consideration of the sum of Five shillings in hand paid and also by the consent of the said LEEMAN & WILLEMS he the said WILLIAM JACKSON hath granted unto the said ELISHA DICKENSON all that parcel of ground and bounded and described as followeth; the sd. two lotts are the same on which the said ELISHA DICKENSON hath already sundry buildings erected and are in that addition of Fredericksburg made by the Honourable JOHN GRYMES Esquire as Executor of Mr. HENRY WILLIS and by Colo. WILLIAM WALLERs plan numbered Fifteen and Thirteen, each lott containing half an acre, the lott numbered Fifteen is on the continuation of CAROLINE STREET and the Lott numbered thirteen on the continuation of PRINCESS ANNE STREET, and both on a Street which divides them from the lotts numbered Thirty three and Thirty four, which were formerly the property of MESSRS. COCKRANE & COMPY., or CUNNINGHAME & COMPY., and confiscated to the use of the Commonwealth to which no name is given in Colonel WALLERs Plan, but is of the same breadth, to wit, sixty six feet as others in the Old Town, To have and to hold the said parcel of Ground and premisses unto the said ELISHA DICKENSON his Executors and assigns during the term of Fifteen years; commencing from the first day of August last and fully to be compleat paying therefore yearly and every year during the said term the full sum of Eight pounds current money of Virginia in Spanish Milled Dollars or other Silver or Gold equivalent thereto; without any deduction for Taxes charged or imposed on the said premisses or to be charged and imposed by Act of Assembly or otherwise; And if it shall happen that the said yearly Rent shall be behind and unpaid for the space of Forty days then and from thence forth it shall be lawful for the said WILLIAM JACKSON his heirs

to reenter as of his former estate and it is agreed between the said WILLIAM JACKSON and ELISHA DICKENSON that the said ELISHA may during the term aforesaid at the proper costs and charges of the said ELISHA in all things be at liberty to erect, build, set up and finish or cause to be made and finished upon the said Ground herein before demised all such houses buildings gardens pailings inclosures and improvements as he may think proper and necessary; And further it is agreed that all such other improvements as are already or may thereafter be made on the premisses the same by the said ELISHA DICKENSON his Executors or assigns shall be kept up and maintained thereon and not at any time removed therefrom, and all manner of needful reparations made and so repaired upheld and kept in good repair will leave the same; at the expiration of this present demise; In Witness whereof the said WILLIAM JACKSON, MESSRS. LEEMAN & WILLEMS and ELISHA DICKENSON have set their hands and affixed their seals
Sealed & Delivered in presence of

O. TOWLE, H. McAUSLAND, WILLIAM JACKSON
GEO: MURRAY, JNO: RICHARDS, CHS. LEEMANS for
JAS: SOMERVILLE, A. BUCHANAN p W. J. LEEMANS & WILLEMS

At a Hustings Court held for the Town and Corporation of Fredericksburg on Monday the Sixth day of February one thousand seven hundred and eighty six
This Deed was proved by the oaths of ANDREW BUCHANAN, GEORGE MURRAY and JOHN RICHARDS witnesses thereto and ordered to be recorded
Test HENRY ARMISTEAD, Clerk

p. 225 THIS INDENTURE made the fourth day of April one thousand seven hundred and eighty five Between JOSEPH WALKER of the Town of Fredericksburg, Carriage Maker, of the one part and JOHN SMITH of the aforesaid Town of the other part; Witnesseth that the said JOHN SMITH of his own free Will and by consent and approbation of the Court of Hustings of the aforesaid Town doth bind himself an Apprentice to the said JOSEPH WALKER until he shall arrive to the age of Twenty one years, he being Thirteen years old the Twelvth day of December last, & during which time the said JOHN SMITH shall truly serve the said JOSEPH WALKER in all things as an Apprentice; And the said JOSEPH WALKER for his part doth agree that he will teach or cause to be taught, the said SMITH in the Trade of making Carriages, and will find and provide for him during the time aforesaid, Also the said JOSEPH WALKER doth agree to teach or cause to be instructed for the said JOHN SMITH to read and write; In Witness whereof the parties have set their hands and seals JOSEPH WALKER
JOHN SMITH

At a Hustings Court held the fourth day of April one thousand seven hundred and eighty five This Indenture of Apprenticeship was acknowledged by the parties, approved of by the Court and ordered to be recorded & is
Test HENRY ARMISTEAD, Clk.
Examined and delivered CHS. TRAVIS.

p. 226 Fredericksburg July 19th 1786. Received full satisfaction for the Mortgage by a full payment of the Bond for which this was a security, as witness my hand the day & date above written
Witness WILLIAM FRENCH, ALEXANDER ROANE CHARLES LEEMANS

At a Court continued & held for the Town and Corporation of Fredericksburg on Tuesday the Eighth day of August one thousand seven hundred & eighty six
This Receipt from CHS. LEEMANS to JOHN REED & STANDISH FORDE was proved by the oaths of WM. FRENCH & ALEXR: ROANE & ordered to be recorded
Test HENRY ARMISTEAD, Clk.

pp. 226-227 THIS INDENTURE made the fifth day of September one thousand seven hundred and eighty five Between RICHARD KENNEY of the one part and BENJAMIN HENDRICK of the other part, both of the Town of Fredericksburg and County of Spotsylvania; Witnesseth that the said RICHARD KENNEY for the sum of Five shillings current money doth hereby let and to farm let unto the said BENJA: HENDRICK a peice of ground situated in the said Town of Fredericksburg Beginning seventy six feet from the corner of HAWKE STREET and the House at present occupied by THOMAS COCKRAN, running along CAROLINE STREET twenty eight feet, thence by a right angle one hundred & twenty feet back, thence upwards towards HAWKE STREET twenty eight feet, thence by a right angle to CAROLINE STREET at the beginning; Together with all benefits; To have and to hold unto the said BENJAMIN HENDRICK his heirs and assigns from the day of the date hereof during the term of Twenty one years to commence on the Fourteenth day of February one thousand seven hundred and eighty five; the said BENJAMIN HENDRICK paying unto the said RICHARD KENNEY his heirs the sum of Seven pounds ten shillings current money in Specie or hard money every year during the term aforesd., and so to continue his annual payments on the fourteenth day of February every year during the term; together with all taxes, charges and incumbrances that shall become due and that the said BENJAMIN HENDRICK shall deliver up the said Grounds with all buildings gardens and appertenances belonging; In Witness whereof they have hereunto set their hands and seals

"THOS: COCKRAN" inserted instead of JOHN RICHESON before signed R. K.

Test WM. ORR, RICHD. KENNEY

SAML. LUCAS, ROBT. WALKER

At a Hustings Court held for the Corporation of Fredericksburg on Monday the Seventh day of November one thousand seven hundred and Eighty five

This Lease indented acknowledged and ordered to be recorded and is truly recorded

Test HENRY ARMISTEAD, Clerk C. F.

pp. 228-229 (On margin: Delivd. the Origl. Deed to H. CHILES)

THIS INDENTURE made the Sixth day of February in the year of our Lord one thousand seven hundred and Eighty six Between JOHN WIGGLESWORTH of the County of Spotsylvania, Gent., and PHILADELPHIA his Wife of the one part and HENRY CHILES of the County of CAROLINE (and both of the State of Virginia) of the other part; Witnesseth that the said JOHN WIGLESWORTH and PHILADELPHIA his Wife in consideration of the sum of One hundred and Twenty nine pounds Ten shillings Specie hath sold unto the said HENRY CHILES his heirs forever a lott of ground in the Town of Fredericksburg and County aforesaid and known by the name and being part of the LONG ORDINARY LOTT and is adjoining on the South side by Mr. THOS: COCKRAN Ground and on the North side by Mr. ATKINSONs Ground and contains Eighteen feet in the front on CAROLINE STREET, and from the Street extending with said breadth one hundred and thirty two feet Westward where it adjoined the COURT HOUSE LOTT, Together with all gardens and trees; To have and to hold the said Lott unto the said HENRY CHILES his heirs and assigns forever; And the said JOHN WIGLESWORTH and PHILADELPHIA his Wife will warrant & forever defend the said Lott against the claims of any other persons; In Witness whereof the said JOHN WIGLESWORTH and PHILADELPHIA his Wife have set their hands and seals

In presence of (no witnesses shown) JOHN WIGGLESWORTH

PHILADELPHIA WIGGLESWORTH

The Commonwealth of Virginia to GEORGE FRENCH and JAMES SOMERVILLE, Gent. of the Corporation of Fredericksburg Greeting; (The Commision for the private examination of

PHILADELPHIA, the Wife of JOHN WIGGLESWORTH); Witness HENRY ARMISTEAD Clerk of our said Court this first day of March 1786 in the Tenth year of the Common Wealth

HENRY ARMISTEAD, Clerk, C. F.

The Corporation of Fredericksburg Sc. Pursuant to this Commission we did examine (the return of the Execution of the private Examination of PHILADELPHIA WIGGLESWORTH), Certified under our hands and seals this twentyeth day of May one thousand seven hundred and eighty six

JAMES SOMERVILLE
GEORGE FRENCH

At a Hustings Court held for the Corporation of Fredericksburg on Monday the Sixth day of February one thousand seven hundred and eighty six
This Deed indented & receipt was acknowledged personally by JOHN WIGGLESWORTH and ordered to be recorded;

And at a Court held the Fifth day of June following; This Commission & Certificate of the acknowledgement of the said PHILADELPHIA WIGGLESWORTH to the said Deed was returned and ordered to be recorded and are truly recorded

Test HENRY ARMISTEAD, Clerk, C. F.

pp. (On margin: Exd. & Deld: ROGER DIXON 5 Mar: 89)
230- THIS INDENTURE made the twenty sixth day of June in the year of our Lord one
231 thousand seven hundred and eighty five and in the Ninth year of the Independence of the United States of Virginia (marked out) America, Between RICHARD PEACOCK, Son and Heir at Law of RICHARD PEACOCK late of the Town of Fredericksburg in the State of Virginia Gent., deceased, of the one part and ROGER DIXON of the said place and State, Gentleman, of the other part; Witnesseth that the said RICHARD PEACOCK for Two hundred and Fifty pounds current money of the State aforesaid hath granted unto the said ROGER DIXON his heirs and assigns forever all that parcel of land containing One hundred and seventy one and a half feet in front on CAROLINE STREET in the Town of Fredericksburg aforesaid being the Northwest part of the Lott numbered Sixteen 16 in the plan of the said Town and extending (blank) feet in Depth from CAROLINE STREET aforesaid to the Lott numbered Fourteen 14, together with all the houses buildings and improvements belonging; To have and to hold unto the said ROGER DIXON his heirs and assigns forever without trouble or denial of him the said RICHARD PEACOCK his heirs or assigns or any persons claiming under him; In Witness whereof the said parties have set their hands and seals
Sealed and delivered in presence of

JOS: WOOD JUNR., RICHARD PEACOCK
JNO: COAKLEY, COLLIN FRAZER

At a Hustings Court held for the Corporation of Fredericksburg on Monday the Fourth day of July one thousand seven hundred and eighty five
This Deed was proved by the oaths of JOHN WOOD JUNR., JOHN COAKLEY & COLLIN FRAZER and ordered to be recorded Test HENRY ARMISTEAD, Clk.

pp. THIS INDENTURE made the twenty fourth day of June in the year of our Lord
232- one thousand seven hundred and eighty five and in the Ninth year of the
233 Independence of the United States of America Between ROGER DIXON, Son and Heir at Law of ROGER DIXON, late of the Town of Fredericksburg in the State of Virginia, Gentleman, deceased, of the one part and MARY GIBBS of the same place and State, Widow, of the other part; Witnesseth that the said ROGER DIXON for the sum of Ten pounds to him in hand paid doth sell unto the said MARY GIBBS her heirs and assigns all that parcel of land contining Twenty six feet in front on CAROLINE STREET in the

Town of Fredericksburg aforesaid being part of the Lott numbered Sixteen in the plan of the said Town bounded by PRUSSIA STREET and extending (blank) feet in depth on the said Street to the lot numbered fourteen, together with all the houses and improvements, To have and to hold unto the said MARY GIBBS her heirs and assigns and the said ROGER DIXON doth promise the said MARY GIBBS her heirs and assigns hereafter shall hold the said premisses without molestation of said ROGER DIXON his heirs or assigns and will warrant and forever defend by these presents; In Witness whereof the said parties have set their hands and seals
Sealed and delivered in presents of
JOS: WOOD JUNR., ROGER DIXON
JOHN COAKLEY, COLLIN FRASER
At a Hustings Court held for the Corporation of Fredericksburg on Monday the Fourth day of July one thousand seven hundred and Eighty five
This Deed was proved by the Oaths of the witnesses and ordered to be recorded
Test HENRY ARMISTEAD, Clk. C. F.

pp. 234-236 THIS INDENTURE made the Twenty sixth day of June in the year of our Lord one thousand seven hundred and eighty five and in the Ninth year of the Independence of the United States of America Between MARY GIBBS of Fredericksburg in the State of Virginia, Widow, formerly the Widow and Relict of RICHARD PEACOCK, late of the same place and State, Gentleman, deceased, and RICHARD PEACOCK, Son and Heir at Law of the said RICHARD PEACOCK deceasded of the one part and ROGER DIXON also of the same place and State, Gentleman, of the other part; Witnessth that the said MARY GIBBS and RICHARD PEACOCK in consideration of the sum of Ten pounds have sold unto the said ROGER DIXON his heirs and all assigns all that parcel of land containing Twenty six feet in front on CAROLINE STREET in the Town of Fredericksburg being part of the Lot number Sixteen in the plan of the said Town, bounded by PRUSSIA STREET and extending (blank) feet in depth on the said Street to the lot numbered fourteen together with all houses and improvements; To have and to hold to the only proper use and behoof of the said ROGER DIXON his heirs and assigns forever; In Witness whereof the parties have set their hands and seals
Sealed and delivered in presence of
JOS: WOOD JUNR., MARY ✕ GIBBS
JOHN COAKLY, COLLIN FRAZER RICHARD PEACOCK
At a Hustings Court held for the Corporation of Fredericksburg on Monday the Fourth day of July one thousand seven hundred and eighty five
This Deed was proved by the oaths of the witnesses thereto and ordered to be recorded
Test HENRY ARMISTEAD, Clk. C. F.

pp. 236-238 THIS INDENTURE made this Seventeenth day of August in the year of our Lord one thousand seven hundred and Eighty four Between JOHN HAWKINS, Merchant, of the Town of Fredericksburg and ANNA GABRIELLA his Wife of the one part and SUSANNA HEATH, Spinster, of the said Town of the other part; Witnesseth that for Seven hundred pounds current money of Virginia the said JOHN HAWKINS & ANN his Wife have sold unto the said SUSANNA HEATH & her heirs all that parcel of land which he bought of MESSRS. HALL & HORNER, being part of a Lott in the said Town of Fredericksburg and numbered in the first plan thereof Forty three and bounded; Beginning on Main Street of said Town called CAROLINE STREET at the intersection of the said Street and GEORGE STREET, thence down CAROLINE STREET to the North end of the LONG ORDINARY, thence at right angle from CAROLINE STREET and parrallell with

GEORGE STREET one hundred and thirty two feet to the COURT HOUSE LOTT, thence with the line of the COURT HOUSE LOTT & parrallell with CAROLINE STREET to GEORGE STREET and along GEORGE STREET to the beginning; Except as much thereof as was sold or intended to be sold to JOHN HAWKINS by GEORGE MITCHELL, which is bounded, Beginning on CAROLINE STREET thirty three feet above the North end of the LONG ORGINDARY, thence along CAROLINE STREET thirty three feet to the end of the LONG ORDINARY, thence at a right angle from the COURT HOUSE LOTT aforementioned, thence with the line of the COURT HOUSE LOTT & parrallell with CAROLINE STREET thirty seven and a half feet, thence by a direct line to the beginning of this last dividend, together with all houses buildigns orchards belonging; To have and to hold unto the said SUSAN: HEATH her heirs and assigns forever; In Witness whereof the said J. HAWKINS and ANN his Wife have set their hands & seals

Signed sealed and delivered in presence of

DAVID BLAIR, WILLIAM PORTER, JOHN HAWKINS

JNO: ANDERSON, WILLIAM LOVELL ANNA GABRIELLA HAWKINS

The Commonwealth of Virginia to ROBERT TALIAFERRO, JOHN ARMISTEAD and JOHN HOOMES Gent., Justices of CAROLINE County (The Commission for the private examination of GABRIELLA, the Wife of JOHN HAWKINS), Witness HENRY ARMISTEAD Clerk of our said Court this Nineteenth day of August one thousand seven hundred and Eighty four in the Ninth year of the Commonwealth

HENRY ARMISTEAD, Clerk

CAROLINE County to wit: (The return of the Execution of the private Examination of ANNA GABRIELLA HAWKINS); Given under our hands and seals this Nineteenth day of August one thousand seven hundred and Eighty four

ROBERT TALIAFERRO
JOHN ARMISTEAD

At a Court of Hustings held for the Corporation of Fredericksburg on Monday the Sixth day of December one thousand seven hundred and Eighty four

This Deed was proved by the oaths of the witnesses which with a Commission and a Certificate of the privy Examination of the said ANNA GABRIELLA HAWKINS are ordered to be recorded Test HENRY ARMISTEAD, Clerk

pp. THIS INDENTURE made the twenty sixth day of October in the year of our Lord
239- one thousand seven hundred and Eighty five Between HUGH McKILLUP of
240 CULPEPER County, Merchant, and JUDITH his Wife (formerly Wife of WILLIAM
HOUSTON deceased), of the one part and LARKIN SMITH of KING & QUEEN County Esqr., of the other part; Whereas the said WILLIAM HOUSTON in his life time by Deed of Bargain and Sale dated the Twentieth day of October one thousand seven hundred and seventy five and recorded in the County Court of Spotsylvania did sell unto OLIVER TOWLES Esqr., two lotts of ground in the Town of Fredericksburg known & described in the plan thereof by the numbers Two hundred & fifty five & Two hundred & Sixty five, which lots the said OLIVER TOWLES hath since sold & conveyed to the said LARKIN SMITH, And Whereas the said JUDITH did not execute the said Deed nor ever relinquish her right of Dower in the Lots aforesaid by which means she is entitled to one third part thereof during her life, And the said HUGH McKILLUP & JUDITH his Wife have agreed to make over & relinquish unto the said LARKIN SMITH & his heirs all her the said JUDITH's right of Dower in the said two lotts; Now This Indenture witnesseth that the said HUGH McKILLUP and JUDITH his Wife in consideration of the sum of Sixty pounds current money of Virginia do sell unto the said LARKIN SMITH all right which the said JUDITH hath in the two lots aforesaid either as Dower of her said Husband,

WILLIAM HOUSTON or otherwise; To have and to hold unto the said LARKIN SMITH his heirs & assigns forever; In Witness whereof the said HUGH McKILLUP and JUDITH his Wife have set their hands and seals
Sealed and delivered in presence of
CHARLES URQUHART, B. FULLER, LAW: BROOKE, JOS: WOOD JUNR. — HUGH McKILLUP, JUDITH McKILLUP

The Commonwealth of Virginia to GEORGE WEEDON, THOMAS MILLER & WILLIAM McWILLIAMS Gent., Justices of the Corporation of Fredericksburg, Greeting; (The Commission for the privy Examination of JUDITH, the Wife of HUGH McKILLU); Witness HENRY ARMISTEAD Clerk of our said Court this Twenty sixth day of October one thousand seven hundred and eight five in the Tenth year of the Common Wealth
HENRY ARMISTEAD, Clerk

Corporation of Fredericksburg to wit; (The return of the Execution of the private Examination of JUDITH McKILLUP); Certified under our hands and seals this twenty seventh day of October one thousand seven hundred and Eighty five
GEORGE WEEDON,
WILLIAM McWILLIAMS

At a Court continued and held for the Town and Corporation of Fredericksburg on Tuesday the Eighth day of November one thousand seven hundred and eighty five This Deed was proved by the oaths of CHARLES URQUHART, JOSEPH WOOD and LAW: BROOKE and the acknowledgement of the said JUDITH appears by a Commission and certificate of the privy examination which with the said Deed are ordered to be recorded Test HENRY ARMISTEAD, Clk.

pp. 241-242 THIS INDENTURE made the Sixth day of March in the year of our Lord one thousand seven hundred and eighty six Between JOHN BROWNLOW of the Town of Fredericksburg of the one part and JAMES BROWN of the same place of the other part; Witnesseth that the said JOHN BROWNLOW in consideration of Seventy five pounds current money hath granted unto the said JOHN BROWN his heirs & assigns the one half or moiety of a Lot of Ground in the said Town of Fredericksburg & described in the plan of the said Town by the number Four, which moiety is bounded, beginning at a Stone on SOPHIA STREET distant one hundred & thirty seven feet and one half foot from the corner of said Lott at the intersection of HANOVER STREET & SOPHIA STREET aforesaid, thence a straight line parallel to HANOVER STREET about ninety nine feet to the River; thence up the River to GEORGE STREET, thence with said Street to SOPHIA STREET aforesaid, thence along the same one hundred and ninety two feet & one half to the beginning; Together with all houses buildings, To have and to hold the said moiety or one half of the lot aforesaid unto the said JAMES BROWN his heirs and assigns forever; without the molestation of the said JOHN BROWNLOW his heirs or any other person claiming under him; In Witness whereof the said JOHN BROWNLOW hath set his hand and affixed his seal
Sealed & delivered in the presence of
(no witnesses shown) JOHN BROWNLOW

At a Hustings Court held for the Town and Corporation of Fredericksburg on Monday the Sixth day of March one thousand seven hundred and Eighty six
This Deed was acknowledged by the said JOHN BROWNLOW and ordered to be recorded
Test HENRY ARMISTEAD, Clk.

Delivered Mr. JAS: BROWN

p. 242 ARTICLES of AGREEMENT made & entered into this twelfth day of July one thousand seven hundred and eighty four Between HENRY VOWLES of the Town of FALMOUTH of the one part and LEONARD PATTERSON of the Town of Fredericksburg of the other part; Witnesseth that the said VOWLES hath for the sum of Six pounds Specie per annum rented unto the said PATTERSON until the first day of January One thousand seven hundred and ninety one, a peice of ground in Fredericksburg (whereon said PATTERSON now dwells) containing Twenty one feet front & eighty eight feet back; But it is to be understood that the said VOWLES does not ensure or to be answerable that the said PATTERSON shall keep possession of the above term only so far as it may be in his power to let him, or has a right to rent out this Ground; It is further agreed that the said PATTERSON may have the liberty of moving off the buildings &c. that he has or my put on this Ground any time before or at the expiration of the term, provided he complies with this contract and leaves the Ground levil and in as good roder as he found it at this interance thereon; In Testimony whereof we have both set our hands the day and date above
Signed in the presence of
PHILIP LIPSCOMB, HENRY VOWLES
BENJAMIN WEEKS LEONARD PATTERSON

At a Hustings Court held for the Corporation of Fredericksburg on Tuesday the eighth day of March one thousand seven hundred and eighty five
These Articles of Agreement was proved by the witnesses and ordred to be recorded
Test HENRY ARMISTEAD, Clerk

pp. 243-244 THIS INDENTURE made the thirty first March in year of our Lord one thousand seven hundred and eighty five Between LAWRENCE SLAUGHTER and SUSANAH his Wife of the County of COULPEPER of the one part and the Honble. JAMES MERCER, Executor and Trustee of the late Majr. ALEXANDER DICK of the County of Spotsylvania of the other part; Whereas the late ALEXANDER DICK and the above named LAWRENCE SLAUGHTER not long since, (to wit, about the month of October last) had contracted with each other for the sale of certain Locations or entries of Land on the Western Waters which the said SLAUGHTER was then entitled to for the consideration of certain lands adjoining the Town of Fredericksburg commonly called the MEADOW and suppose to contain about Six acres which the said ALEXANDER DICK was then entitled to, and for so much money as the said Western Lands might amount to over and above Four thousand acres at Ten pounds the hundred, Exclusive of all charges of Surveys, Pattents &c. in compliance with which contract the said DICK made and executed proper Deeds in Law for conveying the said MEADOW LAND to the said SLAUGHTER in fee as by the said Deed now of record amongst the Records of the Hustings Court for the said City of Fredericksburg may appear, And Whereas the above contract was made mostly upon the sum of mutual advantate, from the opportunity the said DICK expected to have for surveying and clearing the above lands out of the Office & seeing ample justice done to the said LAWRENCE and himself by his personal attendance on the spot which is now impossible through the late death of the said DICK, and the said SLAUGHTER anxious to entrust the securing the above mentioned lands to a person he may have the late good confidence in and upon such times as he may think proper may be compelled to agree to, And Whereas the said ALEXANDER DICK by his last Will has devised his whole Estate to the above named JOHN MERCER, whom he appointed his sole Executor for the purpose of paying of Debts and the said MERCER finding it far more convenient to manage the disposition of the lands called the MEADOW LAND rather than the Lands on the Western Waters which wou'd require more moneys in advance and great trouble, And be slow raising money by sale, It is agreed upon the mutual advantage of the said ALEXANDER DICK his Creditors and Legatees and the said SLAUGHTER to cancel & annul the aforementioend contract as if the same had never been made; Now this Indenture Witnesseth that in pursuance of the wish of the said MERCER and SLAUGHTER, and in consideration of the premisses and also for the further consideration of Twenty shillings to the said LAWRENCE SLAUGHTER in hand paid by the said JAMES MERCER, the said LAWRENCE SLAUGHTER and SUSANNAH his Wife have sold unto the said JAMES MERCER his heirs & assigns forever all the aforementioend parcel of land called the MEADOW, adjoining the Town of Fredericksburg containing about six acres being the whole the said ALEXANDER DICK sold or intended to sell to the said SLAUGHTER by the Deed referred to; To have and to hold the said Land unto the said JAMES MERCER upon Trust to & for the purposes mentioned in the Last Will of the said ALEXANDER DICK and for none other purpose and for the use of the said ALEXANDER DICKs or his Fathers Creditors & Legatees; in the same manner as if the said ALEXANDER DICK never conveyed the said Lands and the same were subject to the said Will as well as his other lands thereby devised freed and discharged from the Dower of the said SUSANNA SLAUGHTER and without the lawful hinderance of the said LAWRENCE SLAUGHTER his heirs or assigns; In Witness whereof the said LAWRENCE SLAUGHTER and SUSANNAH his Wife have set their hands and seals

Sealed and delivered in presence of

HENRY ARMISTEAD, FONTAINE MAURY, LAWRENCE SLAUGHTER
SAML. K. BRADFORD, J. DAWSON,
FRAS: THORNTON

At a Hustings Court held for the Corporation of Fredericksburg on Monday the Fourth day of July one thousand seven hundred and eighty five
This Deed was proved by the oaths of HENRY ARMISTEAD, FONTAINE MAURY and SAMUEL K. BRADFORD and ordered to be recorded

Test HENRY ARMISTEAD, Clerk

pp. (On margin: Delivd. the Origl. Deed to BENJ: DAY)
245- THIS INDENTURE made this first day of December in the year of our Lord one
247 thousand seven hundred and Eighty six Between CALLANDER & HENDERSON
and ELIZABETH, the Wife of ELIEZER CALLENDER, MILDRED the Wife of DAVID HENDERSON, of the Town and Corporation of Fredericksburg in the County of Spotsylvania of the one part and BENJAMIN DAY of the Town and Corporation aforesaid of the other part; Witnesseth that the said CALLENDER and HENDERSON and ELIZABETH and MILDRED their Wives, for the sum of One thousand two hundred and twelve pounds Specie have granted unto the said BENJAMIN DAY his heirs and assigns forever, all that parcel of Ground in the Town and Corporation of Fredericksburg being part of two lots which are marked in the plan of the said Town number Forty seven and Forty eight, as follows, Vizt., One hundred and four feet and six inches on Lot number Forty seven beginning at the North Corner of Lot number Forty five, the property of JOHN BAYLOR, and now occupied by JOHN LEGG, thence Fifty eight feet and six inches back parrallell with AMELIA STREET, thence Twenty two feet South parrallell with CAROLINE STREET, then in a straight line back to PRINCESS ANN STREET; thence Southerly eighty two feet and six inches along PRINCESS ANN STREET on Lot number Forty eight, thence Sixteen poles to the North corner of Lot number Forty five, Together with all houses stables gardens ways to the same belonging; To have and to hold unto the said BENJAMIN DAY his heirs and assigns forever; and the said CALLENDER & HENDERSON and ELIZABETH and MILDRED their Wives will warrant and foreverdefend the said granted Land against

the claims of all persons claiming under them; In Witness whereof the said parties hereunto set their hands and seals
Signed sealed and delivered in presence of

WILLIAM THOMPSON, JOHN PROUDFIT, WILLIAM FRENCH, HENRY DAY

CALLENDER & HENDERSON
ELIZABETH CALLENDER
MILDRED HENDERSON

(Plan of Lot)

The Commonwealth of Virginia to CHARLES MORTIMER, JAMES DUNCANSON and WILLIAM HARVEY, Gent., Justices of the Town and Corporation of Fredericksburg Greeting; (The Commission for the privy examination of ELIZABETH the Wife of ELIEZER CALLENDER and MILDRED, the Wife of DAVID HENDERSON); Witness HENRY ARMISTEAD, Clerk of our said Court this 15th day of February 1787 & in the Eleventh year of the Common Wealth
HENRY ARMISTEAD, Clerk

Corporation of Fredericksburg, to wit: Pursuant to the within Commission (the return of the Execution of the privy Examinations of ELIZABETH CALLENDER and MILDRED HENDERSON), Certified under our hands and seals this 19th day of April 1787
CHARLES MORTIMER
WILLIAM HARVEY

At a Hustings Court held for the Town and Corporation of Fredericksburg on Monday the first day of January 1787
This Deed and Receipt with a plot thereof was acknowledged and ordered to be recorded
Test HENRY ARMISTEAD, Clk.

pp. 248-249 THIS INDENTURE made the first day of December one thousand seven hundred and Eighty six Between WILLIAM TAYLOR of the Town of FALMOUTH and County of STAFFORD of the one part and JONATHAN HARRISS of the Town of Fredericksburg, Merchant, of the County of Spotsylvania of the other part; Witnesseth that the said WILLIAM TAYLOR in consideration of the sum of One hundred pounds current money of Virginia have granted unto the said JONATHAN HARRISS a parcel of Ground being in the Town and Corporation of Fredericksburg containing Forty feet on CAROLINE STREET running back right angles with the line of Mr. JOHN BAYLOR one hundred & fifty (blank) thence parrallell with the said CAROLINE STREET, thence down CAROLINE STREET forty feet to the corner of Mr. BAYLOR and the beginning; And is the Ground purchased by the said WILLIAM TAYLOR of the said BENJAMIN DAY and are the houses late under the Tenure of MESSRS. RITCHIE, CAMPBELL & RUFFIN; To have and to hold the said Ground and premisses unto the said JONATHAN HARRISS his heirs and assigns in the sole and free use of the said hereby sold Ground against the claim and demand of him the said WILLIAM TAYLOR his heirs or any other persons whatsoever; In Witness whereof the said WILLIAM TAYLOR hath set his hand and affixed his seal
Signed sealed acknowledged & delivered in presence of

JAMES SOMERVILLE, DAVID BLAIR, HENRY ARMISTEAD, BENJA: DAY

WILLIAM TAYLOR

At a Hustings Court held for the Corporation of Fredericksburg on Monday the first day of January one thousand seven hundred and eighty seven;
This Deed was proved by the oathes of JAMES SOMERVILLE, BENJAMIN DAY and HENRY ARMISTEAD and ordered to be recorded Test HENRY ARMISTEAD, Clerk

pp. 249-250 THIS INDENTURE made the eighth day of November one thousand seven hundred and Eighty four Between ALEXANDER SPOTSWOOD and ELIZABETH his Wife of the County of Spotsylvania of the one part and JOHN BAYLOR of the County of CAROLINE of the other part; Witnesseth that in consideration of the sum of One hundred thousand pounds of nett crop tobacco in hand paid, they the said ALEXANDER SPOTSWOOD and ELIZABETH his Wife do sell unto the said JOHN BAYLOR Four lotts numbered (blank) situtate in the Town of Fredericksburg on which the said ALEXANDER SPOTSWOOD lately resided being the lott or lotts which the said ALEXANDER SPOTSWOOD purchased of Colonel LEWIS WILLIS as by Deed recorded in the County Court of Spotsylvania may appear, To have and to hold the said lotts of land with all houses buildings & waters belonging free and clear of them the said ALEXANDER SPOTSWOOD and ELIZABETH his Wife their heirs and assigns; In Witness the parties have set their hands and seals

In the presence of HENRY ARMISTEAD, — ALEXANDER SPOTSWOOD
RICHARD WILLIAMSON, — ELIZABETH SPOTSWOOD
R. WELLFORD, G. WM: SPOONER
WM. DAINGERFIELD, JNO: LEGG

The Commonwealth of Virginia to GEORGE WEEDON & GEORGE FRENCH Gent., Justices of the Corporation of Fredericksbur Greeting; (The Commission for the privy Examination of ELIZABETH, the Wife of ALEXANDER SPOTSWOOD); Witness HENRY ARMISTEAD, Clerk of our said Court this twenty ninth day of January one thousand seven hundred and Eighty five in the Ninth year of the Common Wealth

HENRY ARMISTEAD, Clerk

Pursuant to the within Commission, (the return of the Execution of the privy Examination of ELIZABETH SPOTSWOOD); Certified under our hands and seals this twelvth day of June one thousand seven hundred and eighty five — GEORGE WEEDON
GEORGE FRENCH

At a Hustings Court held for the Town and Corporation of Fredericksburg on Monday the third day of January one thousand seven hundred and eighty five,
This Deed was proved by the oaths of JOHN LEGG, RICHARD WILLIAMSON & GEORGE W. SPOONER & ordered to be recorded; with a Commission of Mrs. SPOTSWOODs privy examination — Test HENRY ARMISTEAD, Clk.

pp. 251-253 THIS INDENTURE made the first day of December one thousand seven hundred and Eighty six between BENJAMIN DAY of the County of Spotsylvania and Town of Fredericksburg and EBENEZER his Wife of the one part and WILLIAM TAYLOE of the County of STAFFORD and Town of FALMOUTH of the other part; Witnesseth that BENJAMIN DAY and EBENEZER his Wife for the sum of Three hundred pounds current money of Virginia have sold unto the said WILLIAM TAYLOE his heirs and assigns a parcel of Ground in the Town and Corporation of Fredericksburg containing Forty feet on CAROLINE STREET running back right angles with the line of Mr. JOHN BAYLOR one hundred and fifty feet; thence parrallell with the said CAROLINE STREET forty feet to the line of Division; thence right angles with the said line one hundred and fifty feet to CAROLINE STREET, thence down and with the said CAROLINE STREET to the Corner of Mr. JOHN BAYLOR and the beginning; and is the Ground or part thereof purchased by the said BENJAMIN DAY of ELEAZER CALLONDER and DAVID HENDERSON; To have and to hold the said Ground and premisses unto the said WILLIAM TAYLOE his heirs and assigns; In Witness whereof the said BENJAMIN DAY and EBENEZER his Wife have hereunto set their hands and seals

In presence of (no witnesses shown) — BENJ: DAY

The Commonweath of Virginia to CHARLES MORTIMER, JAMES SOMERVILLE, JAMES DUNCANSON and GEORGE FRENCH, Gent. Justices of the Court of Hustings of the Corporation of Fredericksburg, Greeting (The Commission for the privy Examination of EBENEZER, wht Wife of BENJAMIN DAY); Witness HENRY ARMISTEAD Clerk of our said Court this fourteenth day of February one thousand seven hundred and Eighty seven in the Eleventh year of the Common Wealth HENRY ARMISTEAD, Clerk

Corporation of Fredericksbury to wit; (the return of the Execution of the privy Examination of EBENEZER DAY); Certified under our hands and seals this (blank) day of (blank) one thousand seven hundred and Eighty seven (no signtures)

At a Hustings Court held for the Town and Corporation of Fredericksburg on the 1st day of January 1787;
This Indenture from BENJAMIN DAY to WILLIAM TAYLOE was acknowledged by the said BENJAMIN DAY and ordered to be recorded
Taken from the Minutes p. R. S. CHEW HENRY ARMISTEAD, Clk. C. F.

pp. 253-254 THIS INDENTURE made the fifth day of December one thousand seven hundred and eighty five Between RICHARD KENNEY of the one part & JOHN RICHESON of the other part; both of the Town of Fredericksburg and County of Spotsylvania, Witnesseth that the said RICHARD KENNEY in consideration of the sum of Five shillings current money paid by the said JOHN RICHESON doth lett & to farm lett unto the said JOHN RICHESON a parcel of ground in the Town of Fredericksburg beginning forty eight feet from the Corner of HAWKE STREET and the House at present occupied by THOMAS COCKRAN running along CAROLINE STREET twenty eight feet, thence by a right angle one hundred and twenty feet back, thence upward toward HAWKE STREET seventy eight feet, thence by a right angle to CAROLINE STREET at the beginning; To have and to hold unto the said JOHN RICHESON his heirs & assigns from the day of the date hereof during the term of Twenty one years to commence on the Fourteenth day of February one thousand seven hundred and eighty five, the said JOHN RICHESON paying unto the said RICHARD KENNEY his heirs the sum of Seven pounds Ten shillings current money in specie or hard money in every year the term aforesaid; to wit on the fourteenth day of February one thousand seven hundred and eighty six, and so to continue his annual payments on the fourteenth day of February every year during the term of Twenty oen years, together with all taxes charges and incumbrances that shall become due and that the said JOHN RICHESON shall peaceably deliver up the possession of the said Ground unto said RICHARD KENNEY his heirs and assigns; In Witness whereof the parties of these presents have set their hands and seals

Signed sealed acknowledged and delivered in presence of
JAMES HANSBROUGH, THORNTON MEADE, RICHARD KENNEY
JAMES JULIAN, JAMES BROWN

At a Court of Hustings held for the Corporation of Fredericksburg on Monday the second day of January one thousand seven hundred and eighty six
This Lease was acknowledged and ordered to be recorded
Test HENRY ARMISTEAD, Clk.

pp. 255-256 THIS INDENTURE made the seventh day of November one thousand seven hundred and Eighty five Between JOHN WELCH of the one part and WILLIAM REAT of the other part; both of the Town of Fredericksburg, Witnesseth that the said JOHN WELCH for the yearly rents and covenants hereinafter contained in the part of the said WILLIAM REAT to be paid hath granted and to farm letten unto the said WILLIAM REATT part of a lott of land being in the Town of Fredericksburg aforesaid on CAROLINE STREET and is known and distinguished in a plan of the said Town by the number Two hundred and Fifty eight; which part of the said lott is laid off in a parrellogarm or long Square, containing thirty six feet in front and one hundred and forty two feet in depth and is the North West or upperr part of the said lott number Two hundred

and fifty eight; Together with all appurtenances; To have and to hold unto the said WILLIAM REATT his Executors and assigns from the date of these presents and for and during the term of Seven years and four months thence next ensuing and fully to be compleated and paying yearly unto the said JOHN WELCH his heirs and assigns the yearly rent of Three pounds current money on or before the Twenty sixth day of June in each year and so in proportion for the remaining four months; And if the said Rent be behind for the space of Twenty eight days next after days appointed for the payment (being first damanded) then and from thenceforth it shall be lawful for the said JOHN WELCH into the said premisses to reenter and the same to have again; In Witness whereof the parties have to these presents set their hands and affixed their seals
Signed sealed and delivered in presence of
(no witnesses shown) JOHN WELCH
WILLIAM REATT

At a Hustings Court held for the Town and Corporation of Fredericksburg on Monday the second day of January one thousand seven hundred & eighty six
This Lease was acknowledged and ordered to be recorded
Test HENRY ARMISTEAD, Clerk

pp. (On margin: July 30. 87, deld. to Mr. J. LEGG)
256- THIS INDENTURE made the thirteenth day of January one thousand seven hun-
258 dred and eighty six Between WILLIAM ROBINSON and JOHN ROBINSON, acting Executors of MICHAEL ROBINSON lately of the Twon of Fredericksburg and State of Virginia of the one part and JOHN LEGG, Merchant, of the said Town and State of the other part; Whereas the said MICHAEL ROBINSON by his last Will and Testament in writing duly made and executed the sixth day of January in the year of our Lord one thousand seven hundred and Eighty four and recorded in the Court of Hustings of Fredericksburg on the Sixteenth day of February in the said year; after having made sundry specifick devises directs that all the rest of his Estate real and personal not before particularly bequeathed should be sold by his Executors for the purposes in the said Will mentioned and nominated and appointed his Sons, MICHAEL ROBINSON, WILLIAM ROBINSON, JOHN ROBINSON and BENJAMIN ROBINSON, Executors of his said Will but MICHAEL and BENJAMIN aforesaid refuseing to qualify, WILLIAM and JOHN only proved the said Will and took upon themselves the Executors thereof; Now This Indenture Witnesseth that the said WILLIAM ROBINSON and JOHN ROBINSON by virtue of the said Power by the said Will granted and for the sum of One hundred pounds current money of Virginia have granted unto the said JOHN LEGG his heirs and assigns forever all that parcel of Ground containing about one fourth of an acre lying on the Street called CHARLES STREET in the aforesaid Town of Fredericksburg being part of the lott known by the number one hundred & thirty three in the plan of the said Town which was purchased by the said MICHAEL ROBINSON in his life time together with the lot number One hundred and thirty four of JAMES DUNCANSON as by a Deed indented and acknowledged by the said JAMES DUNCANSON and MARY his Wife and recorded at the Court for Spotsylvania County on the Twenty first of November one thousand seven hundred and Seventy one will more fully appear; the sais Ground intended to be transferred being bounded Beginning where the said lot number one hundred and thirty htree is cornered by CHARLES STREET and AMELIA STREET, thence along CHARLES STREET half way to the line dividing the Lots one hundred and thirty three and one hundred and thirty five, thence at right angles with the said CHARLES STREET to the line dividing the lots number one hundred thirty three and one hundred and thirty four, thence along the said line to AMELIA STREET and from thence along the

said Street to the beginning; comprehending the compleat half of the aforesaid lot number one hundred and thirty three, And also all houses buildings orchards gardens trees paths belonging; To have and to hold unto the said JOHN LEGG against them the said WILLIAM ROBINSON and JOHN ROBINSON and their heirs and also against the claims of the heirs of the several Children of the said MICHAEL ROBINSON deceased, also the several devisees claiming under his Will shall and will warrant and forever defend by these presents In Witness whereof the said WILLIAM ROBINSON & JOHN ROBINSON have set their hands and seals

In presence of (no witnesses shown) WILLIAM ROBINSON
JOHN ROBINSON

At a Hustings Court held for the Town and Corporation of Fredericksburg on Monday the Sixth day of March one thousand seven hundred and Eighty six
This Deed was acknowledged and ordered to be recorded
Test HENRY ARMISTEAD, Clerk

pp. THIS INDENTURE made the Seventeenth day of October in the year of our Lord
258- one thousand seven hundred & eighty five Between CHARLES WASHNGTON of
262 BERKELEY County, Esqr., & MILDRED his Wife & BURGESS BALL of CULPEPER
Esqr. and FANNY his Wife of the one part and JOHN LEGG of Fredericksburg, Merchant, of the other part; Whereas the said CHARLES WASHINGTON some years ago did give to his Son in Law, the said BURGESS BALL, two lots of Ground with the appurtenances lying in the said Town of Fredericksburg known and described in the platt of the said Town by the numbers Seventy nine and Eighty, And Whereas the said BURGESS BALL did afterwards agree to convey the same to ROBERT FORSYTH, then of Fredericksburg, Merchant, and did execute a Bond dated the twenty first day of June in the year one thousand seven hundred & eighty two for conveying two lotts unto the said ROBERT FORSYTH, And Whereas the said ROBERT FORSYTH has since sold the said lots unto the said JOHN LEGG and for that purpose hath made him an Assignment of the Bond from BURGESS BALL aforesaid but as Deeds of Conveyance property recorded have never yet been made by the said CHARLES WASHINGTON for the said Lots, the legal interest therein & interest therein still remains in him the said CHARLES WASHINGTON; Now this Indenture Witnesseth that the said CHARLES WASHINGTON & MILDRED his Wife and the said BURGESS BALL & FANNY his Wife in consideration of the premisses and of the sum of Two hundred & Fifty pounds current money to them paid, have granted the two lots of Ground aforesaid numbered Seventy nine & Eighty, in the said Town of Fredericksburg; To have and to hold unto him the said JOHN LEGG his heirs & assigns forever from the claim & demand of the said CHARLES WASHINGTON and MILDRED his Wife & the said BURGESS BALL and FANNY his Wife and every other person whatsoever; In Witness whereof the said parties have set their hands and affixed their seals

Sealed & Delivered in the presence of
(As to Colo. WASHINGTON) JNO. FRAZER, CHARLES WASHINGTON
THOS: FOXE, WILLIAM CLAYTON MILDRED WASHINGTON
(As to Colo. BALL) JABEZ, LEGG; KEMP HURST, B. BALL
JAMES JULIAN, JAMES JARVIS FRANCES BALL

The Commonwealth of Virginia to WILLIAM LITTLE, JOHN COOKE and WILLM. CHERRY Gent. of the County of BERKELEY Greeting; (Commission for the privy Examination of MILDRED, the Wife of CHARLES WASHINGTON); Witness HENRY ARMISTEAD Clerk of our said Court of Hustings of Fredericksburg this 18 day of October 1788 in the 13th years of the Common Wealth HENRY ARMISTEAD, Clk.

BERKELEY County, to wit; Pursuant to this Commission (the return of the Execution of the

Commission for the privy Examination of MILDRED WASHINGTON); Certified under our hands and seals this 16th day of August 1788 WILLIAM LITTLE
WILLM. CHERRY

The Commonwealth of Virginia to JAMES SOMERVILLE, GEORGE WEEDON and GEORGE FRENCH, Gent. Justuses of the Town and Corporation of Fredericksburg Greeting; (Commission for the privy Examination of FRANCES, the Wife of BURGESS BALL); Witness HENRY ARMISTEAD Clerk of our said Court this 10th day of March 1787 & in the 11th year of the Common Wealth

Teste HENRY ARMISTEAD

PURSUANT to the within Commission (the return of the execution of the Commission for the privy Examination of FRANCES BALL); Certified under our hands and seals this 10th of March 1787 JAMES SOMERVILLE
G. WEEDON

KNOW ALL MEN by these presents that I BURGESS BALL of the County of KING GEORGE am firmly bound unto ROBERT FORSYTH of the Town of Fredericksburg in the full sum of Five hundred pounds lawfull money this twenty first day of June one thousand seven hundred and Eighty two

The Condition of the above obligation is such that whereas BURGESS BALL hath sold unto the sd. ROBERT FORSYTH two certain lotts in the Square lying between Mr. PHILIP LIPSCOMB and Mr. RICHARD KENNEY & known and described in the plan of Fredericksburg by the numbers of Seventy nine & Eighty, Now if the above bound BURGESS BALL at the request of him the said ROBERT FORSYTH his heirs make a good Deed and Conveyance for the said two lotts in fee simple, then the above obligation to be void or else to remain in full force and virtue

Executed in the presence of
CHARLES CARTER, GEO: BUCKNER JR. BURGESS BALL
THOMAS SYDNOR, JOHN LEGG

For value received of Mr. JOHN LEGG, Merchant in Fredericksburg Virginia, I hereby assign and set over unto him the said JOHN LEGG all my right to the within mentioned two lotts of Land, Given under my hand & Seal at AUGUSTA in GEORGIA this twenty seventh day of June 1785

ROBERT FORSYTH

Witness JAMES FONTAINE, DANL. GAINES,
JOHN MEALS, JOHN THRELKILD

CHS:TON, Fifteenth December 1784

Dear Sir I have just time to acknowledge Receipt of your Letter of the Eighth November in answer to mine of the Twenty third September respecting the two lotts adjoining Mr. LIPSCOMBs they are your and you will please provide for the payment of the Thousand Dollars which you gave me leave to draw; I shall contrive it so that you may not be called on sooner than February next; in the meantime please take up a small Note of mine in the hands of Mr. BRUMFIELD, a small Horse who died last night, and I shall draw on you for Eight pounds Ten shillings & ten pence in favor of Mr. NICHOLASON, Richmond, which please honor and further I shall trouble you not for some time; Please take such steps respecting the Lotts as will get you Conveyance from Mr. SMITH instead of to me. In Hast, I am Truly, Your very sincere,

ROBERT FORSYTH

In haste I shall write you by Water in a few days before I move up to AUGUSTA,
Mr. LEGG

pp. (On margin: Delivered SAML. SELDEN Esqr. 24th Febry. 1787)
263 THIS INDENTURE made the second day of September in the year of our Lord one
265 thousand seven hundred and Eighty six Between JAMES MERCER of the Town of Fredericksburg & County of Spotsylvania Esquire, Devisee & Trustee of ALEXANDER DICK, late of the same place, deceased, of the one part and SAMUEL SELDEN of the County of STAFFFORD Esquire of the other part; Whereas CHARLES DICK Esqr. late of the said Town of Fredericksburg & County of Spotsylvania decealsed, by his last Will & Testament duly proved & recorded in the Corporation Court of the said Town, did devise his whole Estate real & personal unto the said ALEXANDER DICK, his only Son & heir, subject to the payment of his, the said CHARLES DICKs Debts and certain Legacies in the said Will & Testament mentioned; And also whereas the said ALEXANDER after the death of the said CHARLES having entered into the Estate so devised departed this life on the seventeenth day of March one thousand seven hundred and eighty five having first made & published his last Will and Testament now of Record in the said Corporation Court & therein devised his whole Estate & Interests unto the above named JAMES MERCER in Fee upon Trust; First for the payment of the said CHARLES DICK's Debts & legacies, Secondly for the payment of the proper Debts of him the said ALEXANDER DICK, & lastly with certain limitations over and also appointed the said JAMES MERCER sole Executor of his said Will & Testament, And Whereas the said CHARLES and ALEXANDER were at the time of their deaths both greatly indebted by Bonds and simple contracts & the personal Estate altogether not amount to one tenth part of the Debts, the said JAMES MERCER thinking it most for the benefit of those interested in the surplus of the said ALEXANDER DICK's Estate to sell the real Estate of which the said CHARLES died seized; & upon Credit to enhance the value thereof (the whole of the said ALEXANDER DICK's own proper real Estate consisting of Entries for Lands on the Western Waters which are neither surveyed nor Pattented & of very inconsiderable value at present, but may greatly appreciate, the said CHARLES DICK's real Estate being now as valuabale as can be expected for a great while yet to come) advertised the same in the *VIRGINIA GAZETTE* to be sold at Publick auction on the sixth day of June last, being the FAIR DAY, and the said SAMUEL SELDEN having at such Publick auction become a purchaser of part of CHARLES DICK's Estate herein after described; for the price of Eight hundred & ten pounds being the highest bid for the same; Now This Indenture Witnesseth that the said JAMES MERCER hath granted unto the said SAMUEL SELDEN his heirs and assigns all that part of the Estate of the said CHARLES DICK deceased purchased as aforesaid being one certain part of certain lots being in the said Town of Fredericksburg whereon the said CHARLES DICK resided; the whole together containing two lotts or half acres of land which he purchased of JOHN ALLEN in his life time & (blank) TODD who purchased part thereof of the Executors of the said JOHN ALLEN and also a slip of Land adjoining thereto which the said CHARLES DICK purchased of FIELDING LEWIS deceased, being twenty three & half feet in breadth & for length the same as the two first mentioned lots which lots are numbered in the plan of the said Town Fifty one & Fifty two and together with the Slip aforementioned bounded by CAROLINE STREET or Main Street on the North East; on the South East by the Lotts of NATHANIEL CHAPMANs Heirs & the Heirs of the late GENERAL MERCER, on the South West by PRINCESS ANN STREET & on the North West by the new Street in the Addition to the said Town called LEWIS STREET being the whole which the said CHARLES DICK claimed in that part of the Town as by the Deeds from the said JOHN ALLEN & (blank) TODD & FIELDING LEWIS now of Record in the County Court of Spotsylvania may appear, excepting there out Five certain parts thereof purchased at the Sale aforesaid by Sir JOHN PEYTON, Baronet, & the two alleys laid out by the said JAMES MERCER for the common use of the expected purchasers of

the said lots as divided in Plat thereof made by the said JOHN MERCER previous to the sale thereof & recorded in the Corporation of Fredericksburg on the Sixth day of June aforementioned, the said SAMUEL SELDENs part being distinguished in the said last mentioned plot by number one; the other five Lots being purchased as aforementioned by Sir JOHN PEYTON Baronet; And all the houses & buildings and appertenances to the same belonging; To have and to hold the said lot of ground unto the said SAMUEL SELDEN his heirs and assigns forever; In Witness whereof the said JAMES MERCER hath set his hand and seal

Sealed & delivered in presence of

ROBERT MERCER JAMES MERCER

At a Hustings Court held for the Corporation of Fredericksburg on Monday the Fourth day of September one thousand seven hundred & Eighty six

This Deed from the Honble. JAMES MERCER Esqr. and Devisee of CHARLES and ALEXANDER DICK deceased to SAMUEL SELDEN was acknowledged & ordered to be recorded

Test HENRY ARMISTEAD Clk.

pp. (On margin: Delivered GODLOVE HEISKILL 24th Febry. 1787)

265- THIS INDENTURE made the Seventh day of August in the year of our Lord one
266 thousand seven hundred and Eighty six Between JAMES MERCER of the Town of Fredericksburg and County of Spotsylvania Esquire, Devisee and Trustee of ALEXANDER DICK, late of the same place deceased, of the one part and GODLOVE HEISKILL of the same place, Blacksmith, of the other part; Whereas CHARLES DICK Esquire late of the said Town of Fredericksburg and County of Spotsylvania deceased by his last Will and Testament duly proved and Recorded in the Corporation Court of the said Town did devise his whole Estate real and personal unto the said ALEXANDER DICK deceased, his only Son and Heir, subject to the payment of his the said CHARLES DICK's Debts and certain legacies in the said Will and Testament mentioned, And also Whereas the said ALEXANDER after the death of the said CHARLES having entered into the Estate so devised departed this life on the Seventeenth day of March one thousand seven hundred and Eighty five, having first made and published his last Will and Testament now of Record in the said Corporation Court and therein devised his whole Estate unto JAMES MERCER in fee upon Trust first for the payment of the said CHARLES DICK's debts and legacies and secondly for the payment of the proper Debts of him the said ALEXANDER DICK and lastly with a certain limitation & also appointed the said JAMES MERCER his sole Executor of his said last Will and Testament; And Whereas the said CHARLES and ALEXANDER were at the times of their deaths both greatly indebted by Bonds and simple contracts and the personal Estate all together not amounting to one tenth part of the said Debts, the said JAMES MERCER thinking it most for the benefit of those interested in the surplus of the said Estate to sell the Real Estate and upon Credit to enhance the value thereof (the whole of the said ALEXANDER DICK's own proper real Estate consisting of Entries for lands on the Western Waters which are neither surveyed nor Pattented and of very inconsiderable value at present but may greatly appreciate and the said CHARLES DICK's real Estate being now as valuable as can be expected for a great whie yet to come) advertized the same in the *VIRGINIA GAZETTE* to be sold at Publick auction on the sixth day of June last being FAIR DAY, And the said GODLOVE HEISKILL having at such publick auction become a purchaser of part of said CHARLES DICK's Estate herein described for the price of Ninety pounds being the highest price bid for the same; Now this Indenture witnesseth that the said JAMES MERCER has sold unto the said GODLOVE HEISKILL his heirs and assigns all that part of the Estate of the said CHARLES DICK deceased purchased as aforesaid being one lot or half acre on the Bank

of the RIVER RAPPAHANOCK and bounded on the North East by the said River, on the South East by the Cross Street called AMELIA STREET, and on the North West by the Lot belonging to the Estate of Doctor JOHN JULIAN deceased, which Lot the said CHARLES DICK purchased of the POT ASH COMPANY and is well known by the description of the POT ASH LOT and is numbered in the plan of the Town number Seven; And all houses buildings ways belonging; To have and to hold unto the said GODLOVE HEISKILL his heirs and assigns forever; In Witness whereof the said JAMES MERCER hath set his hand and seal

in presence of WILLIAM SMITH, JAMES MERCER
JOS: CHRISTY, HENRY MAYFIELD

At a Hustings Court held for the Corporation of Fredericksburg on Monday the Seventh day of August one thousand seven hundred and eighty six
This Deed was proved by the oaths of the witnesses & ordered to be recorded
Test HENRY ARMISTEAD, Clk.

p. 267 TO BE SOLD at Public Auction at Fredericksburg on the first Tuesday in June next being the FAIR and Day of the PURSE RACE

All the Real Estate of the late CHARLES DICK Esquire, deceased, situate in the said Town and County of Spotsylvania to wit; Two hundred and ninety acres of Land about seven miles from the Town adjoining the Lands of LEWIS & DUDLEY being the same Mr. DICK formerly purchased of Mr. SIMON MILLER of ESSEX, this Land is very well timbered, the soil good and quite fresh; Six acres of Land adjoining the Town known by the name of the MEADOW LOT, this is really an elegant situation for a Gentleman of Taste; One quarter of an acre Water Lot on the bank of the River on a line with the BRICK STORE, occupied by Messrs. LILLY & FISHER; half an acre Water Lot known by the name of the POT ASH LOT, this Lot contains many fresh springs and well adapted for a Brewery, Distillery and Tan Yard; Also one acre and a quarter being two lots and part of a lot whereon the late Mr. DICK resided; situate on the Main Street in the best part of the (   ) for Trade; And two on the Hill for private houses; The Terms of sale are one fourth ready cash, another fourth in six months, the other two fourths in twelve months with a proviso that if one moiety thereof shall be paid when due, a further credit of six months will be allowed for the residue; the whole to bear Interest from the day of the sale; And to accomidate the purchaser it is excepted public securities will be accepted for most if not all of the first quarter; The Title is unquestionable but Deeds will not be fully executed until actual receipt of the purchase money; possession will be given immediately and Bond with security required of the purchaser
JAMES MERCER, Trustee

There will also be sold at the COURTHOUSE of ALBEMARLE County on the First day of the Court in July next, Two hundred acres of land belonging to the same Estate, on nine months credit; bearing interest from the day of Sale on Bond and Security. Col. GEORGE NICHOLAS knows the land and will direct the sale for. April Twenty ninth one thousand seven hundred & Eighty six J. M.

p. 268 Plot of Land on North Back Street, South Main Street, East LEWIS STREET, West upper half the late GENERAL MERCERs Lot; half an acre, lower half PEARSON, CHAPMANs lot half an acre division of Mr. CHARLES DICK's lots, whereon he lately resided.

No. 1. Described by figures 1, 2, 3, & 4, is 80 feet on the Main Street & 113 feet on LEWIS STREET,

2. 5, 6, 7, & 8 is 46 1/2 feet on Main Street & 115 feet depth to the 10 foot alley on the Hill

3. 9, 10, 11 & 12; is 54 feet on Main Street & 113 feet deep to the same Alley;

4. 13, 14, 15, & 16 is 99 feet on the Back Street & 140 feet from each back to West side of the same Alley;

5. 17, 18, 19, & 20. is 92 feet on the Back Street & 65 feet on LEWIS STREET;

6. 21, 22, 23, & 24; is 92 feet on the 10 foot Alley & 75 feet on LEWIS STREET

A. A Necessary H. Smoke House
B. School House I. Bale House
C. Dwelling do. K. Coopers Shop
D. Brick Dairy L. Smith's do.
E. Meat House M. Stone Store
F. Kitchen N. Wood do.
G. Corn House O. Water Mill

A Copy of the Plat to which my Bonds and Deeds for the sale of the Lots the property of the late CHARLES DICK Esqr. do refer JAMES MERCER

At a Hustings Court held for the Corporation of Fredericksburg on Monday the Fifth day of June one thousand seven hundred and Eighty six

A Platt of Lotts whereon the late CHARLES DICK Gent., deceased, & which JAMES MERCER intends to dispose thereof was returned and acknowledged by the said JAMES MERCER Gent. and at his request that with the advertisement of the sale thereof is ordered to be recorded Test HENRY ARMISTEAD, Clerk

pp. 269-271 THIS INDENTURE TRIPARTITE Between CHARLES WASHINGTON and MILDRED his Wife of the first part; GEORGE AUGUSTINE WASHINGTON and FRANCES his Wife of the second part of the County of BERKLEY; And ZACHARIAH LUCAS of the County of Spotsylvania and Town of Fredericksburg of the third part; Whereas the said CHARLES WASHINGTON and MILDRED his Wife being possessed of a Lott of Ground in the Town of Fredericksburg and being one half of the Lott numbered (blank) (which the said ZACHARIAH LUCAS now possessed) did as well for Five shillings as for the natural love & affection which they had for the said GEORGE AUGUSTINE WASHINGTON give and grant the same unto him but never made any conveyance of the said half lott or piece of ground, And the said GEORGE AUGUSTINE WASHINGTON hath agreed to the sale of the said ground unto the said ZACHARIAH LUCAS for the sum of One hundred pounds current money; Now This Indenture Witnesseth that for the sum of Five Shillings by GEORGE AUGUSTINE WASHINGTON paid to the said CHARLES WASHINGTON and MILDRED his Wife and for the said sum of One hundred pounds current money by said ZACHARIAH LUCAS paid to the said GEORGE AUGUSTINE WASHINGTON, and for the further sum of Five shillings by said ZACHARIAH LUCAS paid to the said CHARLES WASHINGTON and MILDRED his Wife, they the said CHARLES WASHINGTON and MILDRED his Wife have granted unto the said ZACHARIAH LUCAS the said half lott in the said plan of the Town of Fredericksburg; To have and to hold to the said ZACHARIAH LUCASand his heirs against the claim of CHARLES WASHINGTON and MILDRED his Wife and GEORGE AUGUSTIN WASHINGTON and FRANCES his Wife or any other person whatsoever; In Witness whereof the said CHARLES WASHINGTON and MILDRED his Wife and GEORGE AUGUSTINE WASHINGTON and FRANCES his Wife have set their hands and seals this Sixth day of October one thousand seven hundred and Eighty six

In presence of CHARLES MORTIMER, CHARLES WASHINGTON
GEO: FRENCH, MILDRED WASHINGTON
R. B. CHEW, GEO: A. WASHINGTON
FRANCIS THORNTON FRANCES WASHINGTON

The Commonwealth of Virginia to CHARLES MORTIMER and GEORGE FRENCH, Gent.,

Justices of the Corporation of Fredericksburg ((the Commission for the privy Examination of MILDRED the Wife of CHARLES WASHINGTON and FRANCES, the Wife of GEORGE AUGUSTIN WASHINGTON) Witness HENRY ARMISTEAD, Clerk of our said Court of Hustings for the Town and Corporation of Fredericksburg the sixth day of October One thousand seven hundred & eighty six in the Eleventh year of the Common Wealth

HENRY ARMISTEAD, Clerk

Corporation of Fredericksburg, to wit; Pursuant to the above Commission (the return of the Execution of the Commission for the privy Examination of MILDRED WASHINGTON and FRANCES WASHINGTON); Certified under our hands and seals this Sixth day of October one thousand seven hundred and eighty six

CHARLES MORTIMER
GEORGE FRENCH

At a Hustings Court held for the Corporation of Fredericksburg on Monday the seventh day of November one thousand seven hundred and eighty six
This Deed proved by the oaths of the witnesses with a Commission of the privy Examination of Mrs. MILDRED WASHINGTON and Mrs. FRANCES WASHINGTON returned and ordered to be recorded Test HENRY ARMISTEAD, Clk.

pp. 271-273 THIS INDENTURE Witnesseth that I WILLIAM SCELTON of the Corporation & Town of Fredericksburg & State of Virginia with the consent of my Mother, HANAH SCELTON of the same place, hath put himself and by these presents do voluntarily and of his own free will & accord, put himself Apprentice to WILLIAM SMOCK of the Corporation and Town aforesaid, Sadler, to lern his Art and Mistery, And after the manner of an Apprentice to serve from the day and date hereof during the full term of Six years & five months during all which term the said Apprentice his said Master to serve during the said Term and the said Master shall use the utmost of his Endeavors to teach or cause to be taught the said Apprentice in the Trade of a Sadler, and provide for him during the said Term and the said Master further is to give him Schooling as far as the Double Rule of Three and for the true performance of all the agreements the said parties bind themselves by these presents; In Witness whereof the said parties have set their hands and seals the seventh day of August one thousand seven hundred and eighty six

WILLIAM SKELTON
HANNAH SKELTON
WILLIAM SMOCK

At a Hustings Court held for the Town and Corporation of Fredericksburg on Monday the Seventh day of August one thousand seven hundred & eighty six
This Indenture of Apprenticeship was approved by the Court, acknowledged, and ordered to be recorded Test HENRY ARMISTEAD, Clerk

p. 272 THIS INDENTURE of Apprenticeship Between MARY GRISSHELL and TRACY GRISSHELL her Daughter of the one part and TULLY WHITHURST and POLLY his Wife of the Town of Fredericksburg of the other part; Witnesseth that the said MARY GRISSHELL with the consent and approbation of the Court of Hustings of Fredericksburg do bind her Daughter the said TRACY GRISSHELL an Apprentice to TULLY WHITHURST & POLLY his Wife with them to dwell and serve till she shall arrive to the age of Eighteen years during which time the said TRACEY GRISSHELL shall serve the said TULLY WHITHURST as a faithful Apprentice and the said TULLY WHITHURST and POLLY his Wife on their parts doth promise they will cause her to be instructed and taught to sew, that they will find her sufficient clothing diet and lodging; Moreover that they will cause her to be learnt to Read and in all things treat her as an Apprentice ought to be; Witness our hands and seals this third day of July one thousand seven

hundred and eighty six
TULLY WHITHURST
MARY GRISSHELL

At a Hustings Court held for the Corporation of Fredericksburg on Monday the Third day of July one thousand seven hundred & eighty six
This Indenture of Apprenticeship from MARY GRISSHELL and TRACY GRISSHELL her Daughter to TULLY WHITHURST was approved by the Court & acknowledged and ordered to be recorded Test HENRY ARMISTEAD, Clk.

p. 273 THIS INDENTURE of Apprenticeship made this Twenty ninth day of November one thousand seven hundred and eighty five Between THOMAS USHER of the one part and HENRY SHELTON, Seaman or Sailer, of the other part; Witnesseth that the said THOMAS USHER (by and with the Consent of the Court of Hustings of Fredericksburg) doth put and place himself an Apprentice to the said HENRY SHELTON with him to Dwell and serve during the term of Six years commencing from the date hereof, during which term he shall truly serve his said Master & behave as an Apprentice ought; the said HENRY SHELTON on his part doth promise to provide and furnish the said THOMAS USHER wholesome diet washing cloathing and lodging fitting for such Apprentice and in all things to treat him as an Apprentice ought to be, and doth promise to instruct him in the profession he now useth and moreover to give him one years Schooling; Witness our hands and seals
Witness ARMISTEAD LONG
THOMAS USHER
HENRY SHELTON

(No recording shown)

pp. 273-274 THIS INDENTURE of Apprenticeship made this Six day of November in the year of our Lord one thousand seven hundred and Eighty six Between the Worshipfull the Justices of the Court of Hustings of the Town and Corporation of Fredericksburg of the one part and JAMES SMOCK of the said Town, Saddler and Harness Maker, of the other part; Witnesseth that the said Worshipfull the Justices CHARLES MORTIMER, JAMES SOMERVILLE, GEORGE WEEDON & ELIAZER CALLENDER of the Court of Hustings of Fredericksburg doth put and place a Molatter Boy by the name of Joseph, an Apprentice to the said JAMES SMOCK with him to dwell & serve untill he arrives to the age of Twenty one years during which time he shall well and truly serve his said Master in all things shall do and behave as an Apprentice ought to, the said JAMES SMOCK on his part doth promise to provide and furnish the said Joseph with wholesome diet washing cloathing and lodging and doth promise to instruct him in the profession he now useth and moreover to give him two years Schooling; Witness our hand & seals the day and year first written
D -
O -
JAMES SMOCK

(No recording shown)

pp. 274-275 THIS INDENTURE made this third day of July one thousand seven hundred and eighty six witnesseth that JAMES FEWEL, Son of JOHN FEWEL, hath of his own free will and with the consent and approbation of the Worshipfull Court of Hustings for the Corporation of Fredericksburg placed himself Apprentice unto JOHN ROW of the Corporation aforesaid, Barber, to be taught in the said Trade Science or occupation of a Barber which he the said JOHN now useth and with him as an Apprentice to dwell and serve from the date hereof unto the term of Six years from thence fully to be compleat, during all which said term the said Apprentice his said Master will faithfully serve, in all things as a good and dutifull Apprentice will demean and behave himself towards his said Master and all during the said term and the said Master his said Apprentice the said Trade of Barber will teach and intruct after the best manner & way that he can and will also find his said Apprentice necessaries in Sickness and in Health, meet and convenient for such an Apprentice during the term aforesaid, And at the end of the said Term will give to his said Apprentice over and above his then Cloathing one new suit of Apparel (vizt.) Coat, waistcoat & breeches, hatt & shoes and stockings; with suitable linen as is fit and usual for such an Apprentice; In Witness whereof we have set our hands and seals JOHN ROWE

JAMES FEWELL

At a Court held for the Town and Corporation of Fredericksburg on Monday July 3rd 1786 This Indenture of Apprenticeship between JOHN ROW & JAMES FEWELL was approved of by the Court, Exd. & acknowledged by the parties and ordered to be recorded

Test HENRY ARMISTEAD, Clk.

Delivered J. FEWELL by Order of J. ROWE

pp. 275-276 THIS INDENTURE made this first day of January one thousand seven hundred and Eighty seven Witnesseth that WILLIAM BARBER, Son of WILLIAM BARBER, of the County of RICHMOND placed and bound himself Apprentice unto JAMES BROWN of the Town of Fredericksburg to be taught in the Trade Science and occupation of a Silver Smith, which he the said JAMES BROWN now useth; And with him as an Apprentice to dwell and serve from the day of the date hereof until the full term of Six years from thence next ensuing and fully to be compleat, during all which said term of Six years the said Apprentice his said Master well and faithfully shall serve and in all things as a good and faithfull Apprentice will behave himself towards his said Master and the said Master his said Apprentice the said Trade of a Silver Smith which he now useth with all things thereunto belonging will teach after the best way and anner that he can; and also allow meat drink lodging washing apparel both Linen and Woolen, and all other necessaries in Sickness and in Health for such an Apprentice, And at the end of the said Term will give to his said Apprentice (over and above his then clothing) one new suit of apparel Viz. Coat, waistcoat and breeches, hatt, shoes and stockings with suitable linen as is fit and is usual for such an Apprentice

JAMES BROWN

(No recording shown.)

p. 277 KNOW ALL MEN by these presents that I WILLIAM McWILLIAMS at present of the Town & Borough of Fredericksburg in the State of Virginia have made GEORGE FRENCH of the same Borough, Doctor of Physic, and ANDREW BUCHANAN near the same place, Attorney at Law, my true and lawful Substitutes & Attornies during my soon intended absence from Virginia for my use to receive all money owing to me and on refusal of payment to sue for and recover the same, I do also hereby empower my said Attornies to Lease, Rent & hire out during my absence aforesaid, for one year at a time, all my Estate & property of what kind soever, and to receive the Rents & hires for the same and on failure of payment to take all legal methods for the recovery thereof, And in all respects to act and do in the premisses as fully as I could were I personally present; hereby confirming whatever my said Attornies & Agents shall legally do; And in case of the death, removal out of the State aforesaid or disability or refusal in either of them, I do hereby authorize the other to act in all respects as fully as in the same manner as I have herein mentioned and empowered them both jointly; In Witness whereof I have set my hand and affixed my seal the first day of October in the year of

our Lord one thousand seve hundred and eighty five
Witnesses: WILLIAM FRENCH, WILLIAM McWILLIAMS
THS: GATEWOOD
(No recording shown)

pp. 278-280 THIS INDENTURE made this Sixth day of October in the year of our Lord one thousand seven hundred and Eighty six Between ROBERT JOHNSTON of the Town of PORT ROYAL and County of CAROLINE, Merchant, and JEAN his Wife of the one part and ELEZIER CALLENDER & DAVID HENDERSON of the Town of Fredericksburg & County of Spotsylvania, Merchants, of the other part; Witnesseth that the said ROBERT JOHNSTON and JEAN his Wife for the sum of One thousand five hundred pounds specie doth grnt unto the said ELEIZIER CALLENDER and DAVID HENDERSON their heirs two lotts or one acre of ground in the Town of Fredericksburg numbered Forty seven and Forty eight (as by the Plan to the said Town will appear) together with all buildings and trees; To have and to hold unto the said ELEZIER CALLENDER & DAVID HENDERSON their heirs and assigns forever; In Witness whereof the said ROBERT JOHNSTON and JEAN his Wife have set their hands and seals
Sealed and delivered in presence of
JOHN STEWARD, FRENCH GRAY, ROBERT JOHNSTON
WILLIAM WADDLE, G. G. F. BOSWELL, JANE JOHNSTON

The Commonwealth of Virginia to ROBERT GILCHRIST and JAMES TAYLOR, Gent., Justices of the County Court of CAROLINE (the Commission for the privy Examination of JEAN, the Wife of ROBERT JOHNSTON). Witness HENRY ARMISTEAD Clerk of our said Court this Eighteenth day of October one thousand seven hundred and Eighty six in the Eleventh year of the Common Wealth HENRY ARMISTEAD, Clerk

CAROLINE County, to wit: Pursuant to the above Commission (the return of the Commission for the execution of the privy examination of JEAN JOHNSTON); Certified under our hands and seals this Twenty fifth day of October one thousand seven hundred and eighty six
ROBERT GILCHRIST
JAMES TAYLOR

At a Hustings Court held for the Corporation of Fredericksburg on Monday the Sixth day of November one thousand seven hundred and eighty six
This Deed was proved by the oaths of JAMES STEWARD, WILLIAM WADDLE and FRENCH GRAY with a Commission of privy Examination returned and ordered to be recorded
Test HENRY ARMISTEAD, Clk.

pp. 280-281 THIS INDENTURE made the Third dy of February in the year of our Lord one thousand seven hundred and Eighty six Between MARY SULLIVAN of the Borough of Fredericksburg of one part and JOHN BENSON of the same place of the other part; Whereas ELIZABETH WILKENSON & the said MARY SULLIVAN purchased of BENJAMIN JOHNSTON certain lots of ground in the said Town of Fredericksburg which were conveyed by the said BENJAMIN JOHNSTON to the said WILKENSON & SULIVAN as Tenants in Common by Deed dated the first day of January in the year one thousand seven hundred and seventy nine and recorded in the Court of Spotsylvania County by the said Deed may appear, And Whereas the said MARY SULLIVAN has agreed to sell her moiety or one half of the said Lots & parcels of Ground unto the said JOHN BENSON, Now This Indenture Witnesseth that the said MARY SULLIVAN in consideration of the sum of One thousand pounds current money to her paid, hath sold unto the said JOHN BENSON his heirs & assigns all her moiety or half of the Lots of Ground aforesaid as specified in the Deed from the said JOHNSTON; Together with all houses ways and all right of her the said MARY SULLIVAN to the same; To have and to hold the said moiety of the lots unto the said JOHN BENSON her heirs & assigns from the claim & demand of her the said MARY SULLIVAN & her heirs & every other person & will warrant and defend forever by these presents; In Witness whereof the said MARY SULLIVAN hath set her hand and seal

In presence of JOHN T. BROOKE, MARY × SULLIVAN
R. S. BROOKE, GUST. B. WALLACE

At a Court of Hustings held for the Town and Corporation of Fredericksburg on Monday the Fourth day of April one thousand seven hundred and eighty six
This Deed was proved by the oaths of two witnesses & ordered to be certified;

And at a Court held on Monday the first day of June one thousand seven hundred and eighty seven, the same was further proved by the Oath of JOHN T. BROOKE and ordered to be recorded and is truly recorded Test HENRY ARMISTEAD, Clk.

p. Gentlemen. It is my deisre that Mr. ROBERT BROOKE be permitted to act as
282 Administrator on the effects of my late Husband, Mr. JOSEPH WOOD JUNR.,
Fredericksburg MARY WOOD
December 27th 1785
To the Honble: Court of Hustings

pp. (On margin: Delivd. June 1st 1787 M. C. URQUHART)
282- THIS INDENTURE made this seventh day of May in the year of our Lord one
284 thousand seven hundred and Eighty seven Between WILLIAM ROBINSON and JOHN ROBINSON, acting Executors of MICHAEL ROBINSON, late of the Town of Fredericksburg and State of Virginia of the one aprt and CHARLES URQUHART & RICHARD KENNEY of the Town of Fredericksburg and State aforesaid, assignee of BENJAMIN WEEKS on behalf of his Compromising Creditors of the other part; Whereas the said MICHAEL ROBINSON by his last Will and Testament in writing duly made and executed on the Sixth day of January in the year one thousand seven hundred and eighty four and recorded in the Court of Hustings of the Town of Fredericksburg on the Sixteenth day of February in the said year; after having made sundry specific devices, directs that all the residue not before bequeathed shall be sold by his Executors for the purposes mentioend in the said Will therein appointing his Sons, WILLIAM ROBINSON, MICHAEL ROBINSON, JOHN ROBINSON and BENJAMIN ROBINSON Executors of his said Will; But MICHAEL and BENJAMIN aforesaid refused to qualify the aforesaid WILLIAM and JOHN (only) proved the said Will; and took upon themselves the sole execution thereof; Now This Indenture Witnesseth that the said WILLIAM ROBINSON and JOHN ROBINSON by virtue of the said power and authority by said Will granted and for the sum of Ninety pounds current money of Virginia to them paid by CHARLES URQUHART and RICHARD KENNEY have sold unto CHARLES URQUHART and RICHARD KENNEY, assignees of BENJAMIN WEEKS aforesaid, their heirs and assigns all that parcel of Ground containing about one quarter of an acre of land in the Town and Corporation of Fredericksburg & known in the plan of the said Town as part of the Lott number One hundred & thirty three; which was purchased by the said MICHAEL ROBINSON in his life time together with the Lott number one hundred and thirty four of JAMES DUNCANSON (as by a Deed indented and acknowledged by the said JAMES DUNCANSON and MARY his Wife at a Court held for Spotsylvania County on the Twenty first day of November one thousand seven hundred and seventy one will more fully appear, the said piece of ground being bounded, Beginning at JOHN LEGGs Corner of the Lott number one hundred and thirty three; thence along CHARLES STREET to Lott number One hundred and

Thirty five; thence running back to the Corner of the Lotts number One hundred and Thirty four & One hundred and Thirty six, thence along the one half of Lott number One hundred and thirty four to LEGGs Lott, and thence along LEGGs Lott to the beginning, comprehending the compleat half of the aforesaid Lott number One hundred and Thirty three together with all houses orchards gardens to the same belonging; To have and to hold unto the said CHARLES URQUHART and RICHARD KENNEY (assignees aforesaid) their heirs and assigns forever; In Witness whereof the said WILLIAM ROBINSON and JOHN ROBINSON, Executors as aforementioned, have sett their hands and seals
Signed Sealed and Delvered in presence of
O. TOWLE, WILLIAM WIATT, WILLIAM ROBINSON
ALEXR. ROAN JOHN ROBINSON

At a Hustings Court held for the Town and Corporation of Fredericksburg on Monday the Seventh day of May one thousand seven hundred and eighty seven
This Deed was acknowledged by the said ROBINSONs and ordered to be recorded
Test HENRY ARMISTEAD, Clk.

pp. 284-286 KNOW ALL MEN by these presents that I WILLIAM CUNNINGHAM of LAINSHAW in consequence of Powers vested in me by the whole of the Partners of the Company known by the name and firm of WILLIAM CUNNINGHAM and COMPANY Merchants in GLASGOW, formerly trading to Virginia; as Manager & Teacher for them, and in name and for the said Company have named WILLIAM REID and WALTER COLQUHORN to be the lawfull Attorneys for the said Company within the Commonwealth of Virginia or any other of the United States of America to sue for and receive all such sums of money belonging to the said WILLIAM CUNNINGHAM & COMPANY within the said Commonwealth of Virginia or any other of the United States of America aforesaid; giveing to the said Attorneys sole power about the premisses to perform as fully as I or the said Company might do if personally present holding firm whatsoever the said Attorneys shall lawfully do; hereby revoking in virtue of my foresaid powers, rescinding and declaring null and void the Letter of Attorney executed by the said Company the Nineteenth day of May one thousand seven hundred and Eighty four in favour of said WILLIAM REID and WALTER COLQUHORN and ROBET PATTEN, ALEXANDER MOSSBURGH and ROBERT KENNAN, in so far as it invested the said ROBERT PATTON, ALEXANDE MOSSBURGH and ROBERT KENNAN with powers to act as is thus expressed; In Witness whereof I have set my hand and Seal at LAINSHAW AYRE SHIRE SCOTLAND this Sixth day of May one thousand seven hundred and eighty five
Signed sealed and delivered (being first duly stamped)
in presence of JAMES BLACK, WILLIAM CUNNINGHAM
WILLIAM BOGLE JUNR., ARTHUR BORLAND

I JOHN CAMPBELL Esquire of BLATRICK, present Lord Provost & Chief Magistrate of the City of GLASGOW in North Britain subscribing do hereby certify and attest that upon the day and date hereof JAMES BLACK, WILLIAM BOGLE and ARTHUR BORLAND did personally appear before me and being solemnly sworn made oath that they were present and did see WILLIAM CUNNINGHAM of LAINSHAW Constituant in the Letter of Attorney within written sign seal and deliver the said Letter of Attorney as his act and deed and they themselves witnesses to the execution thereof, subscribed their names as attesting the same; And further made oath that the names of JAMES BLACK, WILLIAM BOGLE and ARTHUR BORLAND appearing subscribed to the said Leter of Attorney as witnesses attesting the Execution thereof are of the respective hand writing of the Deponants; and the name WILLIAM CUNNINGHAME appearing subscribed thereto as the party executing the said Letter of Attorney is the proper hand writing of the said WILLIAM

CUNNINGHAME, In Testimony of which I and the said witnesses have subscribed these presents and I have caused affix the Common Seal of the said City hereunto, at GLASGOW this ninth day of May one thousand seven hundred and eighty five years

JOHN CAMPBELL JAMES BLACK
WILLIAM BOGLE JUNR.
ARTHUR BORLAND

At a Hustings Court held for the Town and Corporation of Fredericksburg on Monday the fourth day of June one thousand seven hundred and eighty seven
This Power of Attorney was presented to the Court by the said WALTER COLQUHOUN & together with a Certificate of the acknowledgement thereof from under the hand and seal of JOHN CAMPBELL Esquire, Lord Provost & Chief Magistrate of the City of GLASGOW in North Britain, are ordered to be recorded

Test HENRY ARMISTEAD, Clk. Teste ARMISTEAD LONG, D: Clk.

pp. 286-289 THIS INDENTURE made this Twenty second day of January in the year of our Lord one thousand seven hundred and Eighty seven Between JOHN LEGG and LUCY LEE his Wife of the Town of Fredericksburg in the County of Spotsylvania and State of Virginia of the one part and ROBERT SCOTT of the County and State aforesaid of the other part; Witnesseth that the said JOHN LEGG and LUCY LEE his Wife for the sum of Two hundred pounds current money of Virignia hath granted unto the said ROBERT SCOTT his heirs and assigns the upper half of two lotts or half acres of land in the Town of Fredericksburg in the County aforesaid known & discribed in the Platt of the said Town by the numbers 79 and 80 and bounded as follows; Westerly by CAROLINE STREET Eighty to & half feet; Northerly by PHILIP LIPSCOMBs Lotts discribed in the Platt aforesaid by the numbers Eighty one & Eighty two, two hundred and sixty four feet; Easterly by SOPHIA STREET Eighty two 1/2 feet and Southerly by the same half of the aforesaid two lotts number Seventy nine & Eighty, two hundred and sixty four feet; Together with all the houses buildings belonging; To have and to hold the said premisses with their appurtenances to the only proper use of him the said ROBERT SCOTT his heirs and assigns; In Witness whereof the parties to these presents have set their hands and seals
Sealed and delivered in presence of us

WILLIAM WIATT, KEMP HURST, JOHN LEGG
COLLIN ROSS, W. S. STONE to do. LUCY LEE LEGG

The Corporation of Fredericksburg, Sct. The Commonwealth of Virginia to WILLIAM HARVEY and BENJAMIN DAY, Gentlement, Greeting (the Commission for the privy examination of LUCY LEE, Wife of JOHN LEGG); Witness HENRY ARMISTEAD Clerk of our said Court at the Court house the 29th day of January 1787 HENRY ARMISTEAD, Clerk

The Corporation of Fredericksburg Sct. Pursuant to the within Commission (the return of the Execution of the Commission for the privy Examination of LUCY LEE LEGG); Given under our hands and seals this Twenty seventh day of March one thousand seven hundred and eighty seven WILLIAM HARVEY
BENJAMIN DAY

At a Hustings Court held for the Town and Corporation of Fredericksburg on Monday the fifth day of February one thousand seven hundred and eighty seven
This Deed is acknowledged by the said JOHN LEGG and ordered to be recorded

Test HENRY ARMISTEAD, Clerk

pp. 289-290 TO ALL TO WHOM these presents shall come Greeting. WILLIAM WIATT of the Town and Corporation of Fredericksburg in County of Spotsylvania and State of Virginia; Whereas the said WILLIAM WIATT is seased in fee of and in all that parcel of Land in County of Spotsylvania and State aforesaid and within twenty miles of the Town of Fredericksburg aforesaid; containing Five hundred and seventy five acres by an old Survey as per Plott hereunto annexed and which land is at present occupied by JOHN MITCHELL as Tenant under a Lease which expires the first day of January in the year of our Lord one thousand seven hundred and Eighty nine and the Land aforesaid is under no other incumbrance whatsoever; And the said WILLIAM WIATT is also interested in Company with JOSEPH CRAIG in a large tract or parcel of Land lying in the County of FAYETTE and State of Virginia containing by Survey made the Tenth day of April one thousand seven hundred & Eighty five, seven thousand six hundred acres as per platt hereunto annexed and which land is held by the said WILLIAM WIATT and JOSEPH CRAIG in fee simple; and as joint tenants and assignes of HENRY CRUTCHER by Patent granted the said WIATT & CRAIG under the Seal of the State aforesaid and signed by PATRICK HENRY Esquire, Governor of the said State, the twenty sixth day of June 1786, and signed by JOHN HARVIE Esqr. Re:lp Land Office on the back of the said Patent; Now Know yee that I the said WILLIAM WIATT have made JOHN WARDER and JOHN DEARMAN both of the City of LONDON in the Kingdom of Great Britain, Merchants, jointly or seperately my true and lawfull Attorneys for me to grant for such a sum of money as they the said JOHN WARDER and JOHN DEARMAN may be directed to such persons as they my said Attorneys shall think convenient, all the above discribed land and premisses with the appurtenances and also for me to deliver such Deeds for the absolute sale and disposal of the above discribed two tracts of land and premisses as my said Attorneys shall think fit; hereby confirming all such sales which shall at any time hereafter be sealed and executed within the space of three years from the day of these presents by my said Attorneys, touching the Land & Premisses aforesaid; In Witness whereof I have sett my hand and affixed my Seal this Third day of March in the year of our Lord one thousand seven hundred and eighty seven

In presence of (no witnesses shown) WILLIAM WIATT

At a Hustings Court held for the Town and Corporation of Fredericksburg on Monday the fifth day of March one thousand seven hundred and eighty seven
This Power of Attorney was acknowledged and ordered to be recorded
Test HENRY ARMISTEAD, Clk.

pp. 291-292 THIS INDENTURE made the Third day of November in the year of our Lord one thousand seven hundred and eighty six Between JOHN LEWIS of the Town of Fredericksburg and County of Spotsylvania Esqr., Eldest Son and Heir at Law of FIELDING LEWIS, late of the same place, Esqr., deced., & one of the acting Executors of the said FIELDING LEWIS deced., of the one part and JAMES MERCER of the same place of the other part; Whereas the said FIELDING LEWIS deced., in his life time, that is to say, upwards of twenty years ago having sold unto the said JAMES MERCER four certain lots or half acres of land herein after particularly mentioned, being in the said Town of Fredericksburg, for the consideration of Eighty pounds current money which the said FIELDING LEWIS some time after reced. payment of with the Interest due thereon from the time of sale, And the said JAMES MERCER in consequence of the said purchase having entered into the possession & occupation of the said four lotts & having continued in the occupation thereof from the time of the purchase aforementioend and being now seized thereof, And Whereas Deeds of Conveyance for the said four lots never having been made in the life time of the said FIELDING LEWIS whereby the legal title thereof remained in the said FIELDING LEWIS, And Whereas the said FIELDING LEWIS so intitled having before his death duly made and published his last Will in Writing now of Record in the County Court of Spotsylvania & therein & thereby having devised all the Estate whereof the said FIELDING dyed possessed in the said Town of Fredericksburg unto the aforesaid JOHN LEWIS, party to these presents, in fee simple whereby the legal interest of the said FIELDING LEWIS in said four lots so sold became vested in the said JOHN LEWIS under the devise aforementioned or the same deeded to the said JOHN LEWIS as heir at Law as not disposed of by any other devises in the Will of the said FIELDING LEWIS; Now This Indenture Witnesseth that in consideration of Twenty shillings current money to him in hand paid hath granted unto the said JAMES MERCER his heirs & assigns forever all and every the four lotts or half acres of ground in the said Town of Fredericksburg being numbered in the plan of the said town 115, 116, 117, and 118; adjoining to each other being one square & commonly known by the name of the said MERCERS PARK LOTS & being the entire square North West of & next to that square of Lots on which the said MERCER resides, by PRINCE EDWARD STREET on the South West; by PITT STREET on the North West & by CHARLES STREET on the North East as by the plan of the said Town may at large appear; to the sole use & behoof of him the said JAMES MERCER his heirs and assigns forever; And the said JOHN LEWIS for himself his heirs doth warrant that he had not since the death of the said FIELDING LEWIS done any thing whereby the Title of the said JAMES MERCER may be altered contrary to the meaning of these presents; In Witness whereof the said JOHN LEWIS hath set his hand and seal

Sealed and delivered in presence of us

MANN PAGE, G. WEEDON, JOHN LEWIS
ALEXR: SPOTSWOOD, JOHN DAWSON,
CHARLES CARTER,

Deld. Mr. MERCER Plot of the position of my 10 Lotts JS: MERCER

At a Hustings Court held for the Town and Corporation of Fredericksburg on Monday the Second day of April 1787

This Deed was acknowledged by the said LEWIS and ordered to be recorded

Truly Recorded Test ARMISTEAD LONG, D: Clk.

pp. 293-295 (On margin: Augt. 24th. Deld. to CHS. URQUHART 1787 & the fees not paid)

THIS INDENTURE made the Fifth day of March in the year of our Lord one thousand seven hundred and eighty seven Between RICHARD KENNEY and MILDRED his Wife of the Town of Fredericksburg and County of Spotsylvania of one part and CHARLES URQUHART of the Town and County aforesaid of the other part; Witnesseth that the said RICHARD KENNEY & MILDRED his Wife for the sum of Eleven thousand & fifty nine pounds of Crop Tobacco havegranted unto the said CHARLES URQUHART his heirs and assigns forever part of a parcell of Ground in the Town of Fredericksburg which is numbered in the plan of the said Town Seventy seven, begining at the South corner of the Lott we sold WILLIAM LOVELL running thence one hundred & ten feet along SOPHIA STREET untill it joins the corner of Lott number seventy five, thence along the line that divides Lotts No. 77 and 75 one hundred and twenty five feet to the corner of the Ally that divides Lott seventy seven from Lott seventy eight, thence along the said ally one hundred and ten feet untill it joins the South boundary of the Lott sold to WILLIAM LOVELL, and thence to the beginning; Together with all houses stables gardens to the same belonging; To have and to hold unto the said CHARLES URQUHART his heirs and assigns against the claim of all persons claiming under them; In Witness whereof the said RICHARD KENNEY and MILDRED his Wife have set their hands & seals

Sealed & Delivered in presence of

WILLIAM LOVELL RD. KENNEY
BURKETT DAVENPORT, G. LACART

The Commonwealth of Virginia to JAMES SOMERVILLE & BENJAMIN DAY Gent. Justices of the Town and Corporation of Fredericksburg Greeting; (The Commission for the privy Examination of MILDRED, the Wife of RICHARD KENNEY); Witness HENRY ARMISTEAD Clerk of our said Court this fifth day of March one thousand seven hundred and eighty seven in the Eleventh year of the Common Wealth HENRY ARMISTEAD, Clerk

The Corporation of Fredericksburg; to wit; Pursuant to the above Commission (the return of the Execution of the Commission for the privy Examination of MILDRED KENNEY); Certified under our hands and seals this Second day of June one thousand seven hundred and eighty seven JAMES SOMERVILL
BENJA: DAY

At a Hustings Court held for the Town and Corporation of Fredericksburg on Monday the Fifth day of March one thousand seven hundred and Eighty seven
This Deed was proved by the oathes of the witnesses which with a Commission and a Certificate of the privy Examination of the said MILLEY KENNEY are ordered to be recorded & is truly recorded Test HENRY ARMISTEAD, Clk.

pp. (On margin: Delivered to Mr. THOS: COCKRAN October 1st. 1787)
295- THIS INDENTURE made this Fourth day of June in the year of our Lord one
297 thousand seven hundred and eighty seven between RICHARD KENNEY of the Town of Fredericksburg Gent. & MILLEY his Wife of the one part & PETER HANSBROUGH of the County of KING GEORGE Gentn., of the other part; Witnesseth that the said RICHARD KENNEY and MILLEY his Wife for the sum of Forty two pounds Five shillings & four pence specie by said PETER HANSBROUGH to said RICHARD KENNEY in hand paid, whereof the said RICHARD KENNEY doth hereby acknowledge & the said PETER HANSBROUGH his heirs and assigns thereof doth hereby forever acquit & discharge; And the said PETER HANSBROUGH, doth warrant and agree with the said RICHARD KENNEY to pay unto JAMES TOOLE of BALTIMORE, Merchant, or to his assigns, Nine thousand four hundred and twenty pounds of Tobacco with Interest arising thereon in full for a Deed or Mortgage bearing date the first day of September in the year of our Lord one thousand seven hundred and eighty six for a piece of Ground as in the said Mortgage and being a part of what is herein after described, hath sold unto the said PETER HANSBROUGH his heirs and assigns forever a certain lot in the Town of Fredericksburg aforesaid being part of Lott number Seventy eight and appears in the plott of the said Town; Begining One hundred and twenty eight feet from the corner of HAWKE and CAROLINE STREETs, thence running along CAROLINE STREET twenty seven feet Southward, thence in right angles one hundred and twenty feet Eastward back to an Ally fifteen feet wide laid off and opened by the said RICHARD KENNEY and leading into HAWKE STREET, thence twenty seven feet along said Alley Northward and from thence one hundred and twenty feet to the begining; being at present occupied by EDWARD WELLS unto the said PETER HANSBROUGH his heirs and assigns, together with all buildings gardens & trees in conjunction with other adjoining lotts arising from the Alley aforesaid with the benefits which the said RICHARD KENNEY & MILLY his Wife do warrant and agree for themselves their heirs to leave open and unmolested in its present extent; In Witness whereof the said RICHARD KENNEY and MILLY his Wife have set their hands and seals
Signed seald and delivered in the presence of
GEORGE FRENCH, RD. KENNEY
WILLIAM HARVEY MILLEY KENNEY

The Commonwealth of Virginia to GEORGE FRENCH, WILLIAM HARVEY Gent., Justices of the Town and Corporation of Fredericksburg Greeting; (The Commission for the privy Examination of MILLEY, the Wife of RICHARD KENNEY; Witness JOHN CHEW JR. Clerk of our said Court this Twenty second day of August 1787 and in the twelvth year of the Common Wealth JNO: CHEW JR., C. F.

Corporation of Fredericksburg to wit; Pursuant to the above Commission (the return of the execution of the Commission for the privy Examination of MILLEY KENNEY); Certified under our hands and seals this Twenty fourth day of August 1787

GEORGE FRENCH
WILLIAM HARVEY

At a Hustings Court held for the Town and Corporation of Fredericksburg on Monday the Fourth day of June one thousand seven hundred & eighty seven
This Deed was acknowledged by the said KENNEY and ordered to be recorded
Truly recorded Teste ARMISTEAD LONG, D. Clk. Teste HENRY ARMISTEAD, Clk.

pp. (On margin: Delivered to Mr. THOS: COCKRAN October 1st 1787)
298- THIS INDENTURE made this Thirteenth day of December in the year of our Lord
300 one thousand seven hundred and eighty six Between RICHARD KENNEY of the Town of Fredericksburg and MILLEY his Wife of the one part and PETER HANSBROUGH of the County of KING GEORGE of the other part; Witnesseth that the said RICHARD KENNEY & MILLEY his Wife for the sum of One hundred and forty pounds specie doth grant unto the said PETER HANSBROUGH his heirs & assigns forever a certain lott of Ground in the Town of Fredericksburg being part of a lot number Seventy eight as appears in the plott of the Town aforesaid and beginning seventy seven feet from the Corner of HAWKE & CAROLINE STREETs thence running along CAROLINE STREET fifty feet Southward, thence right angles one hundred and twenty feet Eastward back to an Alley laid off fifty feet wide, assigned by the said RICHARD KENNEY & leading into HAWKE STREET, thence along said Alley Sixty feet Northward & from thence in a straight line to the beginning; being at present occupied by JOHN ROBINSON and BENJAMIN HENDRICKS, under Leases which are to expire on the Fourteenth day of February in the year of our Lord one thousand seven hundred & Eighty seven & the said Tennants, that is to say, JOHN ROBINSON his heirs is to pay the yearly Rent of Nine pounds specie per anno: and BENJAMIN HENDRICKS his heirs and assigns is to pay the yearly rent of Seven pounds Ten shillings specie current money of Virginia per annum on the Fourteenth day of February in every year untill the expiration of their said Leases; agreeable to the tenor thereby unto the said PETER HANSBROUGH his heirs, together with all buildings and the benefits from the Alley aforesaid; In Witness whereof the said RICHARD KENNEY and MILLEY his Wife have hereunto set their hands and seals

Signed sealed and delivered in presence of
THOS: MILLER, WILLIAM SMITH, RD: KENNEY
JOS: CHRISTY, THOS: COCKRAN MILLEY KENNEY

The Common Wealth of Virginia to JAMES SOMERVILLE and BENJAMIN DAY Gent., Justices of the Corporation of Fredericksburg Greeting (the Commission for the privy Examination of MILLEY, the Wife of RICHARD KENNEY), Witness HENRY ARMISTEAD Clerk of our said Court this sixth day of March 1787 in the Eleventh year of the Common Wealth

HENRY ARMISTEAD, Clerk

Corporation of Fredericksburg to wit; Pursuant to this Commission (the return of the execution of the Commission for the privy Examination of MILLEY KENNEY); Certified under our hands and seals this second day of June one thousand seven hudnred and eighty seven

JAMES SOMERVILLE
BENJAMIN DAY

At a Hustings Court held for the Town and Corporation of Fredericksburg on Monday the Fifth day of March one thousand seven hundred and eighty seven
This Deed was acknowledged by the said KENNEY and ordered to be recorded
Test HENRY ARMISTEAD, Clerk

pp. 300-302 THIS INDENTURE made the Ninth day of January in the year of our Lord one thousand seven hundred and eighty seven Between JOHN WELCH of the County of BALTIMORE Gentn., & ELEANOR his Wife of the one part and EDWARD ROSS of the County of CAROLINE, Mariner, of the other part; Witnesseth that the said JOHN WELCH and ELEANOR his Wife for the sum of Three hundred & twenty five pounds doth grant unto the said EDWARD ROSS his heirs & assigns forever a lott of Ground in the Town of Fredericksburg and adjoined on the North side by JOHN BENSONs Ground and containing Thirty feet in front on CAROLINE STREET, and from the said Street extending with said breadth one hundred & thirty three feet Eastward where it is adjoining by WM. PULLIAMs Ground & numberd: as will appear by the plan of the said Town; together with all buildings gardens and trees with all the advantages to the said EDWARD ROSS his heirs and assigns forever; In Witness whereof the said JOHN WELCH & ELEANOR his Wife have set their hands and seals
Sealed and delivered in presence of
GEORGE FRENCH, DAVID HENDERSON, ALEXR: NAIRNE
JOHN WELCH
ELINOR WELCH

BALTIMORE County Sct. State of MARYLAND. To ABM: VNBIBBER and ISAAC VNBIBBER Justices of the County and State aforesaid Esqrs. Greeting; (the Commission for the privy Examination of ELENER, the Wife of JOHN WELCH); Witness the Seal of our County and in the year Seventeen hundred and eighty seven

BALTIMORE County Sct. We the Subscribers agreeable to the within Order of this County of BALTIMORE; (the return of the execution of the Commission for the Privy Examination of ELINOR WELCH); Given under our hands this (blank) day of (blank) 1787
ABM. VNBIBBER
ISAAC VNBIBBER

State of MARYLAND BALTIMORE County to wit; I hereby certify that ABRA: VN BIBBER & ISAAC VN BIBBER Gentlemen before whome the above acknowledgement was taken and who have thereto subscribed their names were at the day of the date thereof and still remain two of the Justices of the Peace for BALTIMORE County aforesaid and to all Certificates by them signed as such due faith and Credit is and ought to be given as well in Courts of Justice as thereout; In Testimony whereof I have hereunto set my hand & the Seal of Office this 29th day of January 1787
Seal WILLIAM GIBSON, Clerk, BALTO. COTY.

At a Hustings Court held for the Town and Corporation of Fredericksburg on Monday the fifth day of March one thousand seven hundred & eighty seven
This Deed and Commission returned was acknowledged by the said JOHN WELCH and ordered to be recorded Test HENRY ARMISTEAD, Clk.
Truly recorded Teste ARMISTEAD LONG D. Clk.

pp. 303-305 THIS INDENTURE made this first day of January one thousand seven hundred and eighty seven Between ROGER DIXON of the one part and DAVID COYL of the other part, both of the Town of Fredericksburg, witnesseth that the said ROGER DIXON for the Rents and Covenants herein after mentioned doth grant and to farm lett unto the said DAVID COYL and his heirs and assigns a parcel of Ground in the said Town of Fredericksburg on CAROLINE STREET being part of the lott No. (blank) and

now occupied by the said ROGER DIXON who keeps a Blacksmiths Shop on the lower Corner of the said lott; that is to say, twenty four feet front on said CAROLINE STREET beginning at the end of fifty feet on the said Street running from the lower corner of the said Lott where the said Blacksmiths Shop now stands and running thence the said twenty four feet up the said Street towards another Blacksmith Shop belonging to Mr. ELISHA DICKENSON, situate on the same side of the said CAROLINE STREET with the said parcel of ground, thence running at right angles with the said Street one hundred and fourteen feet, thence running paralleli with the first line twenty four feet and thence running parallel with the second line one hundred and fourteen feet to the beginning; To have and to hold the said parcel of ground unto the said DAVID COYL for and during the natrual life of the said DAVID COYL against the claim of the said ROGER DIXON his heirs, the said DAVID COYL paying unto the said ROGER DIXON annually and every year Eight pounds twelve shillings specie for the Rent of the said parcel of ground, the first payment commencing on the first day of January one thousand seven hundred & Eighty eight, the expiration of each and every year the like sum and should it happen that at any time the said DAVID COYL should leave unpaid or be in arrears for Six months one years Rent or not have compleated the covenants herein after mentioned, that then the said ROGER DIXON his heirs retake and occupy the said premisses the same as if this Indenture had never been made; And the said DAVID COYL doth agree for himself with the said ROGER DIXON that he will erect or cause to be erected a good framed House on the whole front hereby granted on CAROLINE STREET and running Eighteen feet back; with a good Stone Walled Cellar, the frame to be at least Eight feet and a half pitch from the under pining which shall be at least two feet high from the level of the Street to the said House to be covered with good feather edge Plank and lay press or Pine shingles all painted; to have two floors and two rooms on each floor lathed plastered and white washed except one room for a Shop to be layed with Plank, a good brick or Stone chimney, good plank floore the above covenants to be compleated by the first day of January one thousand seven hundred and Ninety and kept in good repair at the expiration of the said term herein mentioned under the penalty above mentioned of forfeiting this Lease; And the said DAVID COYL doth oblige his heirs and assigns to pay all damages arising from the nonperformacne of the abovementioned covenants; the said ROGER DIXON doth also agree that when the said DAVID COYL doth erect the House herein covenanted to be on the Street, that he will always allow him a passage of Four feet on one side or the other of the said House as far back as Twenty eight feet so that he doth not debarr himself of the passage to any part of his Lott adjoining; In Witness whereof the parties to these presents have set their hands and seals
Signed sealed and delivered in presence of

WM. PATTIE, ROGER DIXON
JAMES ABBETT DAVID COYL

At a Hustings Court held for the Town and Corporation of Fredericksburg on Monday the Second day of July one thousand seven hundred and Eighty seven
This Deed of Lease was acknowledged by the parties and ordered to be recorded
Deld. DAVID COYL Truly recorded Teste ARMISTEAD LONG, D. Clk.
Test HENRY ARMISTEAD, Clk.

pp. 304-305 KNOW ALL MEN by these presents that I EDWARD SIMPSON of the Corporation of Fredericksburg in Spotsylvania County have made DOCTOR CHARLES MORTIMER and Mr. SAMUEL ABBETT of the Corporation of Fredericksburg and County of Spotsylvania my true and lawfull Attorneys to ask and receive from all persons whom it doth concern all sums of money which are now belonging to me from any

persons whatsoever in any part of Virginia, And in default of payment, to take all lawful ways and means in my name for the recovery thereof; And to do all lawfull things concerning the premisses as fully as I myself could do if I were then personally present, hereby allowing all my said Attorneys shall in my name lawfully do; In Witness whereof I the said EDWARD SIMPSON have set my hand and seal the Eighth day of May in the year of our Lord one thousand seven hundred & eighty seven
Signed sealed & delvered in presence of
GEORGE McCUTCHAN, EDWARD SIMPSON
WILLIAM LOVELL

At a Hustings Court held for the Town and Corporation of Fredericksburg on Monday the second day of July one thousand seven hundred and eighty seven;
This Power of Attorney was proved by the oathes of WILLIAM LOVELL & GEORGE McCUTCHAN and ordered to be recorded Test HENRY ARMISTEAD, Clk.
Truley recorded Teste ARMISTEAD LONG, D. C.

pp. 305-306 THIS INDENTURE made this first day of January one thousand seven hundred and eighty six Between THOMAS POSEY of the County of Spotsylvania and MARY his Wife, Widow of the said late GEORGE THORNTON of the aforesaid County and Guardians to the Children of the aforesaid GEORGE, of one part and ROBERT BROOKE of the said County of Spotsylvania of the other part; Witnesseth that the said THOMAS and MARY his Wife for the Rents and Covenants herein after contained on the part of the said ROBERT have granted and to farm letten unto the said ROBERT all that parcel of Ground being in the Town of Fredericksburg between the lots of JOHN WELCH and THE MARKET HOUSE LOT, containing Fifty five feet front upon CAROLINE STREET & extending one hundred and thirty two feet back making an oblong of Fifty five feet by one hundred and thirty two feet, being the third of a lot formerly sold by the Trustees of St. Georges Parish, To have and to hold the said parcel of Ground and premisses unto the said ROBERT his Executors and assigns during and unto the full term of Thirteen years from thence next ensuing; paying therefore yearly unto the said THOMAS and MARY his Wife the yearly rent of Ten pounds Virginia currency, that is to say, Ten pounds to be paid on the first day of January one thousand seven hundred and Eighty eight and the said sum at the commencement of every succeeding year until the end of the term aforesaid; In Witness whereof the said parties have set their hands & seals
Teste JOHN T. BROOKE, THOMAS POSEY
WILLIAM JARVIS, LAURENCE BROOKE MARY POSEY
RT. BROOKE

At a Hustings Court held for the Town and Corporation of Fredericksburg on Monday the fifth day of March one thousand seven hundred and eighty seven
This Indenture of Lease was proved by two witnesses as to POSEY and acknowledged by the said BROOKE and ordered to be recorded
Truly recorded Test ARMISTEAD LONG, D. Clk.
Test HENRY ARMISTEAD Clerk

pp. 307-208 THIS INDENTURE made this first day of January one thousand seven hundred and eighty six Between ROBERT BROOKE of the Town of Fredericksburg and County of Spotsylvania of the one part and THOMAS POSEY of the said County of Spotsylvania of the other part; Witnesseth that the said ROBERT for the Rents and services herein contained which on the part of the said THOMAS are to be performed hath granted and to farm letten unto the said THOMAS his Executors & assigns all that parcel of Ground in the Town of Fredericksburg between the lots of JOHN

WELCH and the MARKET HOUSE LOT containing Fifty five feet front upon CAROLINE STREET and extending one hundred and thirty two feet back making an oblong of Fifty five feet by one hundred and thirty two feet being the third of a Lot formerly sold by the Trustees of St. Georges Parish; To have and to hold the said ground unto the said THOMAS during the term of Thirteen years from the next ensuing paying yearly unto the said ROBERT the yearly Rent of Ten punds Virginia currency upon the first day of January one thousand seven hundred and eighty eight and the said sum at the commencement of every succeeding year until the end of the Term;

Teste JOHN T. BROOKE, RT. BROOKE
LAURENCE BROOKE, WILLIAM LEWIS THOMAS POSEY

At a Hustings Court held for the Town and Corporation of Frederickburg on Monday the Fifth day of March one thousand seven hundred and eighty seven
This Lease indented was acknowledged by the said BROOKE and proved by two witnesses as to POSEY and ordered to be recorded Test HENRY ARMISTEAD, Clk.
Truly recorded Test ARMISTEAD LONG, D. Clk.

p. 308 THIS INDENTURE made and executed the Twenty third day of August in the year of our Lord One thousand seven hundred & eighty six by WILLIAM REID at present of the Town of Fredericksburg, Witnesseth that the said WILLIAM REID for the sum of Five shillings the receipt whereof he hereby acknowledgeth, but cheifly that he may benefit a certain SARAH REID, Daughter of NANCY ARTHERPE, formerly a resident of Fredericksburg, doth hereby give unto and for the sole use and behoof of the said SARAH REID her heirs and assigns a certain lot of half acre of Ground being in the Town of Fredericksburg situated on the back line of the Town which Lot was purchased by WILLIAM REID from WILLIAM WILLIAMS of COULPEPER as appeares by Indentures dated the seventeenth day of February in the year Seventeen hundred & twenty seven and recorded in the County Court books of Spotsylvania; To have and to hold the said lot or half acre of Ground with all its profits to the said SARAH REID her heirs or assigns; In Witness whereof the said WILLIAM REID hath hereunto set his hand and seal

Signed sealed & delivered in presence of
HENRY MITCHELL, GEORGE HUTCHESON, WILLIAM REID,
NEIL McCOULL, JACOB WHITLER
(no recording shown)

pp. 309-310 THIS INDENTURE made the Eighteenth day of November in the year of our Lord one thousand seven hundred and Eighty six Between JOHN WELCH and NELLY his Wife of the Town of Fredericksburg in County of Spotsylvania of the one part and BENJAMIN ROBINSON of the same County of the other part; Witnesseth that the said JOHN WELCH and NELLY his Wife for the sum of Thirty five pounds current money of Virginia hath granted unto the said BENJAMIN ROBINSON and his heirs and assigns all that parcel of ground in the said Town of Fredericksburg being and is part of the Lott back of Forty feet front and twenty feet back on CAROLINE STREET conveyed by Lease from JOHN DALTON to MICHAEL ROBINSON running with the same right angles to the back of the said lott and the line of ISABELLA MERCER, To have & to hold to the said BENJAMIN ROBINSON his heirs and assigns dureing the life or lives of the said JOHN DALTON and WALTER DALTON, his Son, against the Claim of the said JOHN WELCH and NELLY his Wife; In Witness whereof the said JOHN WELCH and NELLY his Wife have set their hands and seals

Signed acknowledged & delivered in the presence of
ARMISTEAD LONG, THOMAS GOODWIN, JOHN CRUTCHFIELD — JOHN WELCH, ELENER WELCH

At a Hustings Court held for the Town and Corporation of Fredericksburg on Monday the Fifth day of February one thousand seven hundred and eighty seven
This Deed of Lease was acknowledged by the said WELCH and ordered to be recorded
Test HENRY ARMISTEAD, Clk.
Truly recorded Test ARMISTEAD LONG, D. Clerk

pp. 310-311 THIS INDENTURE made sixteenth day of September in the year of our Lord one thousand seven hundred and eighty six Between SAMUEL RODDEY of Fredericksburg of the one part and JAMES SOMERVELLE of the same place, Merchant, of the other part; Witnesseth that the said SAMUEL RODDEY for the sum of Two hundred & sixty pounds Ten shillings and Eleven pence specie with Interest from date now due from the said SAMUEL RODDEY to the said JAMES SOMERVELLE hath granted and made over unto the said JAMES SOMERVELLE his heirs and assigns all judgments which the said SAMUEL RODDEY hath recovered against HAYMAN & MOFFATT and yet unsatisfied for Rents of certain Lotts and Houses in the Town of Fredericksburg known by the name of REIDS STORE, Also all Judgments yet unpaid which said SAMUEL RODDEY hath recovered against GARLAND THOMPSON or any one holding under him for Rents of part of the Lots & Houses aforesaid; And also all Rents issuing out of the said Lots and Houses whether now due or to become due hereafter; To have and to hold the said Judgments, Rents & Profits unto the said JAMES SOMERVELLE his heirs until he and they shall be paid the sum of Two hundred and Sixty pounds, Ten Shillings & Eleven pence with Interest from date hereof and the said SAMUEL RODDEY doth authorize the said JAMES SOMERVELLE either in his own name or in the same of the said SAMUEL RODDEY as may be thought best, to prosecute any action for the recovery of the same & when recovered to receive the Rents aforesaid until the said sum is paid, And whenever the said Debt shall be paid, that the said JAMES SOMERVILLE shall release all claim & title to the same & to the Rents issueing out of the said Lotts & that this Deed shall be void; In Witness whereof the said parties have set their hands & seals
Signed sealed and delivered in the presence of
HENRY MITCHELL, GEORGE HUTCHESON, JOHN HULL — SAMUEL RODDEY, JAMES SOMERVILLE

At a Hustings Court held for the Town and Corporation of Fredericksburg on Monday the first day of January one thousand seven hundred and eighty seven
This Deed of Assignment was proved by the oaths of GEORGE HUTCHESON & JOHN HULL and ordered to be recorded Test HENRY ARMISTEAD
Truly recorded Test ARMISTEAD LONG, D. Clk.
Deld. J. SOMERVILLE

pp. 312-313 KNOW ALL MEN by these presents that I SAMUEL RODDEY of Fredericksburg for the sum of Two hundred Sixty pounds Ten shillings and Eleven pence specie paid by JAMES SOMERVILLE of Fredericksburg, Merchant, have sold unto the said JAMES SOMERVILLE a Negro woman named Pegg, and a younger girl named Pegg the last purchased lately by the said SAMUEL RODDEY of Mr. JOHN DAWSON, To have and to hold all the said slaves Pegg & Pegg Younger unto the said JAMES SOMERVILLE his heirs; In Witness whereof the said SAMUEL RODDEY hath set his hand & affixed his seal this sixteenth day of September one thousand seven hundred and eighty six

Sealed and delivered in presence of
HENRY MITCHELL, GEORGE HUTCHESON, SAMUEL RODDEY

Memdn. The Consideration of this Bill of Sale is one and the same with the consideration of a Deed of Assignment of the Rents due & to become due from MESSRS. HAYMAN & MOFFATT and GARLAND THOMPSON for the Store and Houses on the Lotts known by the name of REIDS STORE the Property of Mr. SAMUEL RODDEY as a security for the payment of Two hundred and sixty pounds Ten shillings & Eleven pence specie which being fully satisfied in virtue of the one or the other, the last to stand void with either of them to be proved at the Election of the said JAMES SOMERVILLE, who is only accountable to the said SAMUEL RODDEY for so much as arises from the Sale of such slaves as they may sell by virtue of the within mentioned Bill of Sale
Test HENRY MITCHELL, SAMUEL RODDEY
GEORGE HUTCHESON

At a Hustings Court held for the Town and Corporation of Fredericksburg the first day of January one thousand seven hundred and eighty seven
This Bill of Sale was proved by the oath of GEORGE HUTCHINSON and ordered to be Certified Test HENRY ARMISTEAD, Clerk

pp. 313-314 TO ALL PEOPLE to whom these presents shall come, I MARY SULLIVAN of the Town of Fredericksburg and County of Spotsylvania send Greeting; Know ye that I the said MARY do for Five shillings grant unto MARY WALKER of the County of CULPEPER one Negroe girl named Jenny, To have and to hold unto the said MARY WALKER her heirs and assigns forever; And I the said MARY the said Negroe girl do warrant and forever defend by the presents and further I the said MARY have put the said MARY WALKER in possession of the said Negroe by the delivery unto her at the sealing hereof; In Witness whereof I have affixed my hand and seal this second day of July one thousand seven hundred and eighty seven
Sealed and delivered in presence of
JOHN T. BROOKE, MARY SULLIVAN her × mark
ROGER DIXON, JOHN DIXON

At a Hustings Court held for the Town and Corporation of Fredericksburg on Monday the second day of July 1787
This Deed of Gift was proved by the oathes of the Witnesses and ordered to be recorded
Test HENRY ARMISTEAD, Clerk

p. 314 KNOW ALL MEN by these presents taht I JOHN McFARLAND of the County of Spotsylvania am about to marry MARGARET SWINNY of the County aforesaid do relinquish any or all claims now or hereafter to all the property of the said MARGARET SWINEY is now possessed of & she is hereby impowered to dispose of the same at all times & in what manner she may think proper; Given under my hand and seal this Fifth day of May 1786
Acknowledged in presence of
HENRY ARMISTEAD, JOHN McFARLAND
ELIZER CALLENDER

A Schedule of the within articles intended to be conveyed.
A Bay Mare and two Colts, a Bed & furniture, two Cows and two Calves
Witness HENRY ARMISTEAD, JOHN McFARLAN
ELEIZER CALLENDER

At a Hustings Court held for the Town and Corporation of Fredericksburg on Monday the fifth day of February one thousand seven hundred and eighty seven
This Bill of Sale was proved by the witnesses and ordered to be recorded
Test HENRY ARMISTEAD, Clk.

pp. (On margin: Delivered this Deed 1st November 1787 to B. BALL)
315- THIS INDENTURE made the sixth day of October one thousand seven hundred
316 and Eighty six Between CHARLES WASHINGTON and MILDRED his Wife of the County of BERKLEY of the one part and GEORGE AUGUSTINE WASHINGTON of the County of FAIRFAX of the other part; Witnesseth that the said CHARLES WASHINGTON and MILDRED his Wife for the natural love and affection which they bear unto their Son, the said GEORGE AUGUSTINE WASHINGTON, as also for the sum of Five shillings, by these presents do sell unto the said GEORGE AUGUSTINE WASHINGTON his heirs and assigns two lotts of ground in the Town of Fredericksburg and by plann of said Town numbered Eighty seven and Eighty eight as by Deed from WARNER LEWIS to the said CHARLES WASHINGTON recorded in the County Court of Spotsylvania may more fully appear; To have and to hold the said lotts number 87 and 88 with all their premisses unto GEORGE AUGUSTINE WASHINGTON his heirs against the claim of him the said CHARLES WASHINGTON and MILDRED his Wife; In Witness whereof the said CHARLES WASHINGTON and MILDRED his Wife have set their hands and affixed their seals
Signed sealed and acknowledged in presence of

R. B. CHEW, ZACHARIAH LUCAS, GEORGE FRENCH, CHARLES MORTIMER, FRANCIS THORNTON

CHARLES WASHINGTON
MILDRED WASHINGTON

The Commonwealth of Virginia to CHARLES MORTIMER and GEORGE FRENCH Gent., Justices of the Corporation of Fredericksburg Greeting; (The Commission for the privy Examination of MILDRED, the Wife of CHARLES WASHINGTON); Witness HENRY ARMISTEAD Clerk of our said Court of Hustings this Sixth October one thousand seven hundred and eighty six and in the Eleventh year of the Commonwealth
HENRY ARMISTEAD, Clerk

Corporation of Fredericksburg to wit: Pursuant to the above Commission (the return of the execution of the Commission for the privy Examination of MILDRED WASHINGTON); Certified under our hands this sixth day of October one thousand seven hundred and eighty six
CHARLES MORTIMER
GEORGE FRENCH

At a Hustings Court held for the Corporation of Fredericksburg on Monday 5th day of February 1787
This Deed was proved by CHARLES MORTIMER, GEORGE FRENCH & ROBERT B. CHEW and a Commission of her examination returned and ordered to be recorded
Test HENRY ARMISTEAD, Clerk
Truly recorded Test ARMISTEAD LONG, D. Clk.

pp. THIS INDENTURE made the Twenty fourth day of May one thousand seven hun-
317- dred and eighty seven Between JAMES HUNTER of the Town of PORTSMOUTH of
318 the one part and JOSEPH JONES of the County of KING GEORGE of the other part; Whereas in or about the month of November in the year one thousand seven hundred and seventy nine the said JAMES HUNTER agreed to purchase of the said JOSEPH JONES his moiety of the BREW HOUSE LOTTS and the Implements of the Trade considered as Specie Value one thousand pounds; but which the said JOSEPH JONES agreed should be then discharged by the payment of Four thousand pounds paper

money and four thousand pounds of Loan Office Certificates of dates prior to the first day of September one thousand seven hundred and seventy eight; And Whereas the said JAMES HUNTER went into possession of the property and continued possessed thereof until the first day of July one thousand seven hundred and Eighty five without having paid for the same agreeable to Contract, other than the Four thousand pounds paper currency, and sundry Certificates tendered to the said JOSEPH JONES but refused as not being agreeable to Contract; And Whereas the said JOSEPH JONES having reserved the legal Title to the BREW HOUSE LOTTS and Implements with the consent of the said JAMES HUNTER as a security for the said JAMES HUNTERs compliance with the Contract and the said JAMES HUNTER having failed to do so, and thinking it out of his power to comply, the said JOSEPH JONES with the privily and consent of the said JAMES HUNTER repossessed himself of the said property and is now possessed thereof and proceeded to sell the same at Public Auction in the Town of Fredericksburg on the Twenty sixth day of December one thousand seven hundred & eighty five after notice thereof repeatedly published in the *VIRGINIA GAZETTE* which when the said JOSEPH JONES purchased the said property as the highest bidder at the price of Eight hundred and seventy five pounds, And Whereas the said JOSEPH JONES & JAMES HUNTER this day settled an account between them respecting the said property whereby it appeares there is a ballance due the said JOSEPH JONES of One hundred and forty eight pounds six shillings & eight pence, This Indenture witnesseth that the said JAMES HUNTER in consideration of the premisses doth discharge the said JOSEPH JONES from all claim and demand respecting the Contract aforesaid and doth relinquish all his calim to the property aforesaid; In Witness whereof the said JAMES HUNTER and JOSEPH JONES have sett their hands and seals

Sealed and delivered in the presence of
JAMES MONROE, ELIZA: MONROE — JAMES HUNTER
JOS: JONES

At a Hustings Court held for the Town and Corporation of Fredericksburg on Monday the second day of July one thousand seven hundred and eighty seven
This Indenture of Release was proved by the oath of JAMES MONROE Gent. and ordered to be Certified Test HENRY ARMISTEAD, Clerk
Deld. Mr. JOS: JONES

pp. 318-319 THIS INDENTURE made the fifth day of October one thousand seven hundred and eighty six Between JOHN WELCH & ELEANOR his Wife of the Town of Fredericksburg in Spotsylvania County of the one part and DAVID SIMONS of the aforesaid Town & County of the other part; Witnesseth that the said JOHN WELCH for the sum of Six hundred pounds lawful money hath granted unto the said DAVID SIMONS his heirs & assigns a certain part of a Lot of Ground in the Town of Fredericksburg containing in front Eighteen feet or rather more thence the same width forty five feet from then twenty feet wide to the extent of the Lott 133 feet or 150 feet being the corner lot on GEORGE STREET up CAROLINE STREET together with the houses kitchen stables and all other improvements and all the profits and advantages; To have and to hold unto the said DAVID SIMONS his heirs and assigns forever; In Witness whereof the said JOHN WELCH and ELEANOR his Wife have hereunto set their hands and seals
JOHN WELCH
ELEANOR WELCH

Received of DAVID SIMONS the sum of Six hundred pounds being the consideration money for the above mentioned lot the date above mentioned
(no witnesses to Deed or Receipt) (No signatures for Receipt)

pp. 320-321 THIS INDENTURE made the fifth day of October one thousand seven hundred and eighty six between DAVID SIMONS of the Town of Fredericksburg in Spotsylvania County in Virginia of the one part & JOHN WELCH of the same place of the other part; Whereas the said DAVID SIMONS by his certain obligation under his hand and seal bearing date the 5th of October aforesaid standeth bound unto the said JOHN WELCH in the sum of Twelve hundred pounds current money of Virginia conditional for the payment of Six hundred pounds like money at or upon the fifth day of October one thousand seven hundred and ninety, Together with lawful Interest for the same as by the said obligation thereof; Now this Indenture witnesseth that the said DAVID SIMONS for the sum of Six hundred pounds & for the better securing the payment unto the said JOHN WELCH and by the further sum of Five shillings hath sold unto the said JOHN WELCH & to his heirs a certain part of a Lot situated in the Town of Fredericksburg containing in front Eighteen feet or rather more thence forty five feet from thence twenty feet wide to the extent of the Lott 133 or 150 feet being the corner of GEORGE STREET up CAROLINE STREET together with all the houses barns stables and all improvements on the said part of a lot; To have and to hold the said part of a Lot hereby granted unto the said JOHN WELCH his heirs and assigns, Provided always nevertheless that if the said DAVID SIMONS his heirs do truly pay unto the said JOHN WELCH the aforesaid Debt on the day and at the time herein before mentioned with lawfull Interest without any further delay then and from thence fourth the said recited obligation shall become absolutely null & void; In Witness whereof the said parties have set their hands and seals DAVID SIMONS
KEATEY SIMONS

At a Court held for the Town and Corporation of Fredericksburg November the 6th 1786 This Indenture was acknowledged by the sd. DAVID SIMONS and Wife, she being first privately examined as the Law directs & ordered to be recorded
Test HENRY ARMISTEAD, Clerk

Deld. Mr. COLSON

pp. 322-323 THIS INDENTURE made this Seventeenth day of November in the year of our Lord one thousand seven hundred and Eighty six Between JOHN SHELBY JUNR. of SULLIVAN County and State of NORTH CAROLINA of the one part and JOHN LEWIS of the County of Spotsylvania & State of Virginia of the other part; Witnesseth that the said JOHN SHELBY for the sum of Four hundred pounds current money of Virginia hath sold a certain parcel of Land containing One thousand acres surveyed the Seventeenth day of July 1774 and Patented the second day of June 1780 in the County of FAYETTE, it being a parcel of land purchased by the said SHELBY of Colo. WILLIAM CRISTIAN deced., as appears by a certain Deed from the said WILLIAM CRISTIAN to the said JOHN SHELBY bearing date the (blank) now recorded in the General Court relation being thereunto had; Beginning at two large Locusts about the middle of THOMAS BARNESes line and running thence South West crossing two branches to a Hickory and Sugar tree; thence North West crossing a branch & small Creek to a Walnut, Locust & Elm, thence North East to an Elm and two Ash trees by a draught, corner to BARNES and with his line thereof South East to the beginning; To have and to hold the said parcel of land unto the said JOHN LEWIS his heirs and assigns; And the said JOHN SHELBY JUNR. will warrant and forever defend the said by these presents In Witness whereof the said JOHN SHELBY JUNIOR hath hereunto set his hand and seal

Sealed & delivered in presence of
RICHARD DIXON, THOMAS BROWN, JOHN SHELBY JR.
FIELDG. LUCAS, JOHN BROWN

At a Hustings Court held for the Town and Corporation of Fredericksburg on Monday the Fourth day of June one thousand seven hundred and eighty seven
This Indenture for Land was proved by three witnesses and ordered to be recorded
Test HENRY ARMISTEAD, Clerk
Truly recorded ARMISTEAD LONG, D. Clerk

pp. 323-327 THIS INDENTURE made the twentieth day of March in the year of our Lord one thousand seven hundred and Eighty seven Between JOHN LEWIS and MARY his Wife of the County of Spotsylvania and State of Virginia of one part and HENRY FITZHUGH of the County of STAFFORD and State aforesaid of the other part; Witnesseth that the said JOHN LEWIS for the sum of Two hundred pounds current money of Virginia have granted unto the said HENRY FITZHUGH and his heirs all that square of two acres of land containing Four half acre lotts of Ground being in the Town and Corporation of Fredericksburg and numbered in the plan of the Town and Corporation 173, 174, 175, 176 described and bounded; Beginning to the West by PRINCESS ANN-STREET three hundred and thirty feet, to the North by FITZHUGH STREET Two hundred and thirty feet; to the East by CAROLINE STREET three hundred and thirty feet; and to the South by PITT STREET Two hundred and sixty four feet to the beginning; And all houses buildings waters profits belonging; To have and to hold the said lands unto the said HENRY FITZHUGH his heirs & assigns forever; In Witness whereof the said JOHN LEWIS & MARY his Wife have set their hands and affixed their seals
Sealed and delivered in the presenceof
WILLIAM WIATT, HUGH BOGGS, JOHN LEWIS
FIELDING LUCAS MARY ANNE LEWIS

The Commonwealth of Virginia to WILLIAM HARVEY and BENJAMIN DAY, Gent., Justices of the Town and Corporation of Fredericksburg Greeting; (The Commission for the privy Examination of MARY ANNE, the Wife of JOHN LEWIS); Witness HENRY ARMISTEAD Clerk of our said court of Hustings this 27th day of March 1787; and in the Eleventh year of the Common Wealth HENRY ARMISTEAD, Clerk

Fredericksburg Corporation Sc. Pursuant to the above Commission (the return of the Execution of the Commission for the privy Examination of MARY ANNE LEWIS); Certified under our hands & seals this twenty seventh day of March in the year of our Lord 1787
WILLIAM HARVEY
BENJAMIN DAY

At the Hustings Court held for the Town and Corporation of Fredericksburg on Monday the second day of April One thousand seven hundred and eighty seven
This Deed together with the Commission annexed and Certificate of the Examination hereof indorsed are ordered to be recorded Test HENRY ARMISTEAD, Clk.
Truly recorded Test ARMISTEAD LONG, D. Clerk

pp. 327-329 THIS INDENTURE made the Seventeenth day of April in the year of our Lord one thousand seven hundred and Eighty seven between HENRY FITZHUGH of the County of STAFFORD and State of Virginia of the one part and JOHN DE BAPTEST of the other part; Witnesseth that the said HENRY FITZHUGH for the Rents and Agreements on the part of the said JOHN DE BAPTIST to be done hath granted unto the said JOHN DE BAPTIST his heirs forever a certain parcel of land in the Town and Corporation of Fredericksburg on FITZHUGH STREET and being part of Lott number One hundred and Eighty in the plan of the said Town bounded; Beginning at Lott one hundred and eighty on a new Street called FITZHUGH STREET and on the upper side of the said Lott, and extending thence down the said Street and parallell to PITT STREET twenty feet, thence parallel to CAROLINE STREET downwards Eighty two and half feet, thence towards the River parallel to PITT STREET forty six feet; then downwards eighty two and an half feet to the line of Lott numbered one hundred and seventy nine, and with the said line towards CAROLINE STREET sixty six feet; thence parallel with CAROLINE STREET to the beginning one hundred and eighty five feet; To have and to hold the said parcel of land to him the said JOHN DE BAPTIST paying for the same on the first day of January next ensuing and on the first day of January yearly and every year forever hereafter unto the said HENRY FITZHUGH his heirs and assigns, the sum of Twenty pounds Ten shillings issuing out of the said premisses and the said JOHN DE BAPTIST doth hereby promise that he every year forevery truly pay the aforesaid sum to be discharged in Gold at the rate of Five shillings and four pence the penny weight or Silver at Six shillings & eight pence the Ounce; unto the said HENRY FITZHUGH on the days appointed for payment thereof and that it shall be lawful for said HENRY FITZHUGH at all times after the said Rent shall come due and the same not paid when demanded to enter upon the said Land and distress and sale make of the goods and chattels which may be thereupon found to pay such rent or part of a Rent as may remain due and if unpaid by the space of thirty days next after the same become due and sufficient goods shall not be found upon the said premisses to satisfy the same, that it may be lawfull for the said HENRY FITZHUGH in and upon the said land to reenter; And the said JOHN DE BAPTIST shall not remove any houses buildings work or improvements that may be built thereon under the penalty of being answerable to the said HENRY FITZHUGH in damages to the full value of such; In Witness whereof the said parties have set their hands and seals

Signed sealed and delivered in the presence of

ZACHARIAS THOMPSON, HENRY FITZHUGH
CHARLES TRAVISS, JOHN BINGY JOHN DE BAPTIST

At a Hustings Court held for the Town and Corporation of Fredericksburg on Monday the seventh day of May one thousand seven hundred and eighty seven
This Deed of Lease was acknowledged by the said FITZHUGH and proved by three witnesses as to DE BAPTIST and ordered to be recorded

Test HENRY ARMISTEAD, Clk.

pp. 330-331 THIS INDENTURE made the fourth day of May in the year of our Lord one thousand seven hundred and Eighty seven Between HENRY FITZHUGH of the County of STAFFORD and State of Virginia of the one part and JOHN NORWOOD of the other part; Witnesseth that the said HENRY FITZHUGH for the Rents and Agreements in this Indenture contained on the part of the said JOHN NORWOOD to be paid, have granted unto the said JOHN NORWOOD his heirs and assigns forever a certain peice of land in the Town and Corporation of Fredericksburg on CAROLINE STREET and being part of Lott number one hundred and seventy five in the plan of the said Town bounded Beginning at twenty seven and an half feet from the lower corner of the said Lott, thence twenty seven and half feet up CAROLINE STREET, thence back one hundred and twenty two feet to KENNEY ALLEY, thence down KENNEY ALLEY twenty seven and half feet, thence one hundred and twenty two feet to the beginning, having an Alley of three & half feet wide on CAROLINE STREET and Forty feet back on the upper corner of the said Lott; To have and to hold the said parcel of Land to the said JOHN NORWOOD his heirs and assigns forever paying for the same the first day of January and on the first day of January yearly and every year forever hereafter unto the said HENRY FITZHUGH his heirs and assigns the annual Rent of Eight pounds good and lawful money of Virginia issuing out of the said hereby demised premisses; And in case any part remain unpaid and no sufficient distress to be found on the premisses that then it may be lawful for the said HENRY FITZHUGH to set up the said land and premisses to the highest bidder and Rent them out till such arrears as may be then due shall be fully satisfied after which the said Land and premisses shall again revert to the said JOHN NORWOOD and if the said Lott of land should lay unimporoved by the space of one year after the first Rent it shall then be lawful for the said HENRY FITZHUGH to reenter and again repossess, he the said JOHN NORWOOD shall at all times hereafter discharge all manner of Taxes and charges imposed upon the said Land and save harmless the said HENRY FITZHUGH from the same; In Witness whereof the parties concerned have set their hands and seals

Signed sealed and delivered in presence of

JOSEPH NORWOOD, GEORGE NORWOOD, HENRY FITZHUGH
(?) DESHMORE, JOHN X SMITH

At a Hustings Court held for the Town and Corporation of Fredericksburg on Monday the seventh day of May one thousand seven hundred and Eighty seven
This Deed of Lease was acknowledged by the said FITZHUGH and proved by three witnesses as to the said NORWOOD and ordered to be recorded

Test HENRY ARMISTEAD, Clerk
Truly recorded ARMISTEAD LONG, D. Clk.

pp. 332-334 THIS INDENTURE made the twenty sixth day of March one thousand seven hundred and eighty seven Between HENRY FITZHUGH of the County of STAFFORD and State of Virginia of the one part and RICHARD KENNEY of the other part;

Witnesseth that the said HENRY FITZHUGH for the Rents and Agreements contained hath granted unto the said RICHARD KENNEY his heirs and assigns forever a certain parcel of Land in the Town and Corporation of Fredericksburg on CAROLINE STREET and being part of Lott number 176, in the plan of the said Town bounded; Beginning twenty seven and a half feet from the upper corner of Lott No. 176 on CAROLINE STREET, running down said Street twenty seven and a half feet, thence one hundred & twenty two feet back to KENNEY ALLEY, thence up KENNEY ALLEY 271 feet, thence one hundred and twenty two feet to the beginning; and the said RICHARD KENNEY is to leave an Alley of Three and a half feet wide on CAROLINE STREET andrunning forty back which is to be the lower corner of the said premisses on CAROLINE STREET, And the said HENRY FITZHUGH doth agree that a Lne or Alley of Twenty feet wide shall extend from PITT STREET to FITZHUGH STREET on the back of the said premisses parallell to CAROLINE STREET which shall forever be open for the advantages of the premisses aforesaid and other; And shall be named KENNY ALLEY, To have and to hold the said Land to RICHARD KENNEY his heirs paying on the first day of January yearly hereafter the sum of Eight pounds to be discharged in Gold at the rate of Five shillings and four pence the penny weight or Silver at Six shillings and eight pence the Ounce; unto the said HENRY FITZHUGH on the days appointed and it may be lawful for the said HENRY FITZHUGH at any time after the said Rent be not paid to enter upon the Land and distress and sale make of the goods and chattels which may be found to pay such Rents as may remain due; In Witness whereof the said parties have set their hands and seals

Signed sealed and delivered in the presence of

WILLIAM WIATT, HENRY FITZHUGH
W. WELLS, EDWD. WELLS RICHARD KENNEY

At a Hustings Court held for the Town and Corporation of Fredericksburg on Monday the seventh day of May one thousand seven hundred and eighty seven
This Deed of Lease was acknowledged by the parties and ordered to be recorded
Test HENRY ARMISTEAD, Clerk
Truly recorded ARMISTEAD LONG, D. Clerk

pp. 334-336 THIS INDENTURE made the first day of May in the year of our Lord one thousand seven hundred and Eighty seven Between HENRY FITZHUGH of the County of STAFFORD and State of Virginia on the one part and SEBASTON LOCK of the other part; Witnesseth that the said HENRY FITZHUGH for the Rents and Agreements in this Indenture contained doth grant unto the said SEBASTON LOCK his heirs and assigns forever a parcel of land in the Town and Corporation of Fredericksburg on CAROLINE STREET and being part of Lott number one hundred and seventy eight in the plan of the said Town bounded beginning at twenty seven and half feet from the lower corner of lott number one hundred and seventy eight and extending on CAROLINE STREET fifty five feet thence back parallel to FITZHUGH and PITT STREETs one hundred and thirty two feet, then parallel with CAROLINE STREET fifty five feet, then parallel to FITZHUGH and PITT STREETs one hundred and thirty two feet to the beginning, the Alley of seven feet wide on CAROLINE STREET and Forty feet back to the middle of the said Lott; To have and to hold the said parcel of land to said SEBASTON LOCK his heirs and assigns forever paying for the same on the first day of January next ensuing and on the first day of January yearly unto the aforesaid HENRY FITZHUGH his heirs and assigns, And if the Rent remain unpaid by space of one month and hath been legally demanded and no sufficient distress to be found on the premisses then it may be lawful for said HENRY FITZHUGH to set up the said Land and premisses to the highest bidder and Rent them out till such arrears be satisfied, he the said SEBASTIAN LOCK shall at all times hereafter pay and discharge all kind and manner of Taxes and Charges imposed upon the said Land

Signed sealed and delivered in the presence of
JOHN NEWTON, HENRY FITZHUGH
ENEAS MURRAY, ANDREW SPECHT

At a Hustings Court held for the Town and Corporation of Fredericksburg on Monday the seventh day of May one thousand seven hundred and Eighty seven
This Deed of Lease was acknowledged by the parties and ordered to be recorded
Test HENRY ARMISTEAD, Clk.
Truly recorded ARMISTEAD LONG, D. Clerk

pp. 336-337 THIS INDENTURE made the fourth day of May in the year of our Lord one thousand seven hundred and eighty seven Between HENRY FITZHUGH of STAFFORD County and State of Virginia on the one part and ANDREW SPECHT of the other part; Witnesseth that the said HENRY FITZHUGH in consideration of the Rentsand Agreements in this Indenture contained hath granted unto the said ANDREW SPECHT his heirs and assigns a parcel of land in the Town and Corporation of Fredericksburg on CAROLINE STREET and being part of lott number one hundred and seventy eight in the plan of the said Town bounded, Beginning at Twenty seven and an half feet from the upper corner of the said lott and extending thence fifty five feet down CAROLINE STREET, thence one hundred and thirty two feet parallel to FITZHUGH and PITT STREETs, thence parallel to CAROLINE STREET fifty five feet, thence one hundred and thirty two feet parallel to FITZHUGH and PITT STREETS to the beginning; leaving an Alley seven feet wide on CAROLINE STREET and forty feet back in the middle of the said lott; To have and to hold the said land unto the said ANDREW SPECHT his heirs and assigns forever; paying on the first day of January next ensuing and on the first day of January every year hereafter unto the aforesaid HENRY FITZHUGH the annual rent of Fifteen pounds Eleven shillings good and lawful money of Virginia, And in case the Rent remain unpaid by one month after the same ought to have been paid, then it shall be lawful for the said HENRY FITZHUGH to set up the said land and premisses to the highest bidder and Rent them out till such arrears shall be paid; In Witness whereof the parties concerned have set their hands and seals

Signed sealed and delivered in the presence of

WILLIAM LOTSPEICK, HENRY FITZHUGH
ENEAS MURRAY, JOSEPH ORMOND ANDREW SPECHT

pp. 338-339 THIS INDENTURE made the twentyeth day of April in the year of our Lord one thousand seven hundred and Eighty seven between HENRY FITZHUGH of STAFFORD County and State of Virginia of one part and GEORGE STRINGFELLOW of the other part; Witnesseth that the said HENRY FITZHUGH for the Rents and Agreements in this Indenture contained doth grant unto the said GEORGE STRINGFELLOW his heirs and assigns a certain parcel of land in the Town and Corporation of Fredericksburg on CAROLINE STREET and being part of Lott number one hundred and seventy six in the plan of the said Town bounded; Beginning at eighty two and half feet from the upper corner of Lot number one hundred and seventy six on CAROLINE STREET, running down the said Street fifty five feet, thence one hundred and twenty two feet back to KENNEY ALLEY, thence up KENNEY ALLEY fifty five feet, thence one hundred and twenty two feet to the beginning, And the said GEORGE STRINGFELLOW is to leave an Alley seven feet wide on CAROLINE STREET and running forty feet back which is in the middle of the said premisses on CAROLINE STREET; And the said FITZHUGH doth agree with the said GEORGE STRINGFELLOW that a Lane or Alley of Twenty feet wide shall extend from PITT STREET to FITZHUGH STREET on the back of the said premisses parallel to CAROLINE STREET, which shall forever be kept open for the advantage of the premisses aforesaid and others and shall be named KENNEY ALLEY; To have and to hold the said Land unto the said GEORGE STRINGFELLOW his heirs and assigns forever paying for the same on the first day of January and on the first day of January yearly forever hereafter unto the aforesaid HENRY FITZHUGH his heirs and assigns the sum of Sixteen pounds good and lawful money of Virginia issuing out of the sd. premisses, And in case the Rent remain unpaid one month and no distress to be found whereby the same might be levied, HENRY FITZHUGH to set up the said land and premisses to the highest bidder and rent them out till such arrears shall be paid; In Witness whereof the parties have set their hands and seals

Signed sealed and delivered in presence of

WILLIAM WIATT, HENRY FITZHUGH
JOHN ANDERSON, JOHN STAMPER GEORGE X STRINGFELLOW

At a Hustings Court held for the Town and Corporation of Fredericksburg on Monday the Seventh day of May one thousand seven hundred and eighty seven
This Deed of Lease was acknowledged by the parties and ordered to be recorded

Test HENRY ARMISTEAD, Clerk

Truly recorded ARMISTEAD LONG, D. Clk.

pp. 340-341 THIS INDENTURE made the first day of May in the year of our Lord one thousand seven hundred and eighty seven Between HENRY FITZHUGH of the County of STAFFORD on the one part and LAZARUS MADDUX of the other part; Witnesseth that the said HENRY FITZHUGH for the Rents and Agreements in this In-

denture contained hath granted unto the said LAZARUS MADDUX his heirs and assigns forever a certain parcel of land in the Town and Corporation of Fredericksburg on CAROLINE STREET and being part of lott number One hundred 76 in the plan of the said Town and bounded, beginning fifty five feet from the upper corner of the said Lott, thence down CAROLINE STREET 272 feet, thence 122 feet back to KENNEY ALLEY, thence up KENNEY ALLEY 277 feet, thence 122 feet to the beginning; leaving an Alley on CAROLINE STREET 3 1/2 feet wide and 40 feet deep on the upper corner of said lott; To have and to hold the said parcel of land to him the said LAZARUS MADDUX his heirs and assigns paying for the same on the first day of January next ensuing and on the first day of January yearly unto the aforesaid HENRY FITZHUGH his heirs and assigns the sum of Eight pounds for the said premisses only to be discharged in Gold at Five shillings and four pence the penny weight or Silver at Six shillings and eight pence the Ounce; In Witness whereof the said parties have set their hands and seals
Signed sealed and delivered in presence of

WILLIAM BALL,	HENRY FITZHUGH
BENJAMIN PETTIT, ZACHARIAH THOMPSON	LAZARUS MADDUX

At a Hustings Court held for the Town and Corporation of Fredericksburg on Monday the 7th day of May 1787
This Deed of Lease was acknowleged by the parties and ordered to be recorded
Test HENRY ARMISTEAD, Clerk

pp. 342-344 THIS INDENTURE made this Fourth day of June in the year of our Lord one thousand seven hundred and eighty seven Between JOHN LEWIS of the Town of Fredericksburg and County of Spotsylvania Gent., and MARY ANN LEWIS his Wife of one part and ELIEZER CALLENDER and DAVID HENDERSON of the Town and County aforesaid of the other part; Witnesseth that the said JOHN LEWIS and MARY ANN his Wife for Three hundred and six pounds hath sold unto the said ELIEZER CALLENDER and DAVID HENDERSON their heirs and assigns forever a parcel of land containing seven acres and twenty six square poles, being in the County of Spotsylvania and is bounded, Beginning at a Stake on Mr. FRANCIS THORNTONs line near a Spring by the side of the FERRY ROAD, thence South West to a Stake on the Main Road to Fredericksburg, thence with the said Road East to the end of a Ditch, thence with the Ditch North East to a Stake by the side of the FERRY ROAD, thence with the FERRY ROAD to the beginning; Together with all buildings gardens & trees; To have and to hold unto the said ELIEZER CALLENDER and DAVID HENDERSON their heirs and assigns forever and the said JOHN LEWIS his heirs will warrant and forever defend the said land against the claims of all persons whatsoever; In Witness whereof the said JOHN LEWIS and MARY ANN his Wife have set their hands and seals
Sealed and delivered in the presence of

ZACHARIAH LUCAS,	JOHN LEWIS
JOHN BROWN, JOHN ROBINSON	MARY ANN LEWIS

The Commonwealth of Virginia to JAMES SOMERVILLE, GEORGE WEEDON, GEORGE FRENCH Esqr. & BENJAMIN DAY Gent., Justices of the Town and Corporation of Fredericksburg (the Commission for the privy Examination of MARY ANN, the Wife of JOHN LEWIS); Witness JOHN CHEW JR. Clerk of our said Court this (blank) day of (blank) one thousand seven hundred and eighty seven and in the Twelvth year of the Commonwealth

Corporation of Fredericksburg to wit: Pursuant to the within Commission (the return of the execution of the privy Examination of MARY ANN LEWIS); Certified under our hands and seals this (blank) day of (blank) one thousand seven hundred and eighty seven

( ) Seal
( ) Seal

(no recording shown)

pp. 344-346 THIS INDENTURE made the Twelfth day of February in the year of our Lord one thousand seven hundred and Eighty seven Between RICHARD KENNEY and MILDRED his Wife of the Town of Fredericksburg and County of Spotsylvania of the one part and WILLIAM LOVELL of the Town & County aforesaid of the other part; Witnesseth that the said RICHARD KENNEY and MILDRED his Wife for the sum of One hundred and Thirty three pounds Six shillings and Eight pence specie have sold unto the said WILLIAM LOVELL his heirs and assigns forever part of a Lott of Ground in the Town of Fredericksburg which is number or marked in the plott of the said Town 77; running from the Corner of HAWK and SOPHIA STREETs down SOPHIA STREET fifty feet till it joins the part of the lott we sold to Mr. JOSIAH WATSON of ALEXANDRIA, from thence in a straight line the full depth of a half acre lott to the Alley, which is to be left open and is between our Lotts and Lott No. 77; thence up the said Alley to HAWK STREET thence down HAWK STREET to the Corner of HAWK and SOPHIA STREETs, it being the Lott where Mr. JOHN FERNEYHOUGH now resides; which I purchased of Mr. JAMES SOMERVELLE, Together with all houses stables gardens waters belonging; To have and to hold unto the said WILLIAM LOVELL his heirs and assigns forever and they will warrant and forever defend the land against the claims of all persons whatsoever claiming under them; In Witness whereof the said RICHARD KENNEY and MILDRED his Wife have set their hands and seals

Signed sealed and delivered in presence of

JAMES JULIAN, WILLIAM SMITH, RD. KENNEY
JOSEPH CHRISTY, THOMAS COCKRAN MILLEY KENNEY

The Commonwealth of Virginia to JAMES SOMERVILLE, BENJAMIN DAY & GEORGE FRENCH Gent., Justices of the Town and Corporation of Fredericksburg Greeting; (the Commission for the privy Examination of MILLEY, the Wife of RICHARD KENNEY); Witness HENRY ARMISTEAD Clerk of our said Court this fifth day of March one thouand seven hundred and eighty seven and in the Eleventh year of the Commonwealth

HENRY ARMISTEAD, Clerk

The Corporation of Fredericksburg, to wit: Pursuant to the within Commission (the return of the execution of the privy Examination of MILLEY KENNEY); Certified under our hands and seals this second of June one thousand seven hundred and eighty seven

JAMES SOMERVILLE
BENJA: DAY

At a Hustings Court held for the Town and Corporation of Fredericksburg on Monday the fifth day of March one thousand seven hundred and eighty seven
This Indenture was proved by three witnesses and ordered to be recorded

Test HENRY ARMISTEAD, Clerk

Truly recorded Test ARMISTEAD LONG, D. Clerk

p. 347 Corporation of Fredericksburg, Hustings Court
Messrs. RODDY & TAYLOR against JOHN WELCH & PHILL: LIPSCOMB December 1784. On a Replevy Bond

Judgment for 50120 lbs. of Tobacco of the Inspection of Fredericksburg or FALMOUTH and L 4..2.. current money & costs; to be discharged by the payment of Twenty seven thousand and sixty pounds of tobo: of Fredericksburg or FALMOUTH Inspections and Two pounds two shillings current money with legal Interest from the 22nd day of May 1784 on the tobacco and cask till paid; cost by Tobo: 15/6;

Copy HENRY ARMISTEAD, Clk.

Received the amount of the within Judgment in full in Cash, tobacco and a Note from WM. FITZHUGH of CHATHAM this 8th day of January 1784

Test JAS: HEATH for RODDY & TAYLOR
WM. ELLIOTT WATSON & URQUHART

p. Received October 24th 1783. Ninety pounds eleven shillings being in full for
348 the within Mortgage JAMES TAYLOR

At a Court of Hustings held for the Town and Corporation of Fredericksburg the 28th of October 1793, A Receipt from JAMES TAYLOR to Mr. HARVEY Gt., was produced in Court and there being no witnesses to the same, CHARLES URQUHART Gt. was sworn who declared he believed the said Receipt together with the name thereto subscribed were the proper hand writing of the said JAMES TAYLOR which is on the motion of the said HARVEY ordered to be recorded

pp. (The following Indenture has been marked out)
349- THIS INDENTURE made this sixth day of March one thousand seven hundred
351 and Ninety Two between JOHN LEGG of the one part and DAVID SIMONS of the other part; Whereas the said JOHN LEGG is entitled to and hath good right to a certain parcel of ground during the term of the natural lifes of JOHN DALTON and his Son, WALTER DALTON, late of the Town of Fredericksburg, which said parcel of ground situated on CAROLINE STREET in the said Town of Fredericksburg being part of the lott in the plan of the Town No. 49; and bounded; Beginning on said CAROLINE STREET at the corner of a piece of ground now the property of DAVID SIMONS & thence running along the said Street twenty feet from thence back from the said Street one lhundred and thirty two feet from thence at right angles with the last line twenty feet & from thence one hundred and thirty two feet to the beginning; making an acre or oblong of one hundred and thirty two feet and twenty feet; Now This Indenture witnesseth that the said JOHN LEGG for the sum of Fifty pounds to him paid and for the Rent hereafter mentioned the said JOHN LEGG has sold unto the said DAVID SIMONS his heirs and assigns all the said parcel of gound and Interest & term of lives of him the said JOHN LOEGG; To have & to hold unto the said DAVID SIMONS for all the rest of the said term of two lives he the said DAVID SIMONS paying yearly the annual rent of Forty shillings to the said JOHN LEGG every year on the Sixth day of March during the said term for lives; In Witness whereof the parties have sett their hands and seals

JNO: LEGG
DAVID SIMONS

At a Court held for the Town and Corporation of Fredericksburg the 23d day of March 1792 This Deed of Lease was acknowledged by the parties and ordered to be recorded Recorded Teste

(This Deed is recorded in next book folio (295), J: C:)

p. (On a scrap of paper)
352 THOS. R. ROOTES, SALLAY P. his Wife to JOHN SCOTT, Deed dated 31st August 1816; conveys a parcel of land adjoining FRIES (?) supposed to contain 31 3/4 acres formerly part of an addition to sd. Land laid off upon the land of DAVID GUINN & the sd. THOS: R. ROOTES commonly known by the name of THE MEADOW, bounded by a new Street which is a continuation of HANOVER, the old County Road, the Ditch running from the TURNPIKE BRIDGE by G. GUNNISANs line and the Alley leaving from the . . . .

Heritage Books by Ruth and Sam Sparacio:

Abstracts of Account Books of Edward Dixon, Merchant of Port Royal, Virginia, Volume I: 1743–1747

Abstracts of Account Books of Edward Dixon, Merchant of Port Royal, Virginia, Volume II

Albemarle County, Virginia Deed and Will Book Abstracts, 1748–1752

Albemarle County, Virginia Deed Book Abstracts, 1758–1761

Albemarle County, Virginia Deed Book Abstracts, 1761–1764

Albemarle County, Virginia Deed Book Abstracts, 1764–1768

Albemarle County, Virginia Deed Book Abstracts, 1768–1770

Albemarle County, Virginia Deed Book Abstracts, 1776–1778

Albemarle County, Virginia Deed Book Abstracts, 1778–1780

Albemarle County, Virginia Deed Book Abstracts, 1780–1783

Albemarle County, Virginia Deed Book Abstracts, 1787–1790

Albemarle County, Virginia Deed Book Abstracts, 1790–1791

Albemarle County, Virginia Deed Book Abstracts, 1791–1793

Augusta County, Virginia Land Tax Books, 1782–1788

Augusta County, Virginia Land Tax Books, 1788–1790

Amherst County, Virginia Land Tax Books, 1789–1791

Caroline County, Virginia Appeals and Land Causes, 1787–1794

Caroline County, Virginia Committee of Safety and Early Surveys, 1729–1762 and 1774–1775

Caroline County, Virginia Land Tax Book Alterations, 1782–1789

Caroline County, Virginia Land Tax Book Alterations, 1792–1795

Caroline County, Virginia Land Tax Book Alterations, 1795–1798

Caroline County, Virginia Order Book Abstracts, 1765

Caroline County, Virginia Order Book Abstracts, 1767–1768

Caroline County, Virginia Order Book Abstracts, 1768–1770

Caroline County, Virginia Order Book Abstracts, 1770–1771

Caroline County, Virginia Order Book, 1764

Caroline County, Virginia Order Book, 1765–1767

Caroline County, Virginia Order Book, 1771–1772

Caroline County, Virginia Order Book, 1772–1773

Caroline County, Virginia Order Book, 1773

Caroline County, Virginia Order Book, 1773–1774

Caroline County, Virginia Order Book, 1774–1778

Caroline County, Virginia Order Book, 1778–1781

Caroline County, Virginia Order Book, 1781–1783

Caroline County, Virginia Order Book, 1783–1784

Caroline County, Virginia Order Book, 1784–1785

Caroline County, Virginia Order Book, 1785–1786

Caroline County, Virginia Order Book, 1786–1787

Caroline County, Virginia Order Book, 1787, Part 1

Caroline County, Virginia Order Book, 1787, Part 2

Caroline County, Virginia Order Book, 1787–1788

Caroline County, Virginia Order Book, 1788

Culpeper County, Virginia Deed Book Abstracts, 1795–1796

Culpeper County, Virginia Land Tax Book, 1782–1786

Culpeper County, Virginia Land Tax Book, 1787–1789

Culpeper County, Virginia Minute Book, 1763–1764

Digest of Family Relationships, 1650–1692, from Virginia County Court Records

Digest of Family Relationships, 1720–1750, from Virginia County Court Records

Digest of Family Relationships, 1750–1763, from Virginia County Court Records

Digest of Family Relationships, 1764–1775, from Virginia County Court Records

Essex County, Virginia Deed and Will Abstracts, 1695–1697

Essex County, Virginia Deed and Will Abstracts, 1697–1699

Essex County, Virginia Deed and Will Abstracts, 1699–1701

Essex County, Virginia Deed and Will Abstracts, 1701–1703

Essex County, Virginia Deed and Will Abstracts, 1745–1749

Essex County, Virginia Deed and Will Book, 1692–1693

Essex County, Virginia Deed and Will Book, 1693–1694

Essex County, Virginia Deed and Will Book, 1694–1695

Essex County, Virginia Deed and Will Book, 1701–1704

Essex County, Virginia Deed, 1753–1754 and Will Book 1750

Essex County, Virginia Deed Abstracts, 1721–1724

Essex County, Virginia Deed Book, 1724–1728

Essex County, Virginia Deed Book, 1728–1733

Essex County, Virginia Deed Book, 1733–1738

Essex County, Virginia Deed Book, 1738–1742

Essex County, Virginia Deed Book, 1742–1745

Essex County, Virginia Deed Book, 1749–1751

Essex County, Virginia Deed Book, 1751–1753

Essex County, Virginia Land Trials Abstracts, 1711–1716 and 1715–1741

Essex County, Virginia Order Book Abstracts, 1695–1699

Essex County, Virginia Order Book Abstracts, 1699–1702

Essex County, Virginia Order Book Abstracts, 1716–1723, Part 1

Essex County, Virginia Order Book Abstracts, 1716–1723, Part 2

Essex County, Virginia Order Book Abstracts, 1716–1723, Part 3

Essex County, Virginia Order Book Abstracts, 1716–1723, Part 4

Essex County, Virginia Order Book Abstracts, 1723–1725, Part 1

Essex County, Virginia Order Book Abstracts, 1723–1725, Part 2

Essex County, Virginia Order Book Abstracts, 1725–1729, Part 1

Essex County, Virginia Order Book Abstracts, 1727–1729

Essex County, Virginia Order Book, 1695–1699

Essex County, Virginia Will Abstracts, 1730–1735

Essex County, Virginia Will Abstracts, 1735–1743

Essex County, Virginia Will Abstracts, 1745–1748

Fairfax County, Virginia Deed Abstracts, 1799–1800 and 1803–1804

Fairfax County, Virginia Deed Abstracts, 1804–1805

Fairfax County, Virginia Deed Book Abstracts, 1799

Fairfax County, Virginia Deed Book, 1798–1799

Fairfax County, Virginia Land Causes, 1788–1824

Fauquier County, Virginia Minute Book Abstracts, 1759–1761

Fauquier County, Virginia Minute Book Abstracts, 1761–1762

Fauquier County, Virginia Minute Book Abstracts, 1766–1767

Fauquier County, Virginia Minute Book Abstracts, 1767–1769

Fauquier County, Virginia Minute Book Abstracts, 1769–1771

Fredericksburg City, Virginia Deed Book, 1782–1787

Fredericksburg City, Virginia Deed Book, 1787–1794

Fredericksburg City, Virginia Deed Book, 1794–1804

Hanover County, Virginia Land Tax Book, 1782–1788

Hanover County, Virginia Land Tax Book, 1789–1793

Hanover County, Virginia Land Tax Book, 1793–1796

King George County, Virginia Order Book Abstracts, 1721–1723

King George County, Virginia Deed Book Abstracts, 1721–1735

King George County, Virginia Deed Book Abstracts, 1735–1752

King George County, Virginia Deed Book Abstracts, 1753–1773

King George County, Virginia Deed Book Abstracts, 1773–1783

King George County, Virginia Will Book Abstracts, 1752–1780

King William County, Virginia Record Book, 1702–1705

King William County, Virginia Record Book, 1705–1721

King William County, Virginia Record Book, 1722 and 1785–1786

Lancaster County, Virginia Deed and Will Book, 1652–1657

Lancaster County, Virginia Deed and Will Book, 1654–1661

Lancaster County, Virginia Deed and Will Book, 1661–1702 (1661–1666 and 1699–1702)

Lancaster County, Virginia Deed Book Abstracts, 1701–1706

Lancaster County, Virginia Deed Book, 1710–1714

Lancaster County, Virginia Order Book Abstracts, 1656–1661

Lancaster County, Virginia Order Book Abstracts, 1662–1666

Lancaster County, Virginia Order Book Abstracts, 1666–1669

Lancaster County, Virginia Order Book Abstracts, 1670–1674

Lancaster County, Virginia Order Book Abstracts, 1674–1678

Lancaster County, Virginia Order Book Abstracts, 1678–1681

Lancaster County, Virginia Order Book Abstracts, 1682–1687

Lancaster County, Virginia Order Book Abstracts, 1729–1732

Lancaster County, Virginia Order Book Abstracts, 1736–1739

Lancaster County, Virginia Order Book Abstracts, 1739–1742

Lancaster County, Virginia Order Book, 1687–1691

Lancaster County, Virginia Order Book, 1691–1695

Lancaster County, Virginia Order Book, 1695–1699

Lancaster County, Virginia Order Book, 1699–1701

Lancaster County, Virginia Order Book, 1701–1703

Lancaster County, Virginia Order Book, 1703–1706

Lancaster County, Virginia Order Book, 1732–1736

Lancaster County, Virginia Will Book, 1675–1689

Loudoun County, Virginia Order Book, 1763–1764

Loudoun County, Virginia Order Book, 1764

Louisa County, Virginia Deed Book, 1744–1746

Louisa County, Virginia Order Book, 1742–1744

Madison County, Virginia Deed Book Abstracts, 1793–1804

Madison County, Virginia Deed Book, 1793–1813, and Marriage Bonds, 1793–1800

Middlesex County, Virginia Deed Book, 1679–1688

Middlesex County, Virginia Deed Book, 1688–1694

Middlesex County, Virginia Deed Book, 1694–1703

Middlesex County, Virginia Deed Book, 1703–1709

Middlesex County, Virginia Deed Book, 1709–1720

Middlesex County, Virginia Order Book Abstracts, 1686–1690

Middlesex County, Virginia Order Book Abstracts, 1697–1700

Middlesex County, Virginia Record Book, 1721–1813

Northumberland County, Virginia Deed and Will Book, 1650–1655

Northumberland County, Virginia Deed and Will Book, 1655–1658

Northumberland County, Virginia Deed and Will Book, 1658–1662

Northumberland County, Virginia Deed and Will Book, 1662–1666

Northumberland County, Virginia Deed and Will Book, 1666–1670

Northumberland County, Virginia Deed and Will Book, 1670–1672 and 1706–1711

Northumberland County, Virginia Deed and Will Book, 1711–1712

Northumberland County, Virginia Order Book, 1652–1657

Northumberland County, Virginia Order Book, 1657–1661

Northumberland County, Virginia Order Book, 1665–1669

Northumberland County, Virginia Order Book, 1669–1673

Northumberland County, Virginia Order Book, 1680–1683

Northumberland County, Virginia Order Book, 1683–1686

Northumberland County, Virginia Order Book, 1699–1700

Northumberland County, Virginia Order Book, 1700–1702

Northumberland County, Virginia Order Book, 1702–1704

Orange County, Virginia, Chancery Suits, 1831–1845

Orange County, Virginia Deeds, 1743–1759

Orange County, Virginia Deed Book Abstracts, 1759–1778

Orange County, Virginia Deed Book Abstracts, 1778–1786

Orange County, Virginia Deed Book Abstracts, 1795–1797

Orange County, Virginia Deed Book Abstracts, 1797–1799

Orange County, Virginia Deed Book Abstracts, 1799–1800

Orange County, Virginia Deed Book Abstracts, 1800–1802

Orange County, Virginia Deed Book Abstracts, 1786–1791, Deed Book 19

Orange County, Virginia Deed Book Abstracts, 1791–1795, Deed Book 20

Orange County, Virginia Land Tax Book, 1782–1790

Orange County, Virginia Land Tax Book, 1791–1795

Orange County, Virginia Order Book Abstracts, 1747–1748

Orange County, Virginia Order Book Abstracts, 1748–1749

Orange County, Virginia Order Book Abstracts, 1749–1752

Orange County, Virginia Order Book Abstracts, 1752–1753

Orange County, Virginia Order Book Abstracts, 1753–1754

Orange County, Virginia Order Book Abstracts, 1755–1756

Orange County, Virginia Order Book Abstracts, 1756–1757

Orange County, Virginia Order Book Abstracts, 1757–1759

Orange County, Virginia Order Book Abstracts, 1759–1762

Orange County, Virginia Order Book Abstracts, 1762–1763

Orange County, Virginia Will Abstracts, 1778–1821

Orange County, Virginia Will Abstracts, 1821–1838

Orange County, Virginia, Will Digest, 1734–1838

Pamunkey Neighbors of Orange County, Virginia (Transcriptions from the original files of County Courts in Virginia, Kentucky and Missouri of wills, deeds, order books & marriages as well as some family lines...)

A Supplement to Pamunkey Neighbors of Orange County, Virginia, Volumes 1 and 2
Ruth and Sam Sparacio, Luretta and Eldon Corkill

Petersburg City, Virginia Hustings Court Deed Book Abstracts, 1784–1787

Petersburg City, Virginia Hustings Court Deed Book Abstracts, 1787–1790

Petersburg City, Virginia Hustings Court Deed Book Abstracts, 1790–1793

Prince William County, Virginia Deed Book Abstracts, 1749–1752

Prince William County, Virginia Order Book Abstracts, 1752–1753

Prince William County, Virginia Order Book Abstracts, 1753–1757

(Old) Rappahannock County, Virginia Deed and Will Book Abstracts, 1656–1662

(Old) Rappahannock County, Virginia Deed and Will Book Abstracts, 1662–1665

(Old) Rappahannock County, Virginia Deed and Will Book Abstracts, 1663–1668

(Old) Rappahannock County, Virginia Deed and Will Book Abstracts, 1665–1677

(Old) Rappahannock County, Virginia Deed and Will Book Abstracts, 1668–1670

(Old) Rappahannock County, Virginia Deed and Will Book Abstracts, 1670–1672

(Old) Rappahannock County, Virginia Deed and Will Book Abstracts, 1672–1673/4

(Old) Rappahannock County, Virginia Deed and Will Book Abstracts, 1673/4–1676

(Old) Rappahannock County, Virginia Deed and Will Book Abstracts, 1677–1678/9

(Old) Rappahannock County, Virginia Deed and Will Book Abstracts, 1678/9–1682

(Old) Rappahannock County, Virginia Deed and Will Book Abstracts, 1682–1686

(Old) Rappahannock County, Virginia Deed and Will Book Abstracts, 1686–1688

(Old) Rappahannock County, Virginia Deed and Will Book Abstracts, 1688–1692

(Old) Rappahannock County, Virginia Order Book Abstracts, 1683–1685

(Old) Rappahannock County, Virginia Order Book Abstracts, 1689–1692

(Old) Rappahannock County, Virginia Will Book Abstracts, 1682–1687

Richmond County, Virginia Deed Book Abstracts, 1692–1695

Richmond County, Virginia Deed Book Abstracts, 1695–1701

Richmond County, Virginia Deed Book Abstracts, 1701–1704

Richmond County, Virginia Deed Book Abstracts, 1705–1708

Richmond County, Virginia Deed Book Abstracts, 1708–1711

Richmond County, Virginia Deed Book Abstracts, 1711–1714

Richmond County, Virginia Deed Book Abstracts, 1715–1718

Richmond County, Virginia Deed Book Abstracts, 1718–1719

Richmond County, Virginia Deed Book Abstracts, 1719–1721

Richmond County, Virginia Deed Book Abstracts, 1721–1725

Richmond County, Virginia Order Book Abstracts, 1694–1697

Richmond County, Virginia Order Book Abstracts, 1697–1699

Richmond County, Virginia Order Book Abstracts, 1699–1701

Richmond County, Virginia Order Book Abstracts, 1714–1715

Richmond County, Virginia Order Book Abstracts, 1719–1721

Richmond County, Virginia Order Book Abstracts, 1721–1725

Richmond County, Virginia Order Book, 1692–1694

Richmond County, Virginia Order Book, 1702–1704

Richmond County, Virginia Order Book, 1717–1718

Richmond County, Virginia Order Book, 1718–1719

Spotsylvania County, Virginia Deed Book, 1722–1725

Spotsylvania County, Virginia Deed Book, 1725–1728

Spotsylvania County, Virginia Deed Book: 1730–1731

Spotsylvania County, Virginia Order Book Abstracts, 1742–1744

Spotsylvania County, Virginia Order Book Abstracts, 1744–1746

Stafford County, Virginia Deed and Will Book, 1686–1689

Stafford County, Virginia Deed and Will Book, 1689–1693

Stafford County, Virginia Deed and Will Book, 1699–1709

Stafford County, Virginia Deed and Will Book, 1780–1786, and Scheme Book Orders, 1790–1793

Stafford County, Virginia Deed Book, 1722–1728 and 1755–1765

Stafford County, Virginia Order Book, 1664–1668 and 1689–1690

Stafford County, Virginia Order Book, 1691–1692

Stafford County, Virginia Order Book, 1692–1693

Stafford County, Virginia Will Book, 1729–1748

Stafford County, Virginia Will Book, 1748–1767

Westmoreland County, Virginia Deed and Will Abstracts, 1723–1726

Westmoreland County, Virginia Deed and Will Abstracts, 1726–1729

Westmoreland County, Virginia Deed and Will Abstracts, 1729–1732

Westmoreland County, Virginia Deed and Will Abstracts, 1732–1734

Westmoreland County, Virginia Deed and Will Abstracts, 1734–1736

Westmoreland County, Virginia Deed and Will Abstracts, 1736–1740

Westmoreland County, Virginia Deed and Will Abstracts, 1740–1742

Westmoreland County, Virginia Deed and Will Abstracts, 1742–1745

Westmoreland County, Virginia Deed and Will Abstracts, 1745–1747

Westmoreland County, Virginia Deed and Will Abstracts, 1747–1748

Westmoreland County, Virginia Deed and Will Abstracts, 1749–1751

Westmoreland County, Virginia Deed and Will Abstracts, 1751–1754

Westmoreland County, Virginia Deed and Will Abstracts, 1754–1756

Westmoreland County, Virginia Order Book, 1705–1707

Westmoreland County, Virginia Order Book, 1707–1709

Westmoreland County, Virginia Order Book, 1709–1712

www.ingramcontent.com/pod-product-compliance
Lightning Source LLC
LaVergne TN
LVHW061250100826
845148LV00008B/1079
9781680344905